STORIES FROM THE STREET

Stories from the Street is a theological exploration of interviews with men and women who have experienced homelessness at some stage in their lives. Framed within a theology of story and a theology of liberation, Nixon suggests that story is not only a vehicle for creating human transformation but it is one of God's chosen means of effecting change. Short biographies of twelve characters are examined under themes including: crises in health and relationships, self-harm and suicide, anger and pain, God and the Bible.

Expanding the existing literature of contextual theology, this book provides an alternative focus to a church-shaped mission by advocating with, and for, a very marginal group; suggesting that their experiences have much to teach the church. Churches are perceived as being active in terms of pastoral work, but reluctant to ask more profound questions about why homelessness exists at all. A theology of homelessness suggests not just a God of the homeless, but a homeless God, who shares stories and provides hope. Engaging with contemporary political and cultural debates about poverty, housing and public spending, Nixon presents a unique theological exploration of homeless people, suffering, hope and the human condition.

Stories from the Street
A Theology of Homelessness

DAVID NIXON
University of Exeter, UK

ASHGATE

806 200 127

Published by
Ashgate Publishing Limited
Wey Court East
Union Road
Farnham
Surrey, GU9 7PT
England

Ashgate Publishing Company
110 Cherry Street
Suite 3-1
Burlington, VT 05401-3818
USA

www.ashgate.com

British Library Cataloguing in Publication Data
Nixon, David.
  Stories from the street : a theology of homelessness.
  1. Homelessness--Religious aspects--Christianity. 2. Homeless persons--Case studies.
  3. God (Christianity)--Will. 4. Christianity and culture.
  5. Church work with the homeless.
  I. Title
  261.8'32592-dc23

The Library of Congress has cataloged the printed edition as follows:
Nixon, David.
  Stories from the street : a theology of homelessness / By David Nixon.
    p. cm.
  Includes bibliographical references and index.
  ISBN 978-1-4094-3745-1 (hardcover) -- ISBN 978-1-4094-3746-8 (pbk.) --
  ISBN 978-1-4094-3747-5 (ebook) 1. Home--Religious aspects--Christianity.
  2. Homelessness--Religious aspects--Christianity. 3. Poverty--Religious aspects--
  Christianity. 4. Church work with the homeless. 5. Church work with the poor.
  6. Homelessness. 7. Storytelling--Religious aspects--Christianity. 8. Autobiography.
  I. Title.
  BR115.H56N59 2013
  261.8'32592--dc23
                                                                        2012028961

ISBN 9781409437451 (hbk)
ISBN 9781409437468 (pbk)
ISBN 9781409437475 (ebk – PDF)
ISBN 9781409474548 (ebk – ePUB)

Printed and bound in Great Britain by the MPG Books Group, UK.

To my parents, John and Elizabeth

Contents

Foreword

This book has taken me back repeatedly to a conversation several years ago with the then Director of Shelter, the UK Homelessness charity that runs a housing helpline, has a network of housing aid centres, and works with a range of other agencies to respond to the needs of the homeless. He spoke of his increasing consciousness of, and consequent unease with, the lack of the voice and the presence of a homeless person at the table of the board of Trustees, where decisions affecting homeless people were made. This was not merely in order to have a better understanding of their needs, but to be informed and corrected by the perspective of reality only to be found from the viewpoint of the hostel or the street.

'He has sent me to bring good news to the poor'. So begins the Gospel of Jesus. But if this is the case then why is it that the Church, in which the Gospel is to be embodied, seems so little to engage the faith and imagination of many of the urban poor and the itinerant homeless?

In this book, David Nixon, drawing on his own experience of urban ministry, has set out to construct a framework in which this question might be answered, and at the same time to bring the religious reflections and spiritual insights of those whom he has met to the table of theology and mission.

Much that follows in these pages is verbatim narrative from the lips of the homeless themselves. Their stories are then placed alongside, and allowed to interact with, the narrative of the Gospel in a dialogue of mutual illumination and critique.

In this way, listening to the voices of homeless men and women is to be pointed towards an exploration and understanding of a larger paradigm which provides a frame of reference for listening to the experience of a wide range of people in many different contexts who increasingly have a sense of their lives being shaped by a space, or spaces, which they have to occupy, but to which they do not belong. In this way the issues of homelessness come to be set in a wider societal context, with a theological critique of globalisation (characterised by privatisation, the freedom of the market, and deregulation) and its impact on individual lives, especially those who are vulnerable and inhabit what society regards as its margins. One result of this process is that individuals become inappropriately perceived as a homogenous, and distanced, mass – invisible as persons and even dehumanised.

In this book an attempt is made to respect personhood and individuality and provide a vehicle through which the voice of homeless people is allowed to be heard not, as so often, as part of a transaction to secure the meeting of needs –

whether of food or shelter, attention or concern. In such transactions the imbalance of power inevitably shapes how a story is told and a voice is heard. But freed from such transactional pressures, there is an authenticity in the voice of those who know that they have little to lose.

In that authenticity there are profound questions raised about what shapes perceptions of God, Church and World, not just for homeless people but for us all.

Michael Langrish,
Bishop of Exeter

Preface

In *Waiting for Godot*, Vladimir and Estragon play language games to pass the time, occasionally revealing the thin separation between survival and despair: 'Come on, Gogo, return the ball, can't you, once in a way?'[1] Although Beckett's characters are a fiction, they reveal the narrative instinct which is an intrinsic part of the human condition. One chance meeting at a local hostel while I worked as a curate in South West England focused a wish to explore more fully the nature of what is meant by storytelling or narrative within the context of belief in the Christian Trinity. The original experience described below limited this exploration to the stories told by those who live on the margins of our society, and especially the stories of homeless people.

My thanks in terms of the original research go firstly to my three supervisors in the Theology Department of Exeter University who saw me through a long-haul project towards a PhD: to Ian Markham who started me off, to Harriet Harris who cajoled and persuaded me that it was worthwhile, and to Tim Gorringe who had the major task of reading and criticising first drafts, middle drafts and final drafts. Thanks too to those in the School of Education who provided moral support, especially Liz Wood and William Richardson; latterly also to Susannah Cornwall who reawakened my interest in the combination of theology and homelessness at such an opportune moment, and introduced me to Contextual Bible Study.

I am particularly grateful to those who provided me with an entry-point to projects in the South West: to all the staff at The Victory, Aubyn Close and St Piran's (all pseudonyms) and in particular to Maureen Castle, Adrian Willcocks and Dave Denham (all very real). Also to Fr. Sam Philpott, Vicar of St Peter's Plymouth, who taught me to open my eyes. St Luke's Foundation Trust enabled me to take study-leave, without which this thesis would never have been completed.

The production of this book would not have been possible without the assistance of my editor Sarah Lloyd and the wonderful support of Russell Cargill.

Above all, thanks go to all those women and men who spent time with me telling the stories of their lives. Some are named here, others contributed indirectly through impression and insight. I hope I have done your stories justice.

---

[1]   Samuel Beckett, *Waiting for Godot* (London: Faber and Faber, 1965), p. 12.

Prologue
Encounter

I should like you to picture a newly-converted direct access hostel in a city in South West England, where homeless men and women can simply turn up, and if there is bedspace, spend the night in warm accommodation with the possibility of a shower and hot food. I should like you to dispel the myth of this city as a tourist town, the departure point for sailings to Brittany, a larger version of a quaint Devon cream-tea village; and instead see the granite-grey buildings as reflecting the harshness of life at the end of the line, literally and metaphorically, for many people. A downstairs room in this hostel with two people seated in conversation – they are about the same age, one a former narcotics user, the other a recently ordained curate trying to understand the work of the hostel situated in an Urban Priority Area (UPA). The details of the conversation are not important; the impression, however, was memorable. The narcotics user (Simon) had been through a local rehabilitation programme, which enabled him to reflect on his life experiences and his addiction. For the priest, the encounter seemed godly, though God was never mentioned. The experiences themselves and the insights into life offered by Simon seemed to speak of God, or at least like the woman with a flow of blood (Luke 8. 43); we touched the hem of Jesus' robe. There was an irony in the reversal of the roles – the priest learning about God from the man who might in other circumstances be seen as a subject for conversion. Surprise, irony, humility, the impact of such an experience, these were the starting points for an investigation into how marginalised people comprehend God, and what they can teach us, the wealthy, about life, about ourselves and about God – their part in our conversion.

PART I
Methods and Mapping

Who could have believed what we have heard? To whom has the power of the Lord been revealed? He grew up before the Lord like a young plant whose roots are in parched ground; he had no beauty, no majesty to catch our eyes, no grace to attract us.

Isaiah 53: 1, 2

Chapter 1
New Clothes for an Old Story? (1)

'But the Emperor has nothing on at all!' said a little child.
'Listen to the voice of innocence!' exclaimed her father; and what the child had said
was whispered from one to another.
'But he has nothing on at all!' at last cried out all the people. The Emperor was
vexed, for he felt that the people were right; but he thought the procession must
go on now. And the lords of the bedchamber took greater pains than ever to appear
holding up a train, although, in reality, there was no train to hold.

Hans Christian Anderson[1]

This encounter is the first story among many stories contained in this book
– principally the stories of homeless people who, with a mixture of courage,
determination, hesitation and hope, have recounted their lives to me. They have
exposed their weakness and vulnerability and, with a few modifications, have
allowed their stories to become public. This is also the story of this writer and his
responses to hearing the stories of others. Some of this story is set down here as
well. By placing these stories out there, in the public domain, they become fixed as
new stories, resonating and conflicting with other stories, part of the ebb and flow
of our desire to make sense of the world through narrative. I now invite you, the
reader, to reflect on your story as you read and react to the stories told here, and so
perhaps form another story which honours the reception of this material.

Part I of this book, therefore, sets out to construct a theology of story, including
the methodological and practical implications of collecting lifestories of homeless
people. Chapter 1 introduces some general themes concerning narrative before
focusing on the claim of liberation theologians that the poor are especially
privileged as storytellers for God, and on the nature of story as a holy conversation.
Chapter 2 concentrates on the place of God in the story: the loving relationship
between God and humanity played out in the narrative of holy scripture in which
we participate as covenantal partners. Chapter 3 looks at the collection of stories
of everyday life and how a qualitative method is best suited to their analysis. There
is an overview of important themes and of the ethical implications of this research,
including the position of the writer/researcher. A second project of Contextual
Bible Reading with homeless people is also described.

Part II (Chapter 4) opens with a return to the significance of context, and situates
these stories within various frames. A brief history of housing and homelessness
takes the reader up to some of the changes intended by the Conservative–Liberal

---

[1]   Hans Christian Anderson, *The Emperor's New Clothes* (London, Blackie: no date),
pp. 109–10.

Coalition Government; an international perspective is provided by situating these comments within the social and economic crisis of 2008 and onwards, which originated in the American housing market. Theologies of place and space, and theologies of equality give further contextual lenses through which to hear, read and interpret what homeless people have recounted. Chapters 5 to 8 analyse these stories of homeless people from various perspectives: short biographies of each interviewee (and biographical details of this writer); common biographical themes under the headings of Causes of Crisis and Results of Crisis; responses centred around emotions and feelings; responses about spirituality and religious experiences. Chapter 9 is an account of how homeless people read and interpreted particular biblical passages, with certain striking results.

Part III offers conclusions by returning to the starting point, and asks in Chapter 10 whether the preceding analysis of the stories of homeless people supports the methodologies described earlier. Chapter 11 examines in more detail Church policy and practice towards homeless people, and what Christian scriptures have said in this regard. Chapter 12 seeks to reconcile these various elements by outlining a theological approach which gives value to the stories which homeless people tell. The central symbol of the Trinity is envisioned not simply as a God of homelessness but as a homeless God who shares the storied experience of the marginalised, while also providing hope of transformation. A theology of story therefore is the crucial access point which uncovers the paucity of our theological and ecclesial response to homelessness, as well as pointing towards a richer and more inclusive future.

Telling stories of the self is dangerous – from an academic point of view, experience tends to be mistrusted and religious experience the more so; there is some personal risk too.[2] However, Jürgen Moltmann uses experience to locate his personal theological existence and to answer the question 'Where do we think theologically?' In *Experiences in Theology*, he describes his reluctant use of the pronoun 'I' in his theological writing, recognising that 'readers of a book want to know not only what the author has to say, but also how he or she arrived at it, and why they put it as they do'.[3] He admits that having studied academic theology, he is now interested in 'the theology of the people' where men and women struggle to bring up families, worry about their children and remember their dead. He begins almost every chapter of the book with a personal introduction: 'My personal access to black theology', 'The beginnings of my personal sensitivity to feminist theology', and so on. Perhaps surprisingly, there is a similar piece of spiritual autobiography in Barth's *Church Dogmatics*, where he reflects on the hymns which he sang as a child:

---

[2]   Brett Smith writes bravely of his depression in 'The Abyss', recognising professionally both advantages and disadvantages of a confessional account. *Qualitative Inquiry* 5/2 (1999): 264–79.

[3]   Jürgen Moltmann, *Experiences in Theology* (English translation. London: SCM, 2000), p. xix.

... as these songs were sung in the everyday language we were then beginning
to hear and speak, and as we joined in singing, we took our mother's hand, as it
were, and went to the stall in Bethlehem, and to the streets of Jerusalem, where,
greeted by children of a similar age, the Saviour made His entry, and to the dark
hill of Golgotha, as the sun rose to the garden of Joseph.[4]

In explicating a theological route map I want first to place this pastoral encounter
with Simon (and others like him) into the broad theoretical framework of practical
theology. The themes I develop are based on an understanding of this encounter
as an event of narrative or story, which whether consciously or not, is always
theological. My first purpose is therefore to produce a theology of story which
comes out of this pastoral experience, and which opens up further possibilities in
the exploration of specific stories of homeless people. My ultimate aim is towards
a theology of homelessness, which includes analysis of these homeless stories in
dialogue with Christian scriptures, Church tradition and other theologies, with
the stories of this writer and this reader also under scrutiny, but secondary to the
main data.

Practical theology includes a number of key characteristics which thread their
way through this book: individual and communal experience of the contemporary
world in dialogue with traditional texts; a postmodern approach which 'retrieves
from the margins the repressed and hidden "Others" of Western modernity'; the
assumption of a 'criterion of love', by which theology and the theologian are
themselves transformed by a spirituality which involves participation of heart and
mind.[5]

I have used the word story or narrative as a descriptive term for recording what
happened in a chance meeting with Simon, the drug-user, with the clarification
that in the recording of it we are now in fact dealing with two stories – his and
mine. A more complex analysis of the encounter soon sees two other constituents,
so that the process begins to look like this: a storyteller tells her story to a listener
or a reader and at this point the story itself takes on some independent life. Some
or all of these elements may be in conversation with the Bible, as the normative
text of Christianity, and with Christian theology. Some parts of the story are
communicated by words, others by body language, silence and so on.

There are a variety of roles or agents here. The first is the role of the storyteller:
liberation theology underscores why special attention should be paid to the stories
told by poor people. The second area focuses on the story itself, so I explain how
a conversation may be described as holy or sacred, give some ground rules for the
reading of texts, and then look beyond the individual to the community nature of
stories. The third area is the place of God and scripture in the telling of stories.
In Chapter 2 *God's Story* I take a broad narrative view of the Bible to include the

---

4   David Ford, *Barth and God's Story* (Frankfurt am Main: Lang, 1981), p. 16.

5   James Woodward and Stephen Pattison (eds), *The Blackwell Reader in Pastoral and Practical Theology* (Oxford: Blackwell, 2000), pp. 113, 201 and 204.

insights of Karl Barth and other theologians, and then concentrate on the stories told by Jesus. The role of listener/reader threads its way throughout this book, especially in references to the reciprocal relationship with text. The significance of this writer's role is recognised by a snapshot of his own life history.

Finally, let me now turn to some introductory remarks about story, and why stories are always theological. 'Narrative as a primary act of mind' is the title of an essay by Barbara Hardy in a collection about children's literature. Her argument is that narrative is not an aesthetic invention of artists but a primary act of mind transferred from life to art. In other words, we function at a fundamental level as human beings through the medium of story:

> For we dream in narrative, daydream in narrative, remember, anticipate, hope, despair, believe, doubt, plan, revise, criticise, construct, gossip, learn, hate and love by narrative. In order really to live, we make up stories about ourselves and others, about the personal as well as the social past and future.[6]

It is not simply children who move between the world of the fairy story and 'real' life but all human beings who inhabit both the world of fantasy and the one of raw events. It is by means of narrative that we impose some order on the unceasing flow of happenings.

From a theological perspective a similar point about the foundational quality of narrative is made by Bernard Lonergan:

> Without stories, there is no knowledge of the world, of ourselves, of others, and of God. Our narrative consciousness is our power for comprehending ourselves in our coherence with the world and other selves; it expresses our existential reality as storytelling and storylistening animals, acting and reacting within our particular world context, overcoming the incoherence of the unexamined life. One man's story is another man's point of departure. We live on stories; we shape our lives through stories, mastering the complexity of our experience through the dynamic of our structured knowing ...[7]

What is a Story? also suggests that it is story which gives form to life, but stresses the presence of emotion – what Cupitt calls 'the production of desire'. Human beings construct lifestories in both these aspects, borrowing magpie-like from any other fiction we can get hold of, often in competition with the stories of others around us.[8] Stories always remain theological because they promise that life can be meaningful; they contain a message or moral imperative; they are value-

---

[6]   Barbara Hardy, 'Narrative as a Primary Act of Mind' in Margaret Meek, Aidan Warlow and Griselda Barton (eds), *The Cool Web* (London: Bodley Head, 1977), p. 13.

[7]   John Navone, *Towards a Theology of Story* (Slough: St. Paul Publications, 1977), p. 18.

[8]   Don Cupitt, *What is a Story?* (London: SCM, 1991), p. 67.

inducing; and they help in maintaining individual identity.[9] More bleakly, Cupitt describes storytelling as equivalent to Scheherazade in *One Thousand and One Nights*: simply 'putting off death by telling tales through the night'. In *How Our Lives Become Stories* Paul John Eakin writes that the autobiographical self is not a single, static entity, but plural, embodied and relational. Narrative form (or story) is not just an appropriate vehicle to express such identity, it is a constituent part of the self, an identity content.[10] Anything which affects our ability to tell the story will touch our identity too. In extreme cases, an inability to narrate (for example, stroke patients and those severely abused in childhood) or an excess of narration (living entirely in a fantasy world) alters our sense of an 'automatic narrative pilot' and consequently damages our identity.[11] This broad understanding of what is meant by story or narrative forms a working definition for this theological route map. It remains to be seen, under the impact of the specific lifestories of homeless people, whether such fundamental assertions are justified.

Stories of Freedom in Liberation Theology

How is it possible that poor, vulnerable or marginalised people become significant storytellers? Liberation theology places the poor at the centre of God's plan for salvation, and explains how telling a story is part of the process of freedom.

Liberation theologians speak of the concept of a preferential option for the poor, a theology from the poor themselves, and a theology which recognises the context in which it is being written. Gustavo Gutiérrez in his introduction to *A Theology of Liberation* refers to the poor having a prior but not exclusive claim on God. He bases this claim not on social analysis, nor human compassion, but on a Christian interpretation of how God operates in human history as recorded by scripture, especially in Matthew 25.[12] Gutiérrez describes two strands of poverty found in the Bible – poverty as a scandalous condition against which to be indignant, and poverty as spiritual childhood, humility before God. The Old Testament prophets Job, Isaiah and Amos all protest against those who 'thrust the poor off the road', 'turn aside the needy from justice', and 'trample the head of the poor into the dust of the earth'.[13] The Levitical and Deuteronomical Laws stand to prevent the injustices of poverty by the provision, for example, of jubilee years. By contrast, the privileged condition of poverty interpreted as abandonment to and trust in God (for example in the Psalms) receives its highest expression in Matthew's version of the Beatitudes and in the imitation of Christ in Philippians 2:

---

[9]   Cupitt, *Story*, p. 77.

[10]   Paul John Eakin, *How Our Lives Become Stories: Making Selves* (Ithaca and London: Cornell University Press, 1999), p. 100.

[11]   Eakin, *Stories*, p. 124.

[12]   Gustavo Gutiérrez, *A Theology of Liberation* (London: SCM, 1988), p. 115.

[13]   Job 24: 2–14; Isaiah 10: 1–2; Amos 2: 6–7.

'Though he was in the form of God, Jesus did not count equality with God as a thing to be grasped ...'.

Juan Luis Segundo uses the concept of priority as a way into reading the gospel, what he calls a 'pre-understanding', so that the option for the poor is not a theme of liberation theology but 'an epistemological premise for an interpretation of the word of God'.[14] The reason and need for this pre-understanding of the gospel is that in Latin America 'literally millions of people are dying because for five centuries the gospel has been interpreted in a particular way'. So the option for the poor becomes a hermeneutical key – or rather a wager on which he stakes himself, his Christian faith and theological work, for he takes the risk of affirming that five centuries of theology in Latin America have been wrong.[15] The option for the poor in concrete terms is to be realised with those who suffer most from material poverty. Segundo moves forward the critical example of the (Lucan) Beatitudes by reminding us that the hungry are not blessed because of their hunger, but because they will cease to be hungry, and so on.

In the Black Theology of Basil Moore and James Cone which focuses on liberation and 'race', the identification of God with the oppressed is such that Christian theology must take the colour of the victims of oppression: 'God's salvation breaks through like a ray of "blackness" upon the "whiteness" of the condition of the oppressed'. The ultimate conclusion of a preferential option for the poor is the complete identification of God with those who are oppressed. For Cone, this is to see the incarnation of the Word in the particular reality of Jesus himself as a black man, but one who would still suffer at the hands of a white Church:

> Christians
> what welcome would they give God's son
> confronted with the classification board
> and identification card stating race
> then consigned to his proper place
> would he be banned for his message
> that love has no colour connotation
> that the brotherhood of man is all-embracing?
>
> Christians
> who deport priests for performing God's work
> will not hesitate to proclaim an order
> declaring the son of God an agitator.[16]

---

[14]   Juan Luis Segundo, *Signs of the Times* (Maryknoll, NY: Orbis Books, 1993), p. 122.

[15]   Segundo, *Signs*, pp. 125 and 126.

[16]   Basil Moore (ed.), *Black Theology: The South African Voice* (London: Hurst, 1973), pp. 55 and 56. The verses are from James Matthew's 'Christians', p. 64.

A theology or a Church from the poor was not the dominant trend of Latin American thinking. The first development of liberation theology sought principally to reveal the ideological weakness of an expression of Christianity which gave support to the ruling classes, and was largely successful among middle-class people (university students and staff in particular); the second, marking a shift around the 1970s and given a different political climate, aimed much more to learn from poor people themselves. This second development was encouraged by the relative failure of the first to find support among precisely those people whom its pastoral practice was designed in the long term to help, largely because this theology was suspicious of popular (Catholic) religious practice. So a painful conversion to be a learner rather than a teacher was the lot of the intellectual including the theologian at this period. Segundo writes:

> It appeared then that if theologians were still to be the 'organic intellectuals' of the common people – that is to say, useful as intellectuals charged with the understanding of popular faith – they were obliged to learn how oppressed people lived their faith.[17]

However, he is quick to point out that there may be an inherent difficulty in evangelising the theologian with an understanding of God which is flawed – 'passive and fatalistic' – one which leaves the poor with no more real hope than before.

To involve poor people themselves, Segundo's second strand of theology is followed when commitment to the poor leads to a realisation that they in turn are a means of evangelising the Church. Gutiérrez writes:

> Commitment to the poor and oppressed and the rise of grassroots communities have helped the Church to discover the evangelising potential of the poor. For the poor challenge the Church at all times, summoning it to conversion; and many of the poor incarnate in their lives the evangelical values of solidarity, service, simplicity and openness to accepting the gifts of God.[18]

The extent to which this challenges the thinking and practice of the Church is illustrated by Samuel Rayan who writes about a theology of the Dalit people in India. His expectation is that all struggle against injustice and brutality is interpreted as a theological event, which is 'provoked and energized by the Holy Spirit, the Father/Mother of the poor'. But such theology is latent and requires the theologian to articulate it, not least so that all are sustained by 'the hope of God's reign on our earth'. Having made this interpretation the Church is then

---

[17] Segundo, *Signs*, p. 74.

[18] Gutiérrez, *Liberation*, p. xlii.

faced with 'the imperative of solidarity and participation'.[19] Rayan re-interprets Hebrews 13: 11–13[20] as a challenge to go with Jesus outside the camp; he sees the essence of Christian spirituality and the identity of the Church in this solidarity with outsiders.

Paulo Freire writes from the perspective of education, both theoretically and from his observations of peasants, urban workers, and the middle-classes. He is concerned with the restoration of humanity to those from whom it has been 'stolen', and also to those who are 'thieves'. Paradoxically, it is the oppressed who will restore the humanity of both themselves and of the oppressor in 'an act of love' on the part of the oppressed.[21] This will restore to both parties the basic vocation of 'becoming more fully human'. By giving back humanity to the oppressor, those who have been victims resist the temptation of becoming oppressors themselves, and cast off a false model of what it is to be human. Yet such liberation is as painful as childbirth since those who suffer injustice have often internalised their role:

> One of the greatest obstacles to the achievement of liberation is that oppressive reality absorbs those within it and thereby acts to submerge men's consciousness. Functionally, oppression is domesticating. To no longer be prey to its force, one must emerge from it and turn upon it. This can be done only by means of the praxis: reflection and action upon the world in order to transform it.[22]

The role of the pedagogue (or theologian) is to work with, and not for, the oppressed, to encourage reflection upon and engagement with the world of oppressive reality.

Liberation theologies are contextual theologies. Gutiérrez asks how can we talk about God given the oppression in Latin America? How can we tell the poor that God loves them in these conditions? Thus there is a movement to favour a particular theological reading as opposed to a universal one, whether the context is Latin America or Black South Africa. Theo Witvliet describes this as a suspicion of the universal:

> Liberation theology is liberation of that theology which supposes itself to be universalist and as such passes over the diversity of human situations and human needs, social tensions and conflicts, and the causes of poverty and wretchedness. It disparages the old association of this pseudo-universality with the dominant

---

[19]   Samuel Rayan, 'The Challenge of the Dalit Issue: Some Theological Perspectives' in V. Devasahayam (ed.), *Dalits and Women* (The Gurkukul Summer Institute, 1992), p. 120.

[20]   For the bodies of those animals whose blood is brought into the sanctuary by the high priest as a sacrifice for sin are burned outside the camp. So Jesus also suffered outside the gate in order to sanctify the people through his own blood. Therefore let us go forth to him outside the camp, and bear the abuse he endured.

[21]   Paolo Freire, *Pedagogy of the Oppressed* (Harmondsworth: Penguin, 1972), pp. 21 and 32.

[22]   Freire, *Pedagogy*, p. 28.

cultures, social classes and races. The epistemological break is the condition for a new form of universality which makes room for these experiences of faith and reflections on faith which are excluded by the dominant traditions of theology and teaching authority.[23]

Moore is pungent in his rewriting of the question:

> What is the meaning of the Gospel for those living not with their white bums in the butter but with their black backs to the wall?[24]

Black Theology, says Moore, 'is situational theology. And the situation is that of the black man in South Africa'.[25] He contrasts this starting point of fear, oppression and hunger with classical Western theology which he describes as 'top-down and doctrinaire'. Gutiérrez situates his theology of sin and redemption firmly in the context of the lives he observes, so that the individual, private or internal dimension of sin gives way to sin as the socio-historical fact of the absence of fellowship and love amongst persons.[26] He contrasts post-Enlightenment European theology with that done in Latin America; the first is concerned with non-believers, the second with non-persons.[27]

Beginning with the role of storyteller, liberation theology discloses how the poor are in a special position to tell stories of God. The stories which they tell of their lives, especially the struggle against injustice and brutality, are seen to be privileged moments with a latent theology awaiting critical articulation. Yet the listener, theologian or pedagogue, is not destined to remain passive. They are called to a variety of different responses. Solidarity and protest in the face of such poverty leads the theologian to a new hermeneutical question in respect of the Bible: who is Jesus for the poor and homeless? This challenge extends uncomfortably to the way in which the Church has lived the gospel for many centuries. In a particularly striking image, theologians are called to go outside the camp and join the poor, to become one of the homeless, who alone are able to set them free from their own oppressive instincts. Yet, the theologian is also called to contest beliefs and practices, which though originating from poor people, are nevertheless instrumental in maintaining unjust structures.

---

[23]   Theo Witvliet, *A Place in the Sun* (English translation. London: SCM, 1985), p. 36.

[24]   Moore, *Black Theology*, p. x.

[25]   Ibid., p. 6.

[26]   Gutiérrez, *Liberation*, chapter 9 'Liberation and Salvation'.

[27]   Ibid., *Liberation*, p. xxix.

Ears to Hear and Eyes to Read

If marginalised people are effective storytellers for God, then perhaps the interviews with homeless people described in later chapters are a kind of holy conversation, one which takes a different form when it is written down, and changes again as it becomes autobiographical. This conversation-story reforms when it is told in public, now sharing ownership as a community possession. God's place in the story is assured by reading the particular text of the Bible, and thereby creating a theology of story in which to place the narratives of homeless people.

Conversations and Texts: Mystery, Love and Suspicion

Martin Buber comes close to affirming that all conversations have the potential to be holy. He defines two different relationships which he calls I–Thou and I–It: I–Thou establishes the world of relations with nature, with other humans and with spiritual beings, whereas I–It is about relations with objects. The building up of the relationship I–Thou with another human is not about sustaining life but helping us 'to glimpse eternity'. The model for this is Jesus as the exemplar of the I of unconditional relationship with the Thou of the Father. Human beings often harden a Thou into an It in their interactions. Conversations with homeless people can be holy when they begin to fashion a discourse which mirrors this I–Thou relationship, allowing free space for exploration by both parties, and with a growing understanding that both I's are affected. For example, in one interview both nervousness and relief were communicated to the interviewer during and after the telling of a painful story. There was also no question of objectivising the interviewee, reducing him to the I–It position, as might have been the case with a quantitative survey.

Conversations are holy too when taken together they become a series of I–Thou relationships which point to a closer relationship with God. Buber does not say that human beings know more about the eternal Thou, simply that they draw closer, the Thou itself remaining a mystery. Indeed, any attempt to define the mystery is in danger of reducing a relationship with God to an I–It position. The mystery turns into paradox when the conversation is with God:

> There is a tale that a man inspired by God once went out from the creaturely realms into the vast waste. There he wandered till he came to the gates of the mystery. He knocked. From within came the cry, 'What do you want here?' He said, 'I have proclaimed your praise in the ears of mortals, but they were deaf to me. So I came back to you that you yourself may hear me and reply'. 'Turn back,' came the reply from within. 'Here is no ear for you. I have sunk my hearing in the deafness of mortals'. True address from God directs man into the

place of lived speech, where the voices of the creatures grope past one another, and in their very missing of one another succeed in reaching the eternal partner.[28]

Human beings are forced back to the world in which they live if they are to have any chance of finding the God who is speaking. God's speech demands response but they are highly likely to be deaf to it. The semi-structured conversations which make up these interviews are an attempt to remove wax from the ears, a theological syringe wielded to the sense of hearing the divine. And although fully conscious that talk is imperfect and encounters fail to connect, yet still in that failure, as in Buber's story, God may be touched.

The adoption here of a critical-realist reading of texts, including raw transcriptions of interviews, implies some both/and statements: that homeless people do reveal some true facts about their lives, and that they also modify their stories for the interview; that the interviewer does operate objectively and that the kind of conversation they have is affected by his stance and ideas; and in a similar vein in the process of transcribing, analysing and reading.[29] This means that while the transcriptions and the analysis will have, to some extent, lives of their own, the interviewer, transcriber and author have an important impact on the final result, the more so when these three roles are held by the same person. This is acknowledged by the inclusion of significant amounts of verbatim text and of the reactions of this author; but to go further, I insist that instead of interpreting this as a weakness, I include the interviewer/transcriber/author as a key storyteller in the theological enterprise around these events. However, by reading a text with a hermeneutic of love, the author will resist the solipsistic temptation simply to reduce it to their own issues.

Love needs to be balanced by suspicion in an analysis of any personal writing. At the root of religious autobiography, the subject (I) is always a literary invention, 'reporting the supreme fiction of memory as fact'.[30] For example, Augustine's *Confessions* begins from early childhood and charts a path through adolescence into adulthood, yet there is a conscious style which draws heavily on the Bible, reflecting the faith of the mature Augustine, the writer. There is a dense interlocking of stories and texts here, further complicated by the realisation of the kind of literary fiction in which there are at least two Augustines, 'the wise narrator and the foolish protagonist'. In other words, the ironic distance between the I of childhood thieving and adolescent lust, and the I of Augustine, monk and

---

[28] Martin Buber, *Between Man and Man* (English translation. London: Routledge & Kegan Paul, 1947), p. 15. See also Martin Buber, *I and Thou* (English translation. Edinburgh: T&T Clark, 1958).

[29] See N.T. Wright, *The New Testament and the People of God* (London: SPCK, 1992).

[30] Eakin, *Stories*, p. 98.

bishop is underscored.[31] Similarly, this author suspects that the I of experiential or 'confessional' mode differs in this text from the I of academic writer and interlocutor, and questions the subsequent implications.

The 'rougher' data of transcriptions are not literary texts, and yet there are sometimes obvious attempts to make sense of the past, to give order to lives which may otherwise appear chaotic. The identity which narrative reveals is thus understood as 'dynamic, changing and plural'. In response to these lifestories, a 'criterion of love' is balanced by a hermeneutic of suspicion: talk of ourselves is less transparent that we would like to think it.

Story as a Community Possession

Turning from the individual or private dimension of narrative, the central feature of Stanley Hauerwas' *A Community of Character* is that stories form and develop communities, and that the viability of a community lies in its ability to tell and re-tell the story of its founder. He uses the novel *Watership Down* by Richard Adams to illustrate his argument, suggesting that the effectiveness of various communities is to be judged by how they maintain the narratives that define them, in this case as rabbits. For example, Part I of *Watership Down* contains 'The Story of the Blessing of El-ahrairah'. El-ahrairah is the founder of the rabbit world, a quasi-mythical figure around whom significant legends are told. This story recalls the way in which Frith (God) has blessed the rabbits with special gifts, but is not to be taken for granted or mocked. Dandelion begins the story in this way:

> Long ago, Frith made the world. He made all the stars too and the world is one
> of the stars. He made them by scattering his droppings over the sky and this is
> why the grass and the trees grow so thick on the world. Frith made the brooks
> flow. They follow him as he goes through the sky and when he leaves the sky
> they look for him all night.[32]

The story is narrated at a crucial early moment when the rabbits escape the danger posed to their original burrow, and exhausted, are in danger of losing courage. They are all familiar with the tale but it is effective in giving them enough strength to hide from immediate danger.

By extension, faith communities are built and formed through the telling and re-telling of foundation stories. Christians learn their parts in the story; they situate

---

[31] T.R. Wright, *Theology and Literature* (Oxford: Blackwell, 1988), pp. 95–100. See also Eric Auerbach, *Mimesis* (Princeton, NJ: Princeton University Press, 1968), pp. 66–76. His analysis of *Confessions* Book vi.8 (Alypius at the gladiatorial games) insists that Augustine is breaking new ground in his writing by abandoning the rule of separated styles and reflecting profoundly on the nature of faith within an earthy and emotional human reality.

[32] Richard Adams, *Watership Down* (Harmondsworth: Penguin, 1974), p. 37.

themselves within the timeframe of the story, and they begin to understand how story works. The best way of doing this, Hauerwas implies in his use of *Watership Down*, is through the medium of story itself. Scripture as performance, however, does not capture sharply enough the 'risk and radical contingency' of the play being enacted. For the Christian, the play is not one she is able to step out of, because it claims to be about a comprehensive interpretation of her identity and future.[33] These stories include the dimension of time since the interpretation of past and present with an eye to the future is also a function of narrative. In the context of Christian ethics, Hauerwas sees narrative as giving the necessary framework for the acquisition of freedom, providing it is a narrative which can 'make sense' of the whole of our lives, including past mistakes:

> we need a story that not only provides the means to acknowledge the blunders as part of our own story, but to see ourselves in a story where even our blunders are part of our on-going grace, that is, are forgiven, and transformed for 'our good and the good of all the church'.[34]

The loss of such narrative is highly significant for the community.

Within a dynamic which moves from private to public I have considered here some aspects of story which pertain to the narratives of homeless people. The sense in which careful listening honours and validates the account of vulnerable lives mirrors the perspective of an I–Thou relationship which Buber describes; but it also points to the paradox of the presence of God. Unless such a conversation, humanly speaking, is to remain in this relatively private domain, the recording and textualising of these sacred encounters is a prerequisite for an exploration of the theology of the stories which homeless people tell. Such texts bring with them the issue of their construction and how we read them. In choosing a critical-realist approach I have sought to combine the holiness of I–Thou with the need for academic rigour, focusing on a twin hermeneutic of love and suspicion, in which love is primary. The possibility of setting these texts before strangers points to the social and moral dimension of storytelling. While the ethics of this enterprise will be viewed in a following chapter, here the focus has been on how stories are the building blocks of community wellbeing and identity, especially in the formation of faith communities. The circle has been closed, as it were, at the end of this section by realising that story can be its own best pedagogue. Entry to the circle is facilitated by a criterion of love, but once there, learning about the significance of story is enabled by our own listening and telling.

---

[33]   Gerard Loughlin, *Telling God's Story* (Cambridge: Cambridge University Press, 1996), p. 134.

[34]   Stanley Hauerwas, *A Community of Character* (London: University of Notre Dame Press, 1981), p. 147.

Chapter 2
New Clothes for an Old Story? (2)

Again Jesus began to teach beside the lake. Such a very large crowd gathered around him that he got into a boat on the lake and sat there, while the whole crowd was beside the lake on the land. He began to teach them many things in parables, and in his teaching he said to them: 'Listen! A sower went out to sow …'.

Mark 4: 1–3

God's Story

The previous chapter focused on the storyteller and then on the form of the story. The next step is to identify God's place in the story, and so establish some conclusions about a theology of story to apply here. We read the Bible in a variety of ways, but I start with a general, but brief, overview about reading scripture in the light of the critical-realist approach mentioned in the previous chapter, and contrast this by looking more closely at Karl Barth's approach to the Bible, especially its narrative qualities. The parables of Jesus, re-read through the lens of a sociopolitical methodology and compared to folktales, are a reminder of the power of all stories (including biblical stories) to transform the human condition.

Reading the Bible

It is not my intention at this point to attempt a detailed description of arguments around how to read the Bible, except insofar as they apply to this particular project – so I adopt the notion of ground rules. These include that reference to the Bible is appropriate here at all; that there are implications of taking a critical-realist stance in relation to scripture; that there are some major advantages in reading the Bible as literature. The first can be disposed of quickly by looking forward to a following chapter about qualitative methodology. Here I draw on an American work of sociology from the 1980s, *Habits of the Heart*, as a reference point for qualitative study. These writers 'dialogued' with de Tocqueville's *Democracy in America* as a quasi-normative text. In turn, scripture is the text with which Christian theology is always in dialogue.

A critical-realist approach to reading the Bible is consistent with the way in which the main research data is analysed, but there are a number of implications. This approach challenges the notion of the Bible as a 'master narrative' in the sense that not only does it provide a resolution to questions of meaning and coherence in human life, but, more significantly, a traditional reading of the Bible claims that the whole world is contained within its particular stories, including the world of criticism and judgement.[1] The literary critic Eric Auerbach summarises this in comparing ancient Greek literature with extracts from Old and New Testaments:

> The Scripture stories do not, like Homer's, court our favour, they do not flatter us that they may please and enchant us – they seek to subject us, and if we refuse to be subjected we are rebels.[2]

Yet, staying within the discipline of literary criticism, Auerbach also points out by implication that scripture itself is the rebel within existing genres. An analysis of the incident in the courtyard of the High Priest's house in which Peter betrays Christ reveals the breaking of the rule of differentiated styles. Authors of this classical period insisted that serious subject matter was treated with the particularly 'high' style of tragedy, almost always involving those of divine or noble birth, and that comedy or popular literature was the correct province for a 'low' style, with characters and situations drawn from everyday life. What is remarkable about the incident in which Peter denies Christ is that the seriousness of the subject matter (love, betrayal, loss of faith, guilt and shame) neither treats with the gods, heroes or nobles, nor places them in a traditional setting, yet nevertheless retains the sublime force of tragedy. But this rule of style is not simply broken as a matter of experiment or whim; rather it reflects the upsurge of a popular religious movement, which was in itself groundbreaking. The Bible may be normative for Christians and for Christian theology, but it need not be a prison – indeed it provides within itself some excuse for rebellion.

On the other hand, the concept of little if any extra textual reality in scripture advanced by writers such as Cupitt and Lindbeck seems a step too far. Terence Wright achieves some balance in asserting that:

> the belief that language does point to a 'real' referent, however indirectly, seems to me to be crucial for Christian faith. And one of the most powerful means of describing this reality, I want to suggest, is necessarily the most indirect: literature. It is through literary devices, narrative, metaphor, symbolism and so on, that we come closest to understanding the human predicament.[3]

Without some notion of a real referent Christianity is in danger of becoming a mere intellectual exercise. What is of significance here is that while Wright advocates clearly a literary approach, this is also Cupitt's answer to the excess of stories with which we are surrounded. His evocative phrase describes life as 'a flowing stream of jostling stories'.[4] He delights in the paradox that while we live and find meaning by stories, we nevertheless attempt to escape from them: we know the attempt is

---

[1]   George A. Lindbeck, *The Nature of Doctrine* (London: SPCK, 1984), p. 117.

[2]   Auerbach, *Mimesis*, p. 15.

[3]   Wright, *Literature*, p. 32.

[4]   Cupitt, *Story*, p. 150.

futile, but we have to keep telling 'anti-stories' about the possibility of freedom. He offers a number of ways out of this dilemma, favouring one which continues to re-interpret stories about Jesus. We tell stories about our yearning for final unity and transcendence, and our failure to find either. His concluding words come full circle, as he wonders whether, after all, not to have a master narrative is also still to have one.

This opens discussion about some major advantages in reading the Bible as literature. A macro view considers that despite the vast range of different material in the Bible – poetry, prophecy, myth and legend, history, legal and liturgical instruction – it is possible to read the Bible as a single text whose subject is God in relationship with the human race in history.[5] The micro view (which is complementary) uses the tools of literary analysis to examine the smaller units within the whole, and speaks for example of characterisation, language, plot and so on. In a similar way a distinction is made between the story of Jesus and the stories told by Jesus.

However, the route of Bible as literature is not without its drawbacks: the importance of 'real referents' has already been mentioned; similarly, the prescriptions of Lindbeck's 'intratextual' interpretation, or those of the earlier critic Ulrich Simon, who speaks of the rebirth of narrative occurring only from within the text itself.[6] A more theological objection to be taken seriously is made by James Barr who writes that a literary reading of the Bible entails a 'poor articulation of theological discussion' around questions like 'Is there a God?' 'Who is Jesus?' and so on.[7] These tensions are made more explicit when Barth's view of biblical narrative is examined.

Karl Barth and Biblical Narrative

Such theological questions are tackled exhaustively in *Church Dogmatics*, but it is Barth's attention to the narrative structure of the Bible which is pertinent for this argument. However, he begins from a point which is almost diametrically opposite to ideas about the Bible as literature. Barth's focus is much less on human stories than on the single story which does interest him: God's story in the person of Jesus Christ. The central span of this story are the years AD 1 to 30, the start marked by the Virgin Birth, its culmination in the resurrection. This stretch of time is made eternal and so embraces the whole of history. Barth underlines the primacy of God's story into which we fit our own:

---

[5] Lindbeck, *Doctrine*, p. 121.

[6] Ulrich Simon, *Story and Faith in the Biblical Narrative* (London: SPCK, 1975), p. 103.

[7] James Barr, *The Bible in the Modern World* (London: SCM, 1973), p. 74.

If the fact that God is with us is a report about the being and life and act of God, then from the very outset it stands in a relationship to our own being and life and acts. A report about ourselves is included in that report about God. We cannot therefore take cognisance of it, be more or less impressed by it, and then leave it as the report of something which has taken place in quite a different sphere in which we ourselves have no place. It tells us that we ourselves are in the sphere of God. It applies to us by telling us of a history which God wills to share with us and therefore an invasion of our history – indeed, of the real truth about our history as a history which is by Him and from Him and to Him … He does not allow His history to be His and ours to be ours, but causes them to take place as a common history. That is the special truth which the Christian message has to proclaim at its very heart.[8]

Barth inserts into his theological analysis two extended literary discussions; the first suggests a three part division of the story of Jesus (Life, Passion, Easter) and the second focuses on the temptations of Jesus in the wilderness and at Gethsemane.[9] Issues of the verification of Jesus' story are not made by reference to any historical accuracy, but through an understanding of the resurrection as Christ alive now. The Easter story becomes the commentary on the other two parts. The hermeneutical circle is thereby closed, with a single one way movement from Christ to us.[10] There is a radical rejection of any exterior criteria for judgement, for we are not outside the story looking in, but actually within the story. The most dangerous enemy is Christian subjectivity – a perspective which shifts emphasis from Jesus to the believer. A similar point is made by Loughlin who considers that the central question posed by narrativist theology to the Church is 'do we start from the Word or the world?'[11] He is keen to indicate that this is not necessarily a single route with two ends, for where we start may determine different end points. With Lindbeck, he sees the world as too problematic a starting point, so favours beginning with the Word.

It is possible to compare Barth's interpretation of biblical narrative with that of the realistic novel; for example, the need for a 'middle-distance perspective' which is neither so close as to miss the whole, nor so far as to blur the details. This allows Barth to pass over inconsistencies and contradictions in the story, and to appreciate it as a literary whole.[12] The story is held together by the central figure of Christ, who gives meaning to the Old Testament, and to history, both before and after the resurrection. The spirituality of *Church Dogmatics* again emphasises that Barth's basic 'rule' for reading the Bible is the recognition that the biblical

---

[8]   Karl Barth, *Church Dogmatics* (Edinburgh: T&T Clark, 1936–77), Volume IV.1 §57 p. 7.

[9]   Barth, *Dogmatics*, IV.1 §59 pp. 224ff and pp. 259ff.

[10]   David Ford, *Barth and God's Story* (Frankfurt am Main: Lang, 1981), p. 37.

[11]   Loughlin, *God's Story*, p. 83.

[12]   Ford, *Barth*, p. 55.

story is the over-arching story, of which our own story is a part. This is 'spiritual' because prayer takes precedence even over exegesis, since prayer recognises the free presence of Jesus and the right ordering between God and humanity. Prayer for Barth has no interest except in revealing the identity of God who is addressed, and our response of amazement and gratitude.[13]

One of Barth's main contributions to theology lies in his appreciation of 'the significance of realistic narrative form in the Bible' and his 'radical attack on post-Enlightenment world views'. This takes the form of:

> the dominance of one story over all others, with the guarantee of the story being the presence of Christ. The story is like a finger which, for all its shaking and its warts, points to Christ; and it is the only witness we have, so that it must be the authority on God and on the new state of the world since the resurrection, and the criterion against which world-views are measured.[14]

Yet it is precisely this dominance which is also the weak point of his theology. Barth gives so little credence to such other factors as historical criticism, subject-centred anthropology and the natural sciences, and humankind is placed in such a secondary position in regard to God, that the story begins to twist under the weight it has to bear. Yet Barth's embrace of the narrative tradition also includes his desire to be surprised by the revelation of God contained in biblical stories, and his wish to 'find some way of making the accustomed unaccustomed again, the well-known unknown, and the old new'.[15]

This desire should also be read alongside a consideration of the Word of God. What emerges strongly here is the significance of the mystery of God, the freedom of God, and that 'the possibility of knowing the Word of God lies in the Word and nowhere else'.[16] This miracle is available to anybody, and the miracle which opens the hermeneutical circle is called faith and grace. Christians stand in faith, being called to fresh hope, fresh promise and a trembling assurance of expectation. Faith is likened to a gift or a loan for exclusive use; it is a point of contact between God and humanity and 'not for inventorying or cataloguing, not for putting on ice or into the museum'.[17]

The tensions remain, however, between arguments advanced so far in support of critical realism (both in the reading of the Bible and of the stories of homeless people) and Barth's views about the primacy of God's story as recited in holy scripture. A suitable way forward may be found in returning to the two parts of Ford's conclusion: Barth's stress on the narrative structure of the Bible, but also that Barth's emphasis on one story to the exclusion of any other is perhaps

---

[13]   Ibid., pp. 166 and 173.

[14]   Ibid., p. 182.

[15]   Barth, *Dogmatics*, IV.1., p. 224.

[16]   Ibid., I.1, p. 255.

[17]   Ibid., I.1, p. 272.

a weakness. A theological route map framed around narrative is strengthened by Barth's analysis, and enriched by his conceptualisation of mystery, grace and faith. However, stories of oppression, poverty and homelessness still remain. They are stories which interest, challenge, and provoke. They cannot be dismissed lightly as simply secondary to God's story; rather we read the story of God with the impact and impression of these stories still buzzing in our minds and shocking our sensibilities.

Further exploration of Barth's writings about Christian freedom show that God's freedom is axiomatic, but cannot to be separated from its close neighbour, human freedom. God does not exist in isolation or as an abstraction, but rather enlists humanity as a partner in a covenantal relationship. Indeed, Barth writes:

> 'Theology', in the literal sense, means the science and doctrine of God. A very precise definition of the Christian endeavour in this respect would really require the more complex term 'The-anthropology'. For an abstract doctrine of God has no place in the Christian realm, only a 'doctrine of God and man', a doctrine of the commerce and communion between God and man.[18]

A fair summary might be that 'the narration of God's mighty deeds cannot proceed without the narration of the corresponding deeds of God's fellow-workers …'.[19] It is the Spirit which wakens human beings to their freedom as God's partner, a God who desires to be with us and to love us.

With this in mind, it is possible to honour the stories of poor people who speak of God and honour the Bible as the normative text for Christian theology. The reading of the mystery of God which abounds in these interactions is accomplished with the freedom of faith and grace, the freedom of the Spirit, and not in the imprisonment of text. It is pertinent to give voice to the deeds and misdeeds of God's fellow-workers; to explore scripture for those whose lack of freedom is real, whose imprisonment is only too concrete; to expose the moments when an uncritical theological approach has permitted or even supported this denial of God.

Parables and Folk Tales

An analysis now of the stories which Jesus tells by means of parables connects the story of the triune God with the possibility of freedom. The Spirit is at work to effect transformation in lives which are not free by suggesting alternative visions in which all can realise their true roles in God's story. The stories of homeless people are not too distant from the lives of first-century Palestinians, subject to similar social, political and economic pressures. This means that parables are worthy of inclusion into a theology of story. However, the question remains of

---

[18]   Karl Barth, *The Humanity of God* (London: Collins, 1967), p. 11.

[19]   John Webster, *Barth's Moral Theology* (Edinburgh: T&T Clark, 1998), p. 90.

how to connect these stories and the realities of two thousand years ago with the accounts of marginalised people now; how are Jesus' words being heard today and who is telling stories about homeless people in the twenty-first century? Answers to these questions point forward to conclusions about a theology of homelessness.

Parables are also of interest from the technical point of view of narrative. As stories within the greater tale of the Bible they can be submitted to the tools of literary analysis.[20] Earlier arguments from liberation theology are brought to bear with a focus on the subversive or 'rebellious' nature of the parable as highlighted by critics such as John Dominic Crossan, Paul Ricoeur and William Herzog.[21] Sally McFague introduces this theme:

> [Parables] do not assume a believing or religious perspective on the part of the listeners to whom they are addressed; they do not assume continuity between our world and a transcendent one; they do not see similarity, connection and harmony between our ways and the ways of God. On the contrary, they are a secular form of language, telling stories of ordinary people involved in mundane family, business and social matters; they assume a non-believing or secular attitude on behalf of their audience; they stress the discontinuity between our ways and the ways of the kingdom; they focus on the dissimilarity, incongruity and tension between the assumptions and expectations of their characters and another set of assumptions and expectations identified with the kingdom.[22]

By comparing Herzog's ideas with those of Jack Zipes on folk and fairy tales we see how the notion of story as conveying the possibility of change and freedom is common to both sacred and secular literature, persisting from pre-modern civilisations to our own day.

For example, the reading of the parable of the Labourers in the Vineyard (Matthew 20: 1–16) usually has the landlord as the God figure and the labourers as ungrateful wastrels.[23] However Herzog sees both landlord and labourers as representatives of the particular social context. The landlord is part of the elite group in this 'advanced agrarian society' who takes advantage of the large

---

[20] For example, Tom Wright uses Jesus' parable of the wicked tenants (Mark 12: 1–11) as the initial vehicle for describing different ways of reading scripture – pre-critical, historical, theological and postmodern. Wright, *New Testament*, pp. 6–9.

[21] For example John Dominic Crossan, *The Dark Interval: Towards a Theology of Story* (Niles, IL: Argus Communications, 1975); Paul Ricoeur, *Time and Narrative* (Chicago: University of Chicago Press, 1984); William Herzog, *Parables as Subversive Speech* (Louisville, KY: Westminster/John Knox Press, 1994).

[22] Sally McFague, *Metaphorical Theology* (London: SCM, 1983), p. 15.

[23] Jeremias calls this the parable of the Good Employer, and so likens God to an 'employer who has compassion for the unemployed and their families'. Joachim Jeremias, *The Parables of Jesus* (New York: Scribners, 1963), pp. 136–9.

number of unemployed day-labourers, the 'expendable' class, 'largely composed of the excess children of peasant households who could afford to pass on their inheritance to only one child, usually the eldest son'.[24] In the second half of the parable, the argument about pay is the landlord's attempt to shame and humiliate the workers more than they can endure. They react and the ringleader is exposed and expelled, more than likely to fall still further in the social hierarchy and end life as a beggar, Lazarus-like at the gate of the rich man. Herzog sees Jesus here as a teacher telling stories, posing problem after problem, to reveal sociopolitical reality and to break the attachment of these rural poor to their oppressors.

The parable which offers most clearly an alternative mode of behaviour is that of the Friend at Midnight (Luke 11: 5–8). This sketch of peasant society emphasises the shared responsibility of the whole community to provide for an unexpected guest. Here the values of the Kingdom of God reside in the extravagant hospitality of the villagers, in contrast to the values of the urban elite. The latter would see such generosity as 'shameless' since it is directed at a stranger for no obvious reward, but it is the shamelessness of Abraham, where the welcome of the sojourner is a foretaste of the messianic banquet.[25] According to Herzog, Jesus also opens up to new possibilities the operation of the debt and holiness codes, as for example in the parable of the Pharisee and Toll Collector (Luke 18: 9–14). The challenge to these redemptive media transforms the place of the lowly toll collector from one of outside subservience to that of questioning the Pharisee's reading of God's judgements. The theology of these stories is created from social, political and economic analysis, and Christians too 'must learn to tell new parables that codify and problematize our world as well as Jesus told parables for his world'.[26]

The parables of Jesus are likened to a mirror held up to the world to help the disciples better understand the narrative of his actions. The ideological dimension of these stories is evidenced by their use when Jesus is under pressure from the Pharisees (Mark 3: 23; 7: 17; 12: 1), and by the theme of 'hearing but not understanding'. The everyday language to which McFague refers underlines that the 'mystery of the Kingdom of God' is utterly mundane – it is to be taken literally as Jesus speaks it. Those who do not understand are not failing to grasp obscure concepts but blinded by the prevailing ideology. It is Jesus, Myers reminds us, who announces that the Parable of the Sower is the key to all the other parables and to the whole of his story (Mark 4: 13). And it is the evangelist Mark who renders the nice fiction of a public and private explanation of the parable by giving both to his readership. There is no 'arcane knowledge' for the image of the lamp and bushel follow on immediately. The yield on the harvest – thirty, sixty, a hundred times greater – is both a demonstration of the plenitude of the divine kingdom and a practical subversion. If such production were possible, it would end the peasant/landlord relationship and undermine the oppressive political economy.

---

24   Herzog, *Parables*, p. 88.
25   Ibid., p. 214.
26   Ibid., p. 265.

'The kingdom is like *this*', says Jesus: it envisions the abolition of the oppressive relationships of production that determined the horizons of the Palestinian farmer's social world.[27]

Jack Zipes also starts from the folk tales told in pre-capitalist agrarian societies. These were transmitted orally with the intention of teaching ordinary people how to cope in an unjust world, and to struggle with some element of hope on their side.[28] However, when these same tales began to be written down towards the end of the seventeenth century, they underwent a change which has continued into the present day. Firstly, they became fairy rather than folk tales, now directed towards a passive public of readers, and losing the brutality of some of the earlier stories.[29] Next, more importantly, there occurred slowly what Zipes calls the 'instrumentalization of fantasy' or the 'commodification of culture'. The original power of these tales to suggest the transformation of society and stimulate the imagination of change gives way to an increasingly dominant culture industry, operating under a different set of values. Whereas folk tales have 'emancipatory potential' and cultivate the 'germs of subversion', we now experience the Disneyfication of culture. Certain utopian views are promoted as if they were possible for us to attain in reality, and theme parks give us a glimpse of a blueprint. Such a development ceases to challenge the status quo. However, this control is not total, and folk and fairy tales still retain some of their magic. The essence of such magic is not in the power to change anything, but instead in the creation of space for thinking, and the stimulation of the imagination.

In J.R.R. Tolkien's *The Hobbit* Bilbo Baggins, the hero of the tale, is a little fellow who through magic (that is, transformation) unlocks new powers within himself, and with others is able to defeat oppression and build a new and better world. Baggins returns home with a profounder understanding of self and of the possibility of cooperating with others, but he remains small and humble despite his new self-confidence. 'He is now in touch with himself through the power of fantasy, and it is Tolkien's fantasy which allows us, too, to glimpse the possibilities of *home*'.[30] While Zipes criticises Tolkien for a limited version of home (there are no women, for example), and also remarks that Tolkien's evident Catholicism places limits on his utopian vision, nevertheless he recognises the importance of 'religious imagination' in the formulation of such a utopia:

---

[27]   Ched Myers, *Binding the Strong Man* (Maryknoll, NY: Orbis, 1988), p. 177.

[28]   Jack Zipes, *Breaking the Magic Spell: Radical Themes of Folk and Fairy Tales* (London: Heinemann, 1979), p. 33.

[29]   Zipes cites as examples versions of 'Beauty and the Beast' told in eighteenth-century France. These have become 'didactic stories which totally corrupt the original meaning of the folk-tale motifs and seek to legitimize the aristocratic standard of living in contrast to the allegedly crass, vulgar values of the emerging bourgeoisie'. *Magic Spell*, p. 8.

[30]   Zipes, *Magic Spell*, p. 154.

> The religious imagination responds to the genuine utopian thrust in [Tolkien's] works, and, whether one considers his fairy tales low or high art, serious fantasy or mere commercial entertainment, it must be recognised that he uncovers a social need of the religious imagination, and points to the widening gap between a technologically constraining society and its alienated individual in search of authentic community.[31]

In a close echo of Barth and Herzog, Zipes also suggests that a counter-balance to this increasing instrumentalisation of culture is that 'the familiar tales must be made strange to us again if we are to respond to the unique images of our own imagination and the possible utopian elements they may contain'.[32]

A further example of this is J.K. Rowling's first novel of the Harry Potter series. *Harry Potter and the Philosopher's Stone* allows the imagination space to focus on typical questions faced by children growing up: unfair treatment of the orphan, learning to cope at school with teachers, rules, friendships and bullying. The world of Hogwarts School of Witchcraft and Wizardry is not so far from the world of the Muggles (ordinary human beings) as to make connections difficult. Hogwarts often takes a familiar experience, school games for example, and exaggerates it wittily. The competitive game of Quidditch is like a three-dimensional rugby played on broomsticks. At another level, however, the novel treats the age-old question of the battle between good and evil. Harry Potter as a baby was able to defeat the renegade wizard Voldemort simply by his presence, although both his parents were killed in the same attack. It is Harry who defeats Voldemort again towards the end of this book, but this time we are given an explanation of how this is possible:

> Your mother died to save you. If there is one thing Voldemort cannot understand, it is love. He didn't realise that love as powerful as your mother's for you leaves its own mark. Not a scar, no visible sign ... to have been loved so deeply, even though the person who loved us is gone, will give us some protection for ever. It is in your very skin. Quirrell, full of hatred, greed and ambition, sharing his soul with Voldemort, could not touch you for this reason. It was agony to touch a person marked by something so good.[33]

Rowling's fantasy seems to tap into what Zipes' has called the 'religious imagination' by presenting in a new and attractive way the fundamental human desire to understand good and evil, love and sacrifice. The enthusiasm surrounding the production of each new Harry Potter novel reinforces the view that there is as strong an appetite as ever for space to explore an answer to these questions,

---

[31]   Ibid., p. 158.

[32]   Ibid., p. 105.

[33]   J.K. Rowling, *Harry Potter and the Philosopher's Stone* (London: Bloomsbury, 1997), p. 216.

among both adults and children. Equally, however, the enormous revenues from associated films and merchandising also display an almost ineluctable tendency to commodification.

The purpose of this book is to focus on the lives of homeless people, perhaps as representatives of other excluded groups, and to ask how theology envisages their lives. In this comparison of Jesus' parables and folk tales, it is evident that both originate from similar social milieux, and following Herzog's interpretation of the parables, both contain similar expectations: to expose the short-comings of existing society and to provide space for the imagination of change. This reveals an aspect of story which has hitherto been undervalued – the power of story to effect transformation. This notion of both power and transformation contrasts with an attempt to dismiss stories as childish playthings, and with a sense that stories are static, immutable (perhaps based on a reading of sacred texts). Stories are, by contrast, dynamic, life affirming and potentially life changing – the stuff of adult lives. The experiences of Alcoholics Anonymous to which several homeless people refer show the power of story in a world of therapy – those who tell aloud their lives not only share with the group their common difficulties, but articulate and have reflected back the possibility of something different and better. This is based on a Twelve Step Programme common to many similar organizations.[34] Both parables and folk tales envision a changed world, and then provide the mental and spiritual space to consider how to realise this. Lastly, it is significant that Barth, Herzog and Zipes all point to the need for recapturing the power of story, in such

---

[34]   *Alcoholics Anonymous* (3rd edn. York: A.A. General Service Office, 1976), pp. 59–60.

We admitted we were powerless over alcohol – that our lives had become unmanageable.

Came to believe that a Power greater than ourselves could restore us to sanity.

Made a decision to turn our will and our lives over to the care of God *as we understood Him*.

Made a searching and fearless moral inventory of ourselves.

Admitted to God, to ourselves, and to another human being the exact nature of our wrongs.

Were entirely ready to have God remove all these defects of character.

Humbly asked Him to remove our shortcomings.

Made a list of persons we had harmed, and became willing to make amends to them all.

Made direct amends to such people wherever possible, except when to do so would injure them or others.

Continued to take personal inventory and when we were wrong promptly admitted it.

Sought through prayer and meditation to improve our conscious contact with God *as we understood Him*, praying only for knowledge of His will for us and the power to carry that out.

Having had a spiritual awakening as the result of these steps, we tried to carry this message to alcoholics, and to practise these principles in all our affairs.

a way as either to revitalise the parables of Jesus, or to tell new tales from our own imagination which suggest the possibility of freedom. Zipes' description of the collapse of the folk tale to the weaker fairy tale may well be paralleled by the domestication of the parables of Jesus: even more reason to re-invigorate them, in Milbank's words:

> The task of such theology is not apologetic, nor even argument. Rather it is to tell again the Christian *mythos*, pronounce again the Christian *logos*, and call again for Christian *praxis* in a manner that restores their freshness and originality. It must articulate Christian difference in such a fashion as to make it strange.[35]

Stories Can Change the World

In Richard Hughes' children's story *The Spider's Palace* a little girl is invited by a spider to live in his crystal palace in order to escape the snakes which are tormenting her. The extraordinary thing about the palace is that not only is it high up in the air, above the tops of the mountains, but also that it is completely transparent; there is one room, however, curtained off from the rest, which is not accessible to her at all. The spider retires into this room nightly. While the little girl is happy playing on the clouds, curiosity at last gets the better of her, and she hides in the curtained room to watch the spider. As he enters he turns into a man, spends an hour there, and turns back into a spider. The little girl goes to bed, and during the night the walls and ceilings of the crystal palace turn into milky-white marble and the palace sinks into the middle of a valley. When the little girl goes to look for the spider, she discovers he has turned into a man permanently. Neither mentions the change, and both continue living in the palace.

An obvious moral from this tale is to be satisfied with enjoying the delights that magic or fantasy provide, and resist the temptation to dismantle the toys to see how they work. Perhaps it is part of the human condition to go one step too far, but in doing so the extraordinary may become ordinary again, the delight is lost. Such are my feelings in regard to story: if the mechanics of story and their working parts are exposed too brutally, we risk the loss of the very thing which captured our imagination at the start. However, by returning to the original purpose of this route map such a risk may be avoided. My purpose here was not to produce a general account of narrative or story, but to give some insights into a theology of story, such as to be useful for understanding the stories which homeless people tell.

I began with a personal experience, both interesting and shocking, which gave rise to an initial process centred on storyteller, story and Christian context. This unique encounter led into the framework of practical theology, which allowed access to such concepts as human experience in the contemporary world, critical dialogue with traditional texts, the importance of the excluded other, and the

---

[35]   John Milbank, *Theology and Social Theory* (Oxford: Blackwell, 1990), p. 381.

possibility of transformation. From this first process more specific questions developed. Why are the poor the storytellers of God? What is to be said about story as it moves from conversation to written text to communal possession? What is God's place in the story? What is our place in God's story? Answers to these questions provide various elements to a theology of story, based on two parts: a theory of listening and a theory of reading.

In a theory of listening, the story of the dispossessed other allows participation in a holy conversation which reaches out to touch the mystery of God and the mystery of our own humanity. In an attempt (but likely failure) to meet truly with the other person we nevertheless succeed in meeting God. A theory of reading recognises a hermeneutic of both love and suspicion, where the first outweighs the second. God's story as revealed in holy scripture and in the stories told by human beings is a principal focus; both recount the autonomy and freedom of God and the humdrum of human life. Narrative form and literary analysis are taken seriously because they break open meaning, confirming and challenging world views. As story comes into public ownership, so the community dimension comes to the fore, in which poor people are seen as the special storytellers of God, both in the stories they tell and in the way those stories confront an affluent Church. As the dispossessed tell stories of pain and suffering, of transformation and recovery, they renew the old stories, create new dynamic narratives and make the Christian story strange again.

Chapter 3

Collecting Stories

If thou didst ever hold me in thy heart,
Absent thee from felicity awhile,
And in this harsh world draw thy breath in pain,
To tell my story.

William Shakespeare, Hamlet V.ii[1]

This chapter moves from theological insights into the nature of story into asking how to collect and analyse the stories of homeless people. Themes from the sociological study of everyday life include the importance and irregularities of conversation, the role of the researcher, the significance of the mundane, and research undertaken with a view to change minds. A range of authors are invoked to provide answers to questions such as 'How do I persuade people to tell their stories to me?' 'What do I do with these stories having heard them?' 'What happens when I start to ask questions about God, or religion or spirituality?' A trajectory from literature to practice must also include a consideration of research ethics, based partly in a comparable study of illness stories, including again the place of the author. This leads into a detailed description of how, where and when these stories were collected, including a reflection on the strengths and weaknesses associated with these particular methods.

Stories of Everyday Life

An overview of sociological research with or without a religious dimension into how people live their lives day to day suggests themes of common interest with this theological exploration of homelessness. Most use some form of interview preceded often by a questionnaire, with results presented both by topic and under individual names. People remain as important as the ideas they express, and via these recorded conversations, their status as co-authors is acknowledged. In the American study *Habits of the Heart*, the authors also acknowledge their own involvement:

> The people who let us into their homes and talked to us so freely during the course of our study are very much part of the authorship of this book. Their words appear in almost every chapter. They made us think things we never thought before. But we have tried to make sense of not only what we saw and

---

[1]   William Shakespeare, *Hamlet* V.ii, in *Complete Works of William Shakespeare* (London: Abbey Library, 1978), p. 882.

heard in our research but also what we have experienced as lifetime members of American society. The story we tell is not just the story of those we interviewed. It is also our own.[2]

Similarly, Nigel Rapport in *Diverse World-Views in an English Village* records the story of his own involvement with the research: his need for a job and accommodation, how to participate in a locally based social life, the attempt at explaining who he was and what he hoped to do in 'Wanet', the difficulties and discomforts he encountered. There may also be involvement with an external 'story': in the case of *Habits*, with the text of Alexis de Tocqueville's *Democracy in America* of the 1830s; in the case of this book, with the Christian scriptures.

Observing, listening to and participating in conversations are central to Rapport's work, but not simply as a methodological tool. He remarks that conversation is the most important way in which reality is maintained, that Doris and Sid make real the multiple facets and possibilities of their personalities through their talk.[3] But just as certain of their world views are corroborated through conversation, so others are deliberately excluded. Conversation becomes a way of constructing or ensuring one's own identity, perhaps at the same time as denying or abasing another's. Miscommunication and misunderstanding amid the plethora of words is a function of the difference between form and meaning. Rapport exposes the superficial interpretation of shared meaning within conversation by contrast with the diverse nature of world views which are revealed beneath the surface. Form and meaning therefore remain distinct, and the writer delights in pointing up inconsistency and difference:

> The beauty of the exchange for me is this confused tension between the surface exchange, the orderly conversational form … and the unique visions, the limitless avenues of thought, the wild disorders of contradiction that can be motivating the exchange, causing its regular re-occurrence, and dancing delightedly but invisibly around its expression.[4]

Without discarding the irregularities of everyday, Rapport defends his decision not to impose a 'specious unity' on the world which Doris and Sid inhabit, or to deny the 'validity of its intricacy and detail'. He wishes to respect the complexity, diversity and idiosyncrasy of the society which he studies, and while by no means averse to analysis, these characteristics are to be left intact. His philosophical approach and style seek to:

---

[2]   Robert Bellah, Richard Madsen, William Sullivan, Ann Swidler and Steven Tipton, *Habits of the Heart* (Berkley: University of California Press, 1985), p. xlv.

[3]   Nigel Rapport, *Diverse World-Views in an English Village* (Edinburgh: Edinburgh University Press, 1993), p. 152.

[4]   Rapport, *World-Views*, p. 163.

keep space open for the sense of wonder which poets can sometimes cause – wonder that there is something new under the sun, something which is *not* an accurate representation of what was there already, something which, at least for the moment, cannot be explained and can barely be described.[5]

Identity, alienation and misunderstanding are also raised as concepts via Wikan's *Life among the Poor in Cairo*. She describes poor people leading their lives surrounded by a culture whose values and attitudes are alien to them. Since they lack the strength to determine their own value system, they are powerless to resist an alien culture being imposed upon them.[6] Some of the same dynamic is evident in Wanet, but the crucial difference is that characters are able to resist the imposition of another system. This study of homeless people indicated that they are much less likely to be able to do so.

The theme of the everyday in contrast to the universal is emphasised in Tim Jenkins' *Religion in English Everyday Life* which contrasts a social anthropological method (which he favours) with that normally used by sociology of religion. In his analysis of the Kingswood Whit Walk he observes a less sharp division between the sacred and profane, and that the religious sphere is seen as part of wider human activity. There is a recognition of the importance of the particular over against the desire to universalise, and of the tendency to trivialise the exceptional:

Usually anomalies – or the lack of fit between the local way of life and the outsider's assumptions – either pass unremarked or are experienced as stereotypic features of the local people, their quaintness, stubbornness and so forth. Yet recourse to such stereotypes explains nothing. It is a form of blindness to the perceptions and motivations that are expressed in everyday life, and which emerge in certain events.[7]

Jenkins is especially keen to point out the paucity of studies which exist about the life of the unrespectable. Those which do exist tend to maintain negative images and underplay any contradictions to these.[8]

Research with a view to shifting dominant world views is exemplified in Elizabeth Stuart's book *Chosen*, which examines the experiences of gay Catholic clergy in Britain in 1993. In the introduction she sketches out a brief history of homosexuality within the Church of Rome and goes on to describe the project of the book. It is clear that this is to be more than just a factual survey. The book is designed so that the experience of gay clergy may be disseminated within the Church, that clergy may feel less isolated, that those in authority may understand

[5]   Ibid., p. 199.

[6]   Unni Wikan, *Life among the Poor in Cairo* (English translation. London: Tavistock Publications, 1980), p. 42.

[7]   Timothy Jenkins, *Religion in English Everyday Life* (Oxford: Berghahn, 1999), p. 77.

[8]   Ibid., p. 192.

the needs of their gay clergy, and that lay people undertake a degree of pastoral care. She explains the origins of the book:

> LGCM [Lesbian and Gay Christian Movement] endeavours to be a voice for the voiceless and so the Roman Catholic Caucus became anxious to provide gay priests and seminarians with a 'safe' opportunity to share their stories. That was how this book was born. It does not claim to be a scientific survey. It does not claim to represent the views of all gay priests in Britain. It simply offers the stories and reflections of a group of British gay priests and seminarians who vary from one another in age, location, background, theology, attitude to sexuality and experience but who seem to share much in common.[9]

Collecting Stories about God

The intention to name God at the heart of this book derived from the encounter described in the Prologue. The fact of God's centrality takes away nothing from the difficulties of analysis. If an account of everyday life based on qualitative methods is a complex process, then the attempt to collect stories about God becomes even more difficult. Trying to pin down the meaning of the words themselves – 'spiritual', 'spirituality', 'religious experience' – is like trying to plait fog, but the endeavour is necessary, not least because interviewees will hear and use all these terms in different ways. Indeed, on reflection, I found that in my own interview questions I had not used terms consistently. A possible pattern emerges that those who write under the aegis of spirituality begin with human experience and try to say more about humanity, whereas writers who talk about religious experience often use the concept of experience (and sometimes single experiences) to say more about God. I want to knit these together more.

Empirical studies like *The Spirit of the Child* draw on the same qualitative methods employed here. David Hay compares the terms 'spiritual' and 'religious', finding that mention of the first prompts a warmer, broader and more inclusive reaction, whereas the word 'religious' brings with it connotations of public institutions and a mixed historical record.[10] His working hypothesis includes the concept of 'spiritual sensitivity', or awareness-sensing, mystery-sensing and value-sensing.

Timothy Beardsworth compiles an account of the first one thousand reports about religious experiences given to the Religious Experience Research Unit (RERU) at Oxford. He puts his finger neatly on some of the ambiguities already illustrated – the difference between a religious experience as an event and

---

[9]   Elizabeth Stuart, *Chosen* (London: Chapman, 1993), p. ix.

[10]   David Hay with Rebecca Nye, *The Spirit of the Child* (London: Fount, 1998), pp. 5–6.

religious experience as a means of interpretation. He also feels the need for some clarification of terms:

> There is an ambiguity about the phrase 'religious experience', depending on how we take the word 'experience'. If we interpret it on the analogy of phrases like 'interesting experience' or 'harrowing experience', then we shall think in terms of episodes occurring at certain times and in certain places; we shall talk of '*a* religious experience' or 'religious *experiences*'. On the other hand, one can argue, as a contributor did, 'Religious experience is not something to be tied down to definite times and places; *it is a way of looking at the world* (and oneself) which colours, or should colour, all one's thoughts and actions'.[11]

He writes that while his research was intended to focus on the second of these, inevitably data arrived with no differentiation. The main drawback of Beardsworth's study is its continued implication of good and bad research subjects, illustrating an important theme for this book. Gender, marital status, age, and age at the time of the experience (if available) are given, but do not provide categories for analysis. In addition, there are designations based on professional employment, for example, 'Rev', 'Major', 'Lt-Col', 'Dr', 'Nun', and so on. There is no mention, for example, of 'mother' or 'private soldier' in the classification system, let alone 'homeless'. The liberation theologies of black people, women and those marginalised by social-political-economic conditions recognise the particularity of experience which underlies all reflective thinking, and so, by extension, that concerned with questions of ultimate meaning.

Other pointers to religious experience which find echoes in these accounts are found in more extensive writing from philosophers of religion. From Swinburne, the concept of God simply being or doing something:

> an experience which seems (epistemically) to the subject to be an experience of God (either of his just being there, or doing something or bringing about something) or of some other supernatural thing. The thing may be a person, such as Mary or Poseidon; or Heaven, or a 'timeless reality beyond oneself', or something equally mysterious and difficult to describe.[12]

And from Sheldrake, a specifically Christian definition of spirituality:

> 'spirituality' is the study of how individuals and groups appropriate traditional Christian beliefs about God, the human person, creation, and their interrelationship, and then express these in worship, fundamental values and

---

[11]   Timothy Beardsworth, *A Sense of Perception* (Oxford: Religious Experience Research Unit, 1977), p. vii.

[12]   Richard Swinburne, *The Existence of God* (Oxford: Oxford University Press, 1977), p. 246.

life-style. Thus, spirituality is the whole of life viewed in terms of a conscious relationship with God, in Jesus Christ, through the indwelling of the Spirit and within the community of believers.[13]

The implication of this rather confused picture is that a generous understanding of terms should be expected, allowing speakers free imagination to create their own figures and themes, and only afterwards and with circumspection subjecting them to analysis. There is one caveat here: it makes little sense to consider religious experience apart from the context in which it occurred, and therefore the identity of the subject, particularly those considered marginal.

Ethics and the Wounded Storyteller

Explorations of the kind described in this book require that a keen critical eye be cast over the ethics of the entire research process, not least because theology demands that a level of ethical judgement be engaged. Without this sort of transparency, any conclusions risk an accusation of moral high ground, or worse of hypocrisy. Honesty is required in terms of the position and status of the researcher, the relationship between the researcher and researched, and the place of such data within an epistemological frame. I recognise already, however, that the statement of such objectives gives away to some extent the choice of such framing, but I will also show that this choice is in line with other narrative enquiry. There is also a risk of some sharp edges coming together between the social justice of liberation theologies and the postmodern analysis of stories. Some of these tensions are resolved in concluding chapters.

Given the importance of identity, my own position is described more fully as one of the characters in the research, whose (auto)biography appears later, forming one of the 12 participants. It is enough to say here that I recognise the inherent tensions arising between those who are homeless and a researcher whose house is automatically provided as a result of his job. In asking detailed and personal questions about someone's lifestory could I also be taking away from those who are already marginalised the little they have to call their own in furtherance of a research project and a publication? In a different context, this is summed up rather well in the title of Kay Hawe's educational article *Exploring the Educational Experience of Muslim Girls: tales Told to Tourists – Should the White Researcher Stay at Home?*[14] Her conclusion is not to remain indoors, but that the kind of ethical discussion envisaged now is a precondition of this work.

---

[13]   Philip Sheldrake, 'Spirituality as an Academic Discipline' in Adrian Thatcher (ed.), *Spirituality and the Curriculum* (London: Cassell, 1999), p. 59.

[14]   K.F. Haw, 'Exploring the Educational Experience of Muslim Girls: Tales Told to Tourists – Should the White Researcher Stay at Home?', *British Educational Research Journal* 22/3 (June 1996): 319–30.

One aspect of this is an awareness that issues of 'voice' and empowerment are far from simple, and that researchers have to learn to walk on uncomfortable ground. This includes the possibility of learning from those being studied, so that there are times 'that I need to be silent, listen, and take responsibility for learning'[15] and that 'we can choose to write so that the voice of those we write about is respected, strong and true'.[16] This is particularly the case here when some participants showed an almost overwhelming desire to tell their story, however painful, and when one interviewee (Caroline) was grateful that somebody was interested enough to ask at all. The responsibility and privilege of entering the world of another person is repaid by the researcher's conscious enjoyment of it: 'Take time along the way to stop and *hear* the roses'.[17]

This respectful process may also avoid further pathologisation of homeless people, in which their position as agents is always reduced to the status of victims. It equally prevents a reinforcement of the solidified category of 'the homeless', which, failing to recognise the variety of people and experiences which are designated by this phrase, adds further to the creation of an alien other.

One of the most comprehensive descriptions of narrative ethics is contained in Arthur Frank's *The Wounded Storyteller*. Although focused on the stories of illness, it is easy to read across from disease to homelessness, including Frank's own vulnerability as a cancer sufferer. He is keen to emphasise that he writes in 'postmodern times' and that one of its principle features is that 'Postmodern times are when the capacity for telling one's own story is reclaimed'.[18] He goes further to describe theoretically the origin of such tensions concerning voice: 'Post-colonialism in its most generalized form is the demand to speak rather than being spoken for and to represent oneself rather than being represented or, in the worst cases, rather than being effaced entirely'.[19] It is by stories that we can reclaim our sense of self, and make sense of the 'narrative wreckage' of our lives during or after illness, and by extension, in the disruption of homelessness.

Frank sees three story types: the restitution narrative which is primarily modernist in its assumptions about cure or return; the chaos narrative and the quest narrative. The chaos narrative describes several of the stories of homeless people which I heard; indeed, Frank refers to them in this section as the 'other', on whom society places the blame for such narratives, and so avoids the massive

---

[15] A. Dewar, Will All the Generic Women in Sport Please Stand Up? Challenges Facing Feminist Sport Sociology, *Quest* 45 (1993): 222.

[16] Lisa Richardson, *Writing Strategies: Reaching Diverse Audiences* (London: Sage, 1990), p. 38.

[17] Michael Patton, *How to Use Qualitative Methods in Evaluation* (London: Sage Publications, 1987), p. 143.

[18] Arthur W. Frank, *The Wounded Storyteller* (Chicago and London: Chicago University Press, 1995), p. 7.

[19] Ibid., p. 13.

social changes required to see the other as part of oneself. While the true chaos narrative may only be present in the silence of the gaps in conversation:

> the mystery of the chaos narrative is its opening to faith: 'Blessed are the poor in spirit, for theirs is the kingdom of heaven' (Matthew 5: 3). The greatest chaos stories are the first despairing verses of many of the Psalms; the Psalms' message seems to be that the redemption of faith can only begin in chaos. Tragically, those who are most destitute are often beyond such solace. For the poor in spirit to recognize their blessedness, some reflective space is required, and that is what poverty, like unremitting pain, denies.[20]

This takes us to the heart of this exploration, and anticipates if not some of the conclusions, then the questions which these homeless stories pose. But there are also quest narratives in these stories – the notion of finding a voice to express oneself and one's experiences, and doing this in a way which will witness to other people. Storytelling becomes an ethical act when it centres on being for the other, in an enterprise which goes beyond the Good Samaritan, or as Frank says: 'Persons live *for* others because their own lives as humans require living in that way'.[21] The telling and the listening mean that there is no longer a 'self-story' but only 'self-other-stories'.

Finally, it is important to state that this work was carried out with the informed consent of participants and of the staff in the centres concerned. Participants were guaranteed confidentiality and anonymity within the remit of a piece of academic writing, and this was recorded at the start of each interview. Pseudonyms have been used for names of participants, other named individuals, and for the particular hostels and centres to which interviewees refer.

Research in South West England

My curiosity and interest having been piqued by the event described in the Prologue, practical questions of how to conduct this research now came to the fore. This experience indicated that a qualitative method with its roots in narrative enquiry was a suitable tool to explore more fully what I had already felt. This approach answers the question: 'Is there a need and desire to personalise the evaluation process by using research methods that emphasize personal face-to-face contact ... [that] feel natural, informal and understandable to the participants?'[22] The fieldwork implied by such methods is personal, direct, and holistic in its approach to the human subject; it also risks methodological imprecision. For example, the

---

[20] Ibid., p. 114.

[21] Ibid., p. 15.

[22] Patton, *Qualitative Methods*, p. 41.

influence of the observer on the observed (the Heisenberg effect) is recognised as both a strength and a weakness, and the notion of reciprocity is also alluded to:

> Observational techniques can be an important part of the methodological repertoire of evaluators, but these techniques are never entirely separate from the individuality of the evaluator doing the fieldwork. The observer always puts his or her mark on the observations, just as the experience of doing fieldwork leaves it mark on the observer.[23]

The valorisation of human existence, both the ordinary and extraordinary, and the possibility of its transformation, makes narrative inquiry a suitable vehicle for the analysis of the lived experience of homeless people: 'Narrative inquirers study an individual's experience in the world, and through the study, seek ways of enriching and transforming that experience for themselves and others.[24]

A very early difficulty lay in access to the subject group, so that notwithstanding my initial experience at the drop-in hostel, it was easier to meet potential interviewees in another housing project. Similarly, the fuzzy definitions of homelessness itself were in part answered by recourse to existing organizations for homeless people. Aubyn House was at the time a purpose-built complex of small one-bed and two-bed flats, with office space and a communal sitting room, managed jointly between the local Anglican Church (where I was curate) and Stonham Housing Association. Its remit was to provide accommodation and support for vulnerable single homeless people, particularly those who had offended and those at risk of offending. It was not a direct access hostel; referral from another agency was needed, though self-referral was possible. The management committee was responsible for the strategic direction of the organization, including the employment of a project director and key workers. I had been a member of this committee for a number of years before approaching the staff with details of what I wished to do. My relationship with the project staff had been developed over the same period, so there was already a degree of trust between us. While I knew few of the residents particularly well, my relations with the staff enabled me to short-circuit the process of getting to know people, though I recognised inherent disadvantages.

By the time I started the process of interviews, I had moved house and job. It made sense to use a second location from a practical point of view, and to provide a wider base of study. The St Piran's Centre for homeless people was then a non-residential drop-in centre, offering hot meals, showers, laundry facilities, clean clothes and basic medical advice. The Centre opened in December 1994 as a part-conversion of a much older city centre church. Its essence was to provide informal support to all who came through its doors and specific advice (for example, on

---

[23]   Ibid., p. 106.

[24]   D. Jean Clandinin and Jerry Rosiek, 'Mapping a Landscape of Narrative Inquiry' in D. Jean Clandinin (ed.) *Handbook of Narrative Inquiry* (London: Sage, 2007), p. 42.

housing, on state benefits, on medical problems) if required or requested. The majority of people who used St Piran's arrived with a background of housing need, but some really sought company and a friendly environment. Following a six-week training course I worked for several months one morning per week as an ordinary volunteer (a floor worker) simply chatting to those who used the facilities. During this period, entry to the Centre was tightened to include only those in real housing need – those sleeping rough and those with no cooking facilities. The staff and other volunteers were aware of my wish to interview users of the Centre. Both Centres have subsequently changed considerably in their remit.

Using semi-structured interviews, I decided therefore to focus on homelessness and spirituality, and ask questions around each. I was particularly interested in how it felt to be homeless, as well as the events that led to homelessness; equally, what feelings were around the issues of spirituality rather than any theoretical discussion. I had four questions in my mind, therefore, which if not asked directly, I wished to cover in the course of the interview: how did you come to be homeless at some point in your life? What did that feel like? Can you describe anything to do with spirituality in connection with when you were homeless? What feelings were associated with these thoughts or experiences?

Given my different involvement in these two projects, the selection of interviewees differed somewhat. At Aubyn House I relied to a large degree on the advice of staff, who having understood the nature of what I wished to achieve, selected residents from a range of experience and age, and a balance of genders. At St Piran's, with first-hand experience of Centre users, I was much more in control of selection, but also used staff guidance about who might wish to speak to me. Since I erred on the side of caution in trying to build up trust before asking for an interview, this limited my pool of potential interviewees to those with whom I talked regularly, and those who used the Centre on a Friday. This is, however, consistent with my desire to maintain respect with the subject group. One indication that this approach was fruitful is perhaps that nobody refused my request for an interview. At St Piran's sustained observation of the users and of the functioning of the Centre was easier than at Aubyn House.

I interviewed eleven people in total, seven from Aubyn House, four from St Piran's; seven men and four women, in an age range of 20 to 60 years old.[25] The practice of the interview was largely similar in both locations. At Aubyn House we used the communal sitting room as a quiet, private place (we were interrupted once), while at St Piran's we used either an upstairs office or a private chapel in the main body of the church. Interviews were tape-recorded with permission of the interviewee, with two exceptions (Tim and Geoff) who preferred written notes.

---

[25]   In alphabetical order of subject the interviews were as follows. Age at the time of the interview is in brackets. These and other names in the text are pseudonyms: Caroline (20) Aubyn House, Charlie (44) Aubyn House, Danni (23) Aubyn House, Fran (25) Aubyn House, Geoff (54) St Piran's, Julie (45) Aubyn House, Jim (43) St Piran's, Marc (30) Aubyn House, Pete (60) Aubyn House, Richard (52) St Piran's, Tim (57) St Piran's.

In each case the interview was opened in a similar way: an introduction to the project, an overview of the kind of areas I was interested in talking about (what led them to Aubyn House or St Piran's, what the experience felt like, whether there was any spiritual insight or reflection they might wish to share in relation to this), and an assurance of confidentiality in terms of changing names and any identifiable reference when circulation of the material widened. My own angle was always clarified – I explained who I was and why I wished to do the interview.

It is in the nature of this kind of research to be criticised on the grounds of objectivity and loose methodology; for example relying (or partly relying) on staff to recommend suitable subjects interposes another layer between the researcher and the interviewee. A more serious theoretical weakness is the verification, or validation, of the data; in other words, the extent to which the analysis of the data can be trusted. The process of triangulation approaches data from different perspectives or with different theories, but part of the verification process is also to be honest about rival explanations and examples which contradict the main conclusions. The ideal would be to check out the results at various stages with those interviewed, but given the transient lives of homeless people, there was little practical possibility of this. An alternative was to use a group of key workers to comment on the findings, and add their own reflections. Two meetings were held at St Piran's with staff who had had the opportunity to review and comment upon the analysis of the research data.

The team broadly supported my analysis, but wished to add a sub-heading of education and literacy (or the absence of it) as an important factor which contributes to why people pass through a Centre like St Piran's. This was mentioned in passing by three interviewees here – Caroline, Geoff and Julie. A further study would probe more deeply into the significance of school within individual life histories. The team suggested starkly the absence of emotional relationships (the numbness suggested here by Charlie and Jim) and the denial of love, and also noted the detrimental effect such an emotional environment has on staff members, not least the average professional burn-out time of two years. One remark about the difficulty in picturing individuals led me to include the short life-history section. I am grateful for the answer to my question about the truthfulness of such clients – that complete confabulation was very rare – which reinforces the impression I had at the time of the interviews and later. Transformation or change, whether of the clients or their situations, was clearly important for all three workers:

> Given my Christian beliefs, I interpret this as meaning 'reform'. Jesus never left the needy person how he found them, for example when he healed the sick. It can be a series of very small steps and a slow process.

> I see this as like the question asked by Jesus, 'What do you want me to do for you?

The last word should go the deputy manager of the project who commented that, 'The group who come here are experts at being homeless'.

A second exploration of homeless people's experience was also undertaken, with more particular emphasis on biblical interpretation, or reading the Bible together. Susannah Cornwall and I used the Contextual Bible Study (CBS) model (as described by Gerald West and John Riches) with a group of homeless and vulnerably housed people at a soup kitchen in South West England.[26] After the initial phase of food and drink, participants were invited to join firstly some icebreaker activities and then to listen to a passage of scripture read aloud, after which they were asked for comments. Conversation and discussion followed. About one-fifth of regular users participated in these study sessions; 13 different people took part over the four study sessions; 11 agreed to their words being used; nobody took part in all four sessions. The passages were all chosen from St Luke's Gospel with an overall theme of justice and exclusion. While there was a little frustration when certain individuals attempted to dominate discussions, the tone overall was good-natured with moments of humour. Concentration and focus were maintained by limiting each study to about 40 minutes. Soup kitchen volunteers were present throughout, but contributed in a minimal way. The sessions were audio-recorded and transcribed.

While methodological issues were recognised concerning the transient nature of users of a soup kitchen and the coherence or not of a 'homeless community', nevertheless the process of CBS is considered valuable, especially with those whose voices and opinions may have been disregarded. There was some evident satisfaction during the sessions, and some participants commented that they had enjoyed them. Riches notes:

> What is striking for most people who encounter the [CBS] method for the first time is that it is a (largely) non-directive form of reading … It enables the group members to make the language and the imagery of the text their own, before they proceed to make connections between it and their own experience. For many this is empowering: people who have lost confidence in their ability to talk about their faith discover that the stories, images and ideas of the Bible can help to illumine their concerns and experience.[27]

Results and analysis of this exploration are found separately in Chapter 9.

[26]   See Susannah Cornwall and David Nixon, 'Readings from the Road: Contextual Bible Study with a Group of Homeless and Vulnerably-Housed People', *The Expository Times* 123/1 (2011): 12–19. John Riches, 'Worship Resources: Contextual Bible Study: Some Reflections', *The Expository Times* 117 (2005): 23–6. Gerald West and Ujamaa Centre staff, *Doing Contextual Bible Study: A Resource Manual* (The Ujamaa Centre for Biblical and Theological Community Development and Research [formerly the Institute for the Study of the Bible and Worker Ministry Project], 2007).

[27]   Riches, 'Worship Resources', p. 23.

This chapter has considered further elements in the pursuit of an analysis of the stories which homeless people tell. Collecting the stories of the vulnerable, even when sometimes there is hope and recovery, has something of the Pied Piper about it. The sense that the appeal of the tune in some way belies the reality of the intention – that these stories are now trapped and open to exploitation – leaves the collector with a sense of unease. *The Wounded Storyteller* does not assuage this, but confronts the moral dimension, allowing the researcher some leeway in the creation of space to allow these utterances of homeless people to be heard, valued and explored. Other writers quoted here from the domain of the social sciences give backing to an inter-disciplinary approach which respects the significance of the human story, its relationship to appropriate 'external' texts and the story of the researchers themselves. Rapport draws conclusions about the multiple world views which his conversations reveal; he delights in the diverse and eccentric, seeing these as akin to poetry in their expression of the human condition. Stuart deals with sensitive, personal material but engages with it in a strongly felt campaign. Jenkins too favours a more discursive, qualitative method than sociology of religion usually allows, with the reminder that poor people are marginalised again as research subjects. They lack the strength to determine and maintain their own value system.

Those who write about spirituality and religious experience tend to have a narrower focus than the one adopted here in respect of story. They have built their arguments around single or multiple experiences which can be designated by subject or researcher as religious; or an interpretation of the world has to be *consciously* in relationship with God, to use Sheldrake's word. This contrasts with the broad view of the previous chapters that we are already within God's story, but the telling and hearing of other human stories adds to knowledge of God and self, and has potential to change the world.

PART II
Results

He was despised, shunned by all, pain-racked and afflicted by disease; we despised him, we held him of no account, an object from which people turn away their eyes. Yet it was our afflictions he was bearing, our pain he endured, while we thought of him as smitten by God, struck down by disease and misery.

Isaiah 53: 3, 4

Chapter 4
Homeless Narratives in Context

I was homeless
    and you sent rockets to the moon
I was homeless
    and you built more office blocks
I was homeless
    and you said I did it on purpose
I was homeless
    and you sent me to yet another official
I was homeless
    and you said I had too many babies
I was homeless
    and you promised to pray for me
I was homeless
    and you said you must write to your MP

Poems from St Piran's

A theology of story affirms that one of the deepest routes into the meaning of God, of God's human creation, and of their mutual loving relationship is through the medium of narrative. It further affirms that story is performative in the changing and improving of the human condition, and that the stories told by Jesus are examples of this. The collection of stories of everyday life requires listening, observing, recording, and analysing, in a framework of loving respect, especially when these stories reveal the painful, hidden aspects of human life. Stories of homeless people are vulnerable stories, narratives of despair and weakness, and also of life, strength and humour; but they are also lives lived in context.

One example of a particular practical context is the Alcoholics Anonymous organisation about which interviewees spoke on several occasions. The social, cultural and legislative history of people without homes is a broader context, updated by an understanding of contemporary politics and policy around homelessness. The changing and problematic nature of how homelessness is defined is thereby disclosed. An international context is recognised by reference to the financial and social crisis in the West deriving from problems in the US housing market in 2007–2008.

The significance of context for the development of theology has been outlined earlier. Recently developed theologies of place by Philip Sheldrake, Tim Gorringe, John Inge, and David Brown inform a context for considering a theology of those who might be considered placeless, or whose place is open to critical contestation. A writer like Duncan Forrester calls for Christian theology to defend the cause of equality in UK society, an equality which would end the destructive poverty reflected in these stories. He demands that Christians be critically aware that they may do little more than pay lip-service to this aspect of their heritage.

Theological context is also at work when John Vincent describes how some aspects of Third World liberation theology are now present in Britain, but that a Church from the poor remains a more distant objective. Evidence here both supports and challenges his findings. A final example of theological context is a more uncomfortable one. It questions the legitimacy and honesty of First World theologians borrowing the language and techniques proper to a theology originating in the Third World. After all, it is First World theology which has contributed to the oppressive conditions from which Third World theologians seek liberation, both political and academic. Ched Myers unravels some of the problematic issues raised by the Latin American or South African theologian's question, 'How can you comfortable theologians write of God on our behalf given your upbringing and your affluence?' Myers calls this the pursuit of theology in the *locus imperii*, the 'place of empire'. The tented cities of the Occupy protests in 2011 and 2012 may be an attempt to answer this question in the context of First World austerity. There is also personal context whereby the life experiences of some of the theologians cited here bear directly on their theology; and it is around the motif of story that Forrester and Myers formulate their ideas.

Scroungers and Scrimshankers:
A Brief History of Homelessness and Housing

In sharp contrast to my desire to respect research subjects whose background is different to mine, it was possible for a Conservative MP as late as 1977 to describe the homeless as 'scroungers and scrimshankers' during discussion of the proposed Housing (Homeless Persons) Act of the same year.[1] Such emotive language is hardly shocking in public debate, for it was not until the late 1960s that serious consideration was given to challenging the commonly held view that those who were homeless had chosen to be so to escape the responsibility of earning a living and maintaining a house. Structural explanations for homelessness – that there were underlying social and economic reasons why people did not access satisfactory housing or were unable to provide a home for themselves – gained ground only slowly. It is from this earlier period that we have the classic picture of a down-and-out, a tramp, a bum, whose life is immortalised albeit in a relatively sympathetic manner by George Orwell:

---

[1]   See R. Burrows, N. Pleace and D. Quilgars (eds), *Homelessness and Social Policy* (London and New York: Routledge, 1997).

At about a quarter to six the Irishman led me to the spike. It was a grim, smoky yellow cube of brick, standing in the corner of the workhouse grounds. With its rows of tiny, barred windows, and a high wall and iron gates separating it from the road, it looked much like a prison. Already a long queue of ragged men had formed up, waiting for the gates to open. They were of all kinds and ages, the youngest a fresh-faced boy of sixteen, the oldest a doubled-up toothless mummy of seventy-five. Some were hardened tramps, recognisable by their sticks and billies and dust-darkened faces; some were factory hands out of work, some agricultural labourers, one a clerk in collar and tie, two certainly imbeciles. Seen in the mass, lounging there, they were a disgusting sight; nothing villainous or dangerous, but a graceless, mangy crew, nearly all ragged and palpably underfed. They were friendly, however, and asked no questions. Many offered me tobacco – cigarette ends that is.[2]

The 1563 Poor Law with its emphasis on parish responsibility was amended in 1834 to establish a system of workhouses which were by design to provide less in the way of conditions than might be possible for the poorest wage earner. Sexes were separated, families divided, unmarked paupers' graves were dug. A Royal Commission of 1905–1909 summarised the principle of 'less eligibility': 'The hanger-on should be lower than him on whom he hangs'.[3] When the Poor Law authorities were made responsible for the housing of those who were victims of bombings in 1939, the inadequacy of such arrangements became clearer. The National Assistance Act of 1948 moved the administration of temporary housing to local authorities, marking the final repeal of nearly four centuries of Poor Law provision. However, since the working experience of those responsible for the new system derived mostly from the former arrangements, actual practice for homeless people remained almost unchanged.

It was only in the 1970s that pressure for change really grew, reflected in the previous decade by the foundation of the charity Shelter and epitomised by the 1966 film *Cathy Come Home*. The result was the Housing (Homeless Persons) Act 1977, which recognised that homelessness was essentially a housing problem, and gave to local authorities statutory duties to provide accommodation in certain circumstances. This Act became Part III of the Housing Act 1985. While recognising the considerable advances since 1948, these pieces of legislation maintained the distinctions of earlier generations. Instead of 'deserving' and 'undeserving poor' homeless people were only entitled to secure, permanent housing if they were deemed to be homeless by virtue of the legislation, in priority need, were not

---

[2] George Orwell, *Down and Out in Paris and London* (Harmondsworth: Penguin, 1987), p. 127. First published by Gollancz, 1933.

[3] Bryan Glastonbury, *Homeless Near a Thousand Homes* (London: Allen & Unwin, 1971), p. 28.

intentionally homeless and had some local connection.[4] Single homeless people, and families without dependants were automatically excluded unless they were 'vulnerable'.

This Act remained in force until 1996, when Part III became a very different Part VII of the Housing Act 1996. The tests of priority remained the same, but those of intentionality and eligibility were strengthened. Under accusations of 'queue-jumping' by homeless people seeking social housing, accommodation was now only provided in hostels and in the private rented sector. Council housing was only available through the normal waiting list. The biggest change was a move from statutory provision of permanent accommodation to temporary housing, potentially for a maximum of two years. Lowe concludes:

> Part VII of the Housing Act 1996 is an historical throwback. Under the new system the punitive attitude of the Poor Law workhouse is re-kindled in modern guise as the hostels and residual private rental accommodation to which homeless families will now be destined, and with no certainty of long-term help. More even than this is the fact that the language and prejudices of the Poor Law (truthfully never far from the 1977 system) are set to recover the lost ground of twenty years.[5]

Throughout this period, there were widely differing interpretations of the Code of Guidance, with, for example Plymouth, accepting 98 per cent of applicants in 1987. Nationally, numbers of those considered homeless rose considerably: in 1976, 33,000; 1978, 53,100; 1992, 184,000.[6] The Homelessness Act (2002) places a responsibility on local authorities to respond to enquiries in a given time period (33 days), with assessment made on five criteria familiar from previous legislation: eligibility, made more complicated by the probable exclusion of asylum seekers; homeless or threatened with homelessness within 28 days (various definitions); a system of priority need, with unclear definitions of vulnerability; intentionality; and a local connection. Only those in priority need are entitled to temporary accommodation provided by the local authority, with assistance to move thereafter.[7]

---

[4]   By the 1985 Act the following persons are defined as having a priority need:
A person with a dependent child or [who] is pregnant.
A person who may be vulnerable on account of their age, mental illness, handicap, physical disability or other special reasons.
Homeless in an emergency, for example fire, flood, and so on.
[5]   Burrows, Pleace and Quilgars, *Homelessness*, p. 34.
[6]   Gerald Daly, *Homeless, Policies, and Lives on the Street* (London and New York: Routledge, 1996), p. 85.
[7]   Cumbria Action for Social Support (CASS), 'A Guide to the Homelessness Act, 2002' (2011). Available at: http://www.cass-cumbria.co.uk/guide-homelessness-act-2002 (accessed 26 January 2012).

In addition, the Social Security Act of 1986 introduced the payment of Housing Benefit in arrears and raised the age of an eligible claimant from 16 to 18. The Rough Sleepers Initiative (1990) aimed to reduce the numbers of homeless and rough sleepers. It was extended beyond London in 1993 and came to the South West in 1996. It was replaced in 1999 by the Homelessness Action Programme which focused on resettlement work and preventative work with vulnerable adults. A continuing focus on rough sleepers by Tony Blair in 1998 witnessed a national reduction from more than 1,800 to 500 by 2007, but the charity Crisis commented that the 'hidden homeless' amounted to a figure nearer 400,000. The number of those defined as statutorily homeless in England at the end of 2011 had increased by 18 per cent to 48,920 compared to the previous year.[8]

Proposals by the Conservative Liberal Coalition Government in the Localism Bill of 2011 will further affect housing provisions in Great Britain, with potentially serious consequences for homeless people. These include a possible limited length tenancy for occupation of social housing, followed by a review; raising social rents to nearer 80 per cent of market rents; capping housing benefit (now called Local Housing Allowance) for certain private rented properties; and greater use by local authorities of the private rented sector. Critics allude to two obvious consequences: a disincentive to improve family income if this entails a forced move of house; and in London and other expensive cities in the south of England, a further 'spatial polarisation' as certain areas become wholly unaffordable by the majority of the population. These factors are exacerbated by more general reductions in government expenditure on welfare following the financial crisis of 2008, and the recession which ensued.

These present proposals reflect two distinct, but connected, trends in housing policy evident since the mid twentieth century. The first is that (with a few exceptions) the market is considered the best provider of housing, and therefore secondly, that a process of 'residualisation' is almost inevitable, that is, that non-market housing is only provided for the most needy. The most common way of analysing housing has been on the basis of tenure, but an alternative lens is to examine how a capitalist market operates. A third theme considers the dynamic of continuity and change. Through most of the post-War period, tenure was for the most part owner occupation, local authority rented, and privately rented. Only in the 1990s did the term 'social rented sector' come into common usage to reflect a mixed economy of local authority and housing association ownership. The original tenants of local authority housing were better-off, mostly white, traditional working-class families, with the less well-off in the poorer quality private rented sector. From the 1970s a process of residualisation began, with a decline in private renting forcing these tenants into the public sector, while better-off families were becoming owners. Other factors contributed to these changes: a general improvement in income and living standards, an increase in women in

---

8   Shelter. Available at: http://england.shelter.org.uk/news/march_2012/homelessness_up_18 (accessed 2 April 2012).

the labour market, an increase in divorce and separate living, a growth in total population, and the recognition of housing for previously overlooked groups like single mothers, the elderly and BME (black and minority ethnic) people. These changes were crystallised in the Right to Buy legislation of 1980.

This quintessentially Thatcherite privatisation policy sold around 1 million council houses in the period 1980–88, and in the period 1980–86 raised more receipts than all the other privatisations together. It reflected both a distrust of local authorities per se, who moved from being seen as the solution to housing problems to their source, as well as a belief in the market, with post 1979 'a particularly aggressive intensification of this view'.[9] The contemporary rhetoric emphasised the merits and virtues of home ownership and denigrated the provision of public housing. While not the cause of residualisation, this policy certainly contributed to its becoming chronic, so that the majority of these tenants are now society's most vulnerable, and as a result it is a tenure most often linked to poverty and social exclusion. Peter Malpas comments that for the poorest, 'Having been excluded from social renting, they are now excluded by it'.[10] While the specific Right to Buy policy was introduced by a Conservative government, New Labour also embraced such changes as the transfer of local authority housing to housing associations, thus also continuing a policy of suspicion towards the local. There remains, however, the tension between the allocation of a scarce resource to the most vulnerable, and the problems which ensue from a concentration of people with educational, health and social needs. The Devonport local regeneration partnership (one of the 39 New Deal for Communities programmes) sought to address this by the demolition of old and tired council flats, and the introduction of mixed tenure developments including owner occupied housing, socially rented and part ownership. One government initiative was ironically trying to correct the problems caused by another.

In a market based analysis, the perspective of the consumer (or occupier) is compared to that of the producer. House builders, the production and retail of white goods and the DIY sector are major components of the British economy, so that there is an arguable government role in ensuring the profitability of this industry. It was only perhaps in the need for a rapid expansion of housing post-War when the private sector could not respond sufficiently that serious government support for public provision was forthcoming. Housing as part of the Welfare State settlement was always more questionable than the inclusion of education or health. Yet market orientated systems of distribution of such a 'basic determinant of well-being' as housing (with their in-built flexibility and insecurity) reveal and contribute to a new set of inequalities. Thus within a dynamic of continuity and change, despite many apparent shifts and manoeuvres, the dominant theme of the last half century has been to balance the population's housing need with sector

---

[9]   Peter Malpas, *Housing and the Welfare State* (Basingstoke: Palgrave Macmillan, 2005), p. 110.

[10]   Malpas, *Housing*, p. 183.

profitability, where state invention becomes ever more restricted to those who cannot provide homes for themselves. The majority of citizens have to rely on the market.

The charity Plymouth Access to Housing (PATH) provides one example of how homelessness is managed at a local level. Their remit includes work with rough sleepers, tenancy and rental support and advice, engagement with refugees, ex-offenders and those with mental health issues.[11] Having presented at PATH and registered as a homeless person, a three-stage process is initiated. There is a maximum stay of four or six weeks at two direct access hostels (Open Doors and The Victory) during which an assessment is made. Stage two is admission to the Salvation Army's hostel for a maximum of two years, funded by the Supporting People programme (national government funding from the Department of Communities and Local Government, locally administered). This hostel has 62 individual rooms for men, of which 60 are part of this funded scheme, and two are retained for emergencies and non-funded places. There is also the possibility of 'safe sleep' in a sitting room where occupants are provided with a box containing pillows and blankets, and breakfast vouchers are provided. There is no access during the day to the rest of the premises. The third stage is a supported tenancy in one of three accommodation units in Plymouth. A conversation with a manager at the local Salvation Army hostel reports that everybody is almost always working to maximum capacity.

This local snapshot reflects the national initiatives described earlier concerned principally with sleeping on the streets. But such funding comes with conditions, is evidence-based and time limited. Two years is a relatively short time to address chaotic lives, and while assessment is now more focused, there was at one time a possibility that the most needy people were not accepted because they might not contribute to a successful assessment. Prison was designated a bad outcome in funding terms, as was the death of a service user. (I suppose that death could hardly be regarded as a good outcome, but more importantly, the limits of assessment regimes are revealed starkly and blackly.) One advantage, however, of time restrictions is to address the risk of institutionalization in hostels run by organisations like the Salvation Army; on the other hand the need for long-term supported housing for some people is further underlined. The Salvation Army believes that its distinctive faith-based ethos, while challenging to some residents at first, leads to a more hopeful and forgiving regard for homeless people, which contributes to the success of changing lives.

---

[11] Plymouth Access to Housing. Available at: www.plymouthpath.org (accessed 28 May 2012).

Housing and the Financial Crisis of 2008: An International Perspective

It is instructive to look back to the banking crisis of 2008 not simply because of its origins in the US housing market, but because it reveals what may happen when residential property is fully commodified in an almost unregulated market. While these events happened in America, the ethical questions which arise are more universal; such events may also hold up a mirror to what is happening currently in the UK.

The collapse of the technology bubble in 2000–2002 and the consequent lowering of US interest rates led almost inevitably, perhaps deliberately, to a boom in domestic consumption and in real estate prices. Deregulation in the financial sector was exemplified by the repeal in 1999 of the Glass-Steagall Act separating retail from investment banking, and large institutions knowing that they were 'too big to fail' took greater risks. The notion of 'moral hazard' which was applied to individuals (that is, the concept that the incentive to repay is weakened if you know that you will be rescued) was reversed for the banking industry. A third factor was a failure to understand the extent of inter-connectedness of property markets across the US, and of financial institutions across the world.

Banks manufactured ever more complex mortgage products with a maximisation of fees which would benefit executives whatever happened to the underlying property and property owner. Such products included 100 per cent non-recourse mortgages (if there was a default, debts only applied to the property itself, and not to other assets), introductory low rates demanding a later re-financing and further fees, 'liar loans' for which proof of income was not required (known in the UK as self-certified loans). These were often sold to those who may never have owned property previously, and whose financial circumstances were potentially shaky. Such mortgages attracted the now infamous moniker of subprime. They were based on two false assumptions, fully supported by the public rhetoric in favour of owner occupation: the promise of constantly increasing prices, and the easy availability of credit. Mortgage holders were encouraged by low interest rates to borrow more to finance further retail consumption, and banks sold bundles of loans (securitised products) imagining that they were spreading risk rather than contagion. The complexity of such products was also designed to bypass regulation. The warning signs were ignored when there was a peculiar alignment of interest – all parties including those holding the mortgage, those selling the mortgage, those selling on derivative mortgage products, were encouraged to take on the biggest loan possible and therefore the greatest risk. But this was entirely dependent on the 'greater fool theory', as near as possible to a legal Ponzi scheme, a kind of reverse pass-the-parcel.

When the music stopped, perhaps with the collapse of the bank Lehman Brothers in 2008 (the biggest bankruptcy in American history), the aphorism attributed to Warren Buffet came true: 'It's only when the tide goes out that you learn who's been swimming naked'. The catastrophe was not simply economic but social, as the loss of a house represented a loss of future for retirement or children's education, above all the loss of the American Dream. Already in 2007 there had been 1.3 million property foreclosures, by 2009 15.2 million US mortgages were in negative equity ('underwater') about one third of all mortgages, which had reduced by 2010 to about one quarter. Prices had declined by 30 per cent from their peak, and by 50 per cent in some areas. By the end of this cycle, home ownership will be lower than at the start. Joseph Stiglitz commented in 2009 that the UK system is yet more reliant on its financial and property sector than the US, and that he reckons on a possible contraction of consumption of 10 per cent.[12] The Royal Bank of Scotland became Europe's biggest bank, but also saw the world's largest financial losses in 2008. America had exported its recession just as it has exported its market philosophy.

Such events provide an opportunity for reflection and reckoning about the kind of society people want, with the suggestion that markets have not simply shaped the economy, but in doing so have shaped society, and therefore individual behaviour. In contrast to solving economic problems, too little attention has been paid to the 'moral deficit' which has also been revealed; that 'financial institutions discovered that there was money at the bottom of the pyramid and did everything they could within the law (and many went beyond the law) to move it towards the top'.[13] The spirit of rugged American individualism manifest in financial markets took (and takes) little account of its effect on others, being expert at gaining credit for success, but denying responsibility for failure. Such focus on the individual can lead to a breakdown of community and the erosion of trust, yet ironically the need for trust was never more apparent than when the credit systems froze over. Stiglitz is not overly optimistic about the future, seeing that the moment for a new kind of social contract may have passed without the necessary reforms in place, and that Wall Street and Main Street (both non-financial corporations and workers) are further apart, with an ability to solve problems thereby diminished.

The recognition that globalisation, (characterised loosely to include privatisation, free trade and deregulation) has an effect on the well-being of communities is in many ways self-evident; less so, is that homelessness is a by-product of such processes. Policies on housing and homelessness are choices, and therefore ideologically and politically motivated. Gerald Daly writes: 'A central unifying concept is the notion of global economic shifts and their reflection in political decisions to limit social spending'.[14] Sociological research enquires how such decisions about homeless people are made by reference to classifications and language attributed to different groups, how such attributions arise and how they in turn reconstitute and reinforce these same ideologies. The notion of 'the homeless' as a homogeneous group which can then be distanced from everybody else with an accumulation of other negative epithets is summarised thus:

---

[12]   Joseph Stiglitz, *Freefall Free Markets and the Sinking of the Global Economy* (London: Penguin, 2010), p. 292.

[13]   Stiglitz, *Freefall*, p. 279.

[14]   Daly, *Homeless*, p. 5.

'They' become an amorphous, remote, alien mass lacking indivisibility or even humanity. A sense of community is lost. Definitions and descriptions of 'the homeless' expose our personal values and beliefs, especially when homelessness is characterized by what it is not.[15]

A significant flaw in the agenda around homelessness, including attempts to formulate policies is the lack of engagement with homeless people themselves, so that public officials, voluntary and statutory agencies feel able to speak on behalf of homeless people in 'a web of interdependent communities based on self-interest' – a kind of homelessness industry. Stories of homeless people are routinely sidelined or ignored, and the question of contextual knowledge dodged. It is easier to present simple cause-and-effect linear relationships than to examine the complex processes connecting economic change, deinstitutionalization (that is, the closing of long stay hospitals and the placing of former patients in the community), national and international demographic shifts and marginalisation. A closed and orderly system may lend itself to politically acceptable quick solutions but if it bears little connection to the alternate reality of homeless people, it will be considerably less effective. Instead, a dynamic social model which respects the context of life on the streets begins to answer the epistemological issues raised by homelessness. However, to rely overmuch on extensive quotations from homeless people themselves may be to pass over underlying structural problems within wider society. The same tension underpins this theological endeavour, with the added factor of theology's own preference to start from the abstract. Yet without a preference for the stories of homeless people, albeit with a critical reading attached, the cycle of marginalisation will never be broken.

Theologies of Place and Space

A relatively recent development theologically has been the exploration of place and space. The extent to which space has become a commodified and therefore contested concept is relevant here, especially when joined to a consideration of those deemed out of place or placeless. John Inge suggests an Enlightenment movement from the particularity of place to the abstraction of space, matched by a growing theological preference for the abstract over the particular. Linked to the development of capitalist economies during the same period of the eighteenth century, and especially to its recent intensification, a growing divide is witnessed between the wealthy and the poor in terms of place and space. While the better-off appreciate the benefits of abstract space as expatriates working for multinational corporations, the refugee or migrant worker faces the same phenomenon as

---

[15]   Ibid., p. 8.

a malign loss of place and dislocation from the familiar.[16] Uncertainty of place is a contemporary practical issue for governments and communities faced with desperate population flows from global south to north, as well as an intellectual one with postmodernity implying a crisis of place: we no longer know where we are individually, socially and relationally. The traditional 'knowing one's place' has given way to the discomfort of shifting sands, as place is discovered as a plural concept constructed by politics and power. If mobility is preferred over stability in this spatial economy, then such freedoms tend to be restricted to those with access to money and education. Groups marginalised by poverty or age become 'stuck' rather than stable. They face increasing fragmentation, and the growth of non-places described by Marc Augé: supermarkets, airports, hotels, motorways, televisions and computers.[17]

The sharp end in Western society of being out of place is to be without a home. Homelessness and homeless people reveal much about the conceptual construction of both place and home which is often taken for granted. Tim Creswell confirms place as an epistemological factor, given how place frames our way of understanding and seeing the world, so that those without place are viewed in a specific way: 'Homelessness is very much defined by a certain kind of disconnection from particular forms of place'.[18] Home is frequently an idealised form of place, loaded with ideological and moral baggage: bricks and mortar carrying contested ideas about heteronormative families, employment and secure futures. As a category which tends to define normality, its opposite – homelessness – is sometimes used as a term of abuse for those who fail to conform to an ever-narrowing definition of social acceptability. Homelessness also needs to be understood in relation to the places in which it is situated, so that periodic political attempts to 'clean up' certain city areas are intimately linked to neo-liberal ideas: 'Homelessness is produced through the push to reconstruct the city as a cohesive place according to middle class/elite values'.[19] Human beings are reduced to the level of detritus to be removed like any other litter.

An alternative view is to remap the city in terms of homeless people, and discover the 'performative and affective geographies' that emerge.[20] Not only are certain spaces determined as prime (for example, shopping centres and retail space where homeless people are often deliberately excluded) or marginal, but also as disciplinary/regulated space (for example where homelessness services are provided) or unregulated. Homeless people move between these spaces in a fairly

---

[16]   John Inge, *A Christian Theology of Place* (Aldershot: Ashgate Publishing, 2003), p. 13.
[17]   Marc Augé, *Non-Places: Introduction to an Anthropology of Supermodernity* (English translation. London/New York: Verso, 1997).
[18]   Tim Creswell, *Place: A Short Introduction* (Oxford: Blackwell, 2004), p. 111.
[19]   Ibid., p. 113.
[20]   Paul Cloke, Jon May and Sarah Johnsen, 'Performativity and Affect in the Homeless City', *Environment and Planning D: Society and Space* 26 (2008): 241–63.

predictable rational way, but also in a non-rational, affective mode, finding 'places of care, generosity, hope, charity, fun, and anger'.[21] This second mapping may enable a re-inscription or re-reading of the homeless city to give a fuller and richer picture of both the city and homeless people.

A theological response to concepts of place and space frames the more specific exploration of homelessness which is the subject of this book. Initially, there is a call by theologians for a greater recognition of how cultural and social shifts have changed the meaning of these concepts. They wish to return theology to the particular away from the abstract, or as Tim Gorringe phrases it, away from the 'great tradition' towards the 'little tradition'.[22] The way in which narrative gives shape and meaning to place is also significant, so that easy narratives may be eschewed and alternatives adopted, especially those which reflect a multiplicity of voices:

> It is only by enabling alternative stories to be heard that an elitist 'history' may be prised open to offer an entry point for the oppressed who have otherwise been excluded from the history of public spaces.[23]

The reading of scripture (especially stories about or told by Jesus) in different places and with different audiences opens the potential to hear different interpretations of the familiar, away from the 'scribal classes' towards a more popular voice. Louise Lawrence recommends Contextual Bible Study as a 'transformative ritual' which provides tools to discover new identities and hidden transcripts.[24] Similarly, the reading of place as text opens the possibility of re-reading with homeless people as main protagonists rather than as marginal players.[25] Lastly, David Brown encourages the re-enchantment of place and the re-invigoration of the sacramental, in other words the possibility of encountering God in unlikely places. He comments that the Church has made a serious mistake in withdrawing from large areas of human experience, and although God speaks only faintly outside traditional revelation, yet the potential to meet God in the modern city still remains.[26]

---

[21]   Cloke, 'Performativity', p. 245.

[22]   T.J. Gorringe, *A Theology of the Built Environment* (Cambridge: Cambridge University Press, 2002), p. 9.

[23]   Philip Sheldrake, *Spaces for the Sacred* (London: SCM Press, 2001), p. 19.

[24]   Louise Lawrence, *The Word in Place: Reading the New Testament in Contemporary Contexts* (London: SCM, 2009), p. 122.

[25]   See Chapter 9.

[26]   David Brown, *God and Enchantment of Place* (Oxford: Oxford University Press, 2004).

Theologies of Equality

In the light of liberation theology rooted in the experiences, reflections and sociopolitical reality of South America, South Africa and the Global South, theologians situated in the affluent North are faced with questions of legitimacy and authenticity: how to do liberation theology (Third World Theology) in the First World. A process common to several theologians seems to begin with the kind of personal experience which is replicated at the start of this book. Reflection on such an experience leads naturally to look at other stories, particularly the stories told by Jesus. For example, the biblical leitmotif for Ched Myers is the story of Peter in the Courtyard of the High Priest (Mark 14: 54ff). This represents those First World Christians, who when confronted with oppression at home and abroad and their complicity in it, take refuge in Denial (Myers' capital): 'I neither know nor understand what you mean' (14: 68). Christians are torn like Peter between being with Jesus in the cells or remaining with the police and soldiers in the courtyard.

> Given the benefit of the doubt, we love Jesus and have vowed, perhaps even stridently, to follow him. We have recognised him as Messiah – it is just that we don't understand what that really means. Of course, we First World Christians are more comfortable in the Palace Courtyard than Peter could ever have been. We participate obediently in its political mechanisms (and machinations). Presidents and military leaders sit in our churches.[27]

His response to Denial is to recommend an interrogatory theology, based on an image of Jesus who questions both his contemporary world and its religious culture. Mark's gospel reflects a wide range of questions to, by or about Jesus, so that Jesus is not a sage of the ancient world but an 'interlocutor of reality'. The central example of this stance is Jesus' question to his disciples at Caesarea Philippi about his own identity (8: 27). In their turn the disciples begin to ask questions, the interlocutees become interlocutors. The Church, then, is potentially empowered to question all authority, but prefers a different bargain.

> Mark's gospel, the prototype of Christian narrative theology, suggests that the church's own theological discourse should also be interrogatory. But if we wish to discover such a discourse, our reconstructive task is formidable, for ecclesial doctrine long ago buried the voice of Jesus the Interlocutor.[28]

Denial of the voice of the poor is reinforced by two Faustian pacts which the Church and theology have entered into. The older one dates back to Constantine, when Jesus of the poor is replaced by the Jesus of the throne – Christians take on the trappings of empire. A more recent bargain underpins our current ambivalence

---

[27] Ched Myers, *Who Will Roll Away the Stone?* (Maryknoll, NY: Orbis, 1994), p. 11.
[28] Myers, *Stone*, p. 29.

between remaining with Jesus or standing outside in the Courtyard. Myers sees that Christian theology has conceded authority over the public sphere to the state (secular capitalism) in the hopes of retaining a modicum of authority over the private sphere. The Church's response to an issue like homelessness is thus impoverished, reduced to a commentary on private morality.

A theology which interrogates is also the response of Duncan Forrester to the parable of the Good Samaritan, for the lawyer's academic question 'Who is my neighbour?' is answered by Jesus with a story from daily life. This shift from abstraction to the existential, from theory to concrete, is a model set up by Jesus for how Christians should live in any age. Forrester's particular daily experience of meeting a leper (Munuswamy) on the way to the South Indian college where he is teaching brings to mind the chasm of equality described by the parable of Lazarus and Dives in Luke's Gospel. Forrester reacts to this by wishing to present 'the human meaning of inequality'. He supports approaches which favour hearing the voices of the victims of poverty, and which privilege feelings and emotions as 'vital ingredients of meaning alongside the statistics and sharp social analysis'. His précis of what inequality means on a human scale foreshadows what is revealed by interviews with homeless people. 'The human meaning of inequality is thus often experienced as oppression and exploitation, powerlessness and the destruction of relationships. It is often an experience of shame and humiliation'.[29] By contrast, a Christian commitment to equality derives from God's affirmation of each human being as of infinite and therefore equal worth, irrespective of differences of colour, gender, social class and so on. His battle cry is for a theology which is less elegant than people centred, more able to hear the stories of the poor than represent the interests of the powerful:

> Theology has a responsibility to represent Munuswamy to the intellectual and political 'powers', to speak for him in situations where his voice is not heard, where he cannot as yet speak for himself. Munuswamy should haunt these powers as he haunts me. This kind of theology is rooted in the real world and its issues and its suffering. It is intended to arouse conviction and lead to action. It cares for people more than for intellectual coherence, or literary elegance, or academic respectability.[30]

The trajectory of this interrogatory theology follows two paths; the first is to repudiate the pacts to which Myers refers and insist that theology re-enters the public realm. The image of Jesus as the man who asks questions about society is emphasised. The second is to understand that theology needs to move from the centre to the periphery, just as the ministry of Jesus, was for the most part not at the metropolitan centre of Israel, but at its margins, both geographically and anthropologically. Myers pursues these ideas via the image of the Temple,

---

[29]   Duncan Forrester, *On Human Worth* (London: SCM Press, 2001), p. 20.
[30]   Forrester, *Human Worth*, p. 72.

God's House, at which the disciples marvel, but Jesus intends to deconstruct (13: 1f). The metaphor of a house needing to be built afresh stands for the difficult desire of First World Christians to bridge the gulf which separates them from their Third World neighbours.[31]

> The architecture of entitlement prevents us from encountering what is 'on the other side'. Yet if we are ever to be motivated to join Jesus in the deconstructive struggle, it will be because we have seen and been moved by the human faces of those condemned by the *locus imperii* to live on the other side of those walls.[32]

Such separation risks being compounded by two further factors. For the First World Christian, the systems of oppression which operate against poor people are invisible, but they are only too obvious for poor people themselves (see, for example, Danni's experience of trying to gain a tenancy). Secondly, witness the irony that many churches spend more time, money, and energy with poor overseas communities than with the communities in their own locality.[33] Like Rayan's imperative to follow Jesus 'outside the camp', Myers likens crossing this divide to the journey made by Jesus across the sea of Galilee, going 'to the other side' in Mark 4: 35. As I attempt to demonstrate my own vulnerability as one of the life histories included here, so Myers talks of his drawing closer to the poor as merely an 'ap-proximation' since he can never be wholly identified as poor. He charts his own journey from the comfortable Los Angeles of childhood to the 'Latino barrio' of committed adulthood, only a few miles away, via a number of expeditions overseas. He remarks that 'I had to travel a long way to overcome four miles of distance'.[34] The motif of journey is continued via the image of the empty tomb – Jesus has already gone ahead of them to Galilee where the disciples are to follow. The 'site and strategy' for doing theology is firmly returned to our own location, providing the same short/long journey is undertaken in the company of Jesus.

Liberation theology in the UK remains, however, in the shadows. Explanations for this include a virtual absence of popular consciousness among poorer people because of their minority status (perhaps 15 per cent) and their fragmentation into smaller, almost independent groups (for example poor whites, single parents,

---

[31] In a footnote on p. 39 Myers clarifies his terms. The First World contains all those characterised by 'entitlement' so will exclude, for example, poor whites. The Third World (whether situated in the USA or Africa) contains those who are structurally marginalised, but excludes elites of colour.

[32] Myers, *Stone*, p. 202.

[33] Myers calls this 'hypermetropic solidarity' and explains it by suggesting that abroad is exotic and help is appreciated, by contrast with home which is suspicious and more challenging of our own preconceptions. I remember a teacher at a girls' independent school in Plymouth being very pleased with an overseas charity collection. The school was situated in the same inner city parish as The Victory and Aubyn House housing projects referred to here, though there seemed to be little contact between the school and the local area.

[34] Myers, *Stone*, p. 224.

redundant workers, Afro-Caribbeans, and so on). Poor people tend not read the Bible, which is seen as the province of the middle classes and divorced from the concept of human freedom. There is little popular movement for liberation where political parties, even of the left, are largely middle-class and participation is expensive. Lastly, there is no specific church of the poor, since 'the Christian story is appropriated by the ruling powers' and effectively policed by the denominations. John Vincent hopes that 'there is a submerged history of popular Christianity somewhere: but its relics are hardly visible today'.[35] The evidence of these stories will be seen to support such an analysis. Popular Christianity is also reflected in these texts, but the extent to which it is in fact helpful to those who profess such beliefs and ideas is discussed later. Vincent concludes that British liberation theology is 'from the poor' inasmuch as it touches their situations, even though they are rarely its main advocates; and 'alongside the poor' when those who do create this theology are middle-class theologians who live and work with poor people, particularly in the inner cities. More recently, the Church of England's disagreements about women's ordination to the episcopate and the place in the Church of gay and lesbian people have tended to focus energy internally, while at the same time exacerbating external issues of credibility and relevance. There has been less room for issues of social justice, especially concerning social marginalisation. A renewed emphasis on the concept of mission is welcome, but this is often constructed around church attendance and financial survival; the link between mission and social justice has been weakened, and God's mission to the world (and especially to the poor) has been decentred by the role of the Church in and of itself.

Centres for people without homes in South West England are exactly the right location, therefore, from which to discover and create theology. This chapter seeks to draw attention to the personal, political, economic and theological context which lies behind the specific life histories which now follow. Homelessness and housing policy in the UK is perceived as primarily focused around capitalist markets rather than individual or societal needs, apart from a restricted social rented sector. Recent US experience suggests what is possible if commodification is taken a stage further, and how the implosion of this market has global repercussions. Moral hazards and moral deficits require further theological explication. Theologies of place highlight the constructed and contested nature of place, and the particular fate of those deemed by others as placeless or out of place. Nevertheless it is the stories told by and of these people, and their re-interpretation of both city and scripture which may enliven understanding of God. Forrester and his espousal of Christian equality reclaims some of the public domain which Myers accuses the Church and theology of having sold. In doing so he answers in part the ethical question of 'armchair liberation theology'.

---

[35]   John Vincent, 'Liberation Theology in Britain, 1970–1995' in Christopher Rowland and John Vincent (eds), *Liberation Theology UK* (Sheffield: Urban Theology Unit, 1995), pp. 24–5.

Vincent, too, while describing certain characteristics of Third World theology now present in Britain, also gives to the theologian the task of enunciating creative thinking on behalf of the poor. Nowhere is this more true than in suggesting renewed images of Jesus which accompany us from the centre to the periphery, asking awkward questions about where our real commitment lies. Lastly, it is the vehicle of story again which inspires: the sight of Munuswamy begging at a railway bridge or Myers' short journey across the city to another socioeconomic culture. The anonymous poem from St Piran's at the start of this chapter reminds us of society's inadequate response to the homeless person: armchair theology gives way before the cardboard box.

Chapter 5
Life Histories of Homeless People

And a voice came from the cloud saying, 'This is my Son, my Chosen; listen to him!'

Luke 9: 35

I have analysed the stories of homeless people in various ways. In this chapter, there is a brief character sketch of each person interviewed, which values their unique individuality, and allows the reader some access into their lives. I have included here also a sketch of self as researcher. Although on one level this is an artificial construction since I was not able to interview myself, yet it does recognise that to shy away from personal involvement is equally artificial. The previous chapters contained enough theological and sociological material to make this adventure both permissible and desirable. This project began with a personal encounter, and continues here with some more insight into why this project is important, and how personal vulnerability can sometimes be advantageous.

In the three chapters which follow, I provide a thematic analysis of interviewees' replies structured around the areas covered in the conversations: on common themes in the biography of the 11 men and women involved; on related emotional issues; and about experience of God or spirituality. All names except my own are pseudonyms. A fourth chapter describes what happened when a different group of homeless people began to read the Bible together. The biblical quotations from St Luke's gospel which stand at the head of Chapters 6 to 8 are intended to ground this analysis in the stories which Jesus tells to his disciples concerning wealth, poverty, community and the Kingdom of God. The account of the Transfiguration of Jesus (this heading) is extended to include all people as chosen sons and daughters of God, not least the lives which now follow.

Caroline

Caroline begins her story at the age of seven, recalling a dysfunctional family, divorced parents, her mother always out at the pub, and sexual abuse. At the age of 13 she was shoplifting to buy food, and at 15 she left home and moved in with a friend. She admits that she 'was hanging around with the wrong people', drinking, smoking, missing school and feeling suicidal. She once tried to phone Childline but the line was engaged. After a number of unsuccessful relationships, she was married at 18. Her husband assaulted her badly, and although they tried a reconciliation, this too failed. She became addicted to valium and attempted to kill herself. She was made homeless when she was evicted for non-payment of rent on the flat she was sharing with another boyfriend. Unable to obtain any drugs, she visited the local Health Centre in a state of collapse, and was advised to move into The Victory hostel, remembering the date precisely. This began a process of recovery, which enabled her to talk about her life with a key worker, and, with the help of the Community Drugs Service, to reduce her dependency. She is pleased that she is now on a reducing 'script' of valium. From The Victory, needing more independence, she moved to Aubyn House about a month before the interview:

> I had a key worker, never had one before. I told him everything, from when I was young, from the age of six and upwards. It was the first time in my life, I got it out. I had someone to speak to, I had a roof over my head, my own room, meals everyday, what I always wanted. It was the only thing I really wanted. I had it but then it was my independence was getting between it, you know, 'cause I was having friends in my room, and you're not allowed to have anybody in your room. So that's why they moved me into here. I've got a counsellor now, so I see him each week.

She is starting to pick up on her missed education with a computer course, and is looking forward to organising herself for job interviews. Her one major concern is that her younger brother (then aged 15/16) would go through the same process that she had experienced, that he will be pressured by his peers and others into taking drugs, and start the same destructive cycle. She tries to advise him how to avoid this.

Caroline is agnostic about belief in God, but still calls herself a Roman Catholic. She attended Mass as a child and as part of her schooling, but as an adult she sees almost no connection between her life and the life of the Church; she is hardly aware of the Church at all.

Charlie

The earliest point Charlie refers to in his interview is the death of both parents: 'I had already lost my father in a fire and my mother with multiple sclerosis ...' but it was the death of his wife which was the prime cause of his homelessness. Prior to this he had 'worked in one place for eleven and a half years' and had known 'a normal, orderly existence'. After her death, her parents asked him to leave. This began eight or nine years of life on the road with increasing dependence on alcohol.

He decided to move down to the West Country because he had always liked it, and by the time he actually moved (four and a half to five years before the interview) he was addicted to pethidine as well. His recovery from these addictions began at the same time as he moved into the Salvation Army hostel, about 18 months from his first arrival. He had also started to attend the clinics of the local

Community Drugs Service and had been prescribed methadone. As he recovered, he found that he had done some permanent physical damage:

> I've just, it's taken time, but gradually I've got better over the years, the last two to three years. I found once I was more or less on the road to recovery, it got easier, obviously it would be, physically. Unfortunately, I'd already done the damage in a lot of ways. My pancreas, I've had half of that taken out, so I still suffer from the physical effects of what I've done to myself.

His residence at Aubyn House and its key worker support system has been part of a continuing recovery process. He feels that he is almost back to a point before his marriage except for the intervening experience:

> Before I couldn't stand my own company, whereas now, I'm quite happy with my own company. I wouldn't have had the patience to sit down and talk to you for half an hour before – no way, unless I was getting something out of it at the end. Yes, I've changed a lot. My attitudes have changed. I'm more or less coming back. I'm back where I was before I got married really, in many ways, except I'm a hell of a lot more experienced now than I was then. I found it very difficult to ask for other people's help before as well. But the main thing I think I did discover is before you can look after anybody else in this life, you've got to look after yourself.

Charlie frequently repeats the phrase 'I'm not a conventionally religious person', expressing his dislike of organised religion, but recognising the existence of a Higher Being. He makes a link between a spiritual side of life and emotional awareness, which is now coming back to him.

David

David comes from a middle-class family. While his father claims a working-class background from Birmingham, he was educated at a grammar school and went to university; his mother went away to school and became a PE teacher. David passed the 11 plus exam and went to the local grammar school, which in the course of his time there became comprehensive. He excelled academically, but was the last to be chosen for the football team on wintry games afternoons. 'Fitting in' was quite difficult, but he did not really care; he had a small group of friends and very supportive family. Like lots of nicely spoken, able children, the others retaliated by shouting 'poof' which could be embarrassing on occasions.

He did fit in at university – or in other words, there were sufficient like-minded people around to feel comfortable, and to realise that he was, at last, part of the in-crowd. The college chapel and the Cathedral enabled him to begin an appropriation of Christian faith and its integration into the rest of life. A rather painful year in Paris as a language assistant led to a concrete decision to be confirmed in the Church of England after his finals at the age of 21.

His first permanent job was teaching languages in a smallish independent school in Shropshire, part of the Woodard Corporation – again, hardly an encounter with the underprivileged. David observed that the size and quality of cars which came at the end of term to take children home increased each year Margaret Thatcher was Prime Minister. His interest in and work with the college chapel grew and the chaplain encouraged him to consider ordination. He jumped through the hoops, was recommended by a selection conference and started another round of university classes in Oxford. St Stephen's House is in the east of the city, in a mixed area of students and an Asian population, a lively but relatively poor community. His first term-time pastoral placement was as a volunteer with an AIDS/HIV charity.

His curacy at St Peter's Plymouth involved him working alongside the City Council, the Probation Service, and Stonham Housing Association, managing together a direct access hostel, a housing project for single homeless people, a community centre and development workers, a home-makers group, and so on. Working here, with the marginalised for the first time, David saw poverty and heard poverty, listening to the stories of the entrapment of the poor and sometimes reflecting upon them.

There was a sharp contrast between this situation and that of being a chaplain in the University of Exeter, his next job. There he experienced a sort of conversion. David invited his next-door neighbour and family for tea. He was curate of the local Anglican evangelical powerhouse. He prevaricated. When he finally came round, he explained that they could not have tea with him since he had heard of his (David's) liberal views about homosexuality, and David detected perhaps an undertow of something more personal that was left unstated. The result of his anger with this was a series of articles and conference papers about sexualities, including a reflection on the failed tea party experience.

He moved jobs after nearly a decade in Exeter, returning to be a parish priest in Plymouth. He commented that the increasingly polarised debates in the Church of England about sexuality left him feeling compromised in a sort of ethical and theological way: ethically, the question was about being representative of an institution which was perceived as, and might well be, intrinsically prejudiced; theologically, because for him issues of justice and equity were of the essence of Jesus' life and teaching, and the Church of England seemed tarnished in this respect. He needed a way of retaining some authenticity and even self-respect. One way of achieving this was to be engaged in part-time paid research work about sexualities (including within ministerial training) at the same time as parish work.

The experience of inner city regeneration and linked housing issues, the economic downturn and related political and social changes, and a small joint project about contextual Bible reading brought him back to previous study and reflection about homelessness and homeless people. This complex and paradoxical matrix of marginalisation and 'at-homeness' is his current dwelling place; David wonders to what extent he has chosen it, or it has chosen him.

Danni

Danni lived in a children's home in Milton Keynes up until the age of 17 when she was asked to leave. The home arranged a flat on a six month tenancy, but since she was still only 17 when the tenancy finished none of the local housing associations was prepared to offer her a place. Her best memories of this time concern trips to the nearby countryside:

> When I used to live in Milton Keynes, you only travel a couple of miles and you're out in the country and that's what I used to do when things got too hard at the children's home. I used to just jump on a push bike and go out to the country. I used to just sit out there and after a couple of hours there, I felt calmer.

Although she had been in trouble with the police a lot when she was younger, she had imagined that living in the flat would be an opportunity for personal growth: in fact she did succeed in curtailing her heavy drinking. However as the end of the tenancy drew nearer, with no other accommodation in sight, she began to panic, started drinking again and returned to crime. She describes the early part of her life in these words:

> I was homeless on and off for a lot of years, was living in a children's home when I was younger and they threw me out when I was seventeen. And they did give me a flat, but that was only for six months. Now when the six months was up I was still seventeen. All the housing associations, the Milton Keynes ones, down there, they wouldn't take me until I was eighteen. So when the six months tenancy of this flat finished, I was homeless.

She then spent four or five years in and out of prison, being jailed in London 13 times. Often she would be released on Friday, re-offend and be back in prison again on Monday. In that period her alcohol dependency and criminal activity became more serious. Danni spoke of a recurrent kidney problem from the age of 14, made worse by alcohol. She felt that in prison she was looked after in this respect with good medical treatment; but as soon as she was released her resumed drinking would lead to kidney problems again. This continued until a particular severe deterioration in health when she was hospitalised outside prison. A doctor made it very clear to her that she was seriously ill and needed to change her behaviour. This led to a decision to change her lifestyle, and helped by the sister of her solicitor she was put in touch with rehabilitation centres around the country.

Staff at Akron House (a residential centre for alcohol and drug treatment) were prepared to interview her over the phone, and she was offered a place which would remain until she was able to take it up. There was some uncertainty as to when this would happen as she was still awaiting sentence, but being released from prison sooner than she had imagined, she went straight to there. She had spent four months this time in prison and spent nine weeks at Akron House. She had experience there of the Twelve Step rehabilitation programme, and so when asked about spirituality refers in vague terms to a Higher Power. On being discharged from Akron it was intended that she would spend six months in a secondary treatment centre in Weston-super-Mare, but she left after three days. With only £15 in her pocket the only option was to return to the city she had come from. She contacted a friend who was supportive but unwilling to take her as a lodger; she recommended The Victory hostel where Danni stayed for six weeks. Her second application to Aubyn House was successful and she moved in. At the time of the interview she was living elsewhere in the city, but because of trouble with her neighbours she wanted to move out of this area, but stay in the city. She still sees a therapist once a week.

Fran

Fran presents the most confused life history of all these subjects, with only passing reference to a number of potentially important events, and sometimes appearing to contradict herself. It is easier to start from her current situation and work backwards. She had been at Aubyn House for two weeks at the date of the interview and prior to that at The Victory hostel, although she initially says that she is still at The Victory. She explains these moves like this:

> So this Christmas I was going over to Portugal I was flying from Manchester to Bara and there was a misprint on the ticket so there was another date booked in for me for the following week but during that week, I was attacked, my belongings were stolen, luckily enough I still had my coach ticket to get back. As soon as I arrived, I booked there and at the beginning of January, no at the beginning of December, two members of staff from here came to visit me. One of them, can't remember who it was, it was Mike, Mike said that … I had actually gone through this channel before, I'd tried to get in before and when I say get in I was offered a place but I didn't take it, something else came. … I told them what I'd been doing for the last two years, that I'd become a life saver, the accommodation and money was not sufficient.

Fran says she has stayed at The Victory hostel on four separate occasions, arriving there after she had been travelling around the country, and being unable to stay where she wished to. She gives no indication as to where she was living previously and I do not ask.

> I travelled a lot up and down the country, hitch-hiking which was quite a sporty thing, open air, fresh air all the time … Plenty of sky really. I can't exactly remember why I moved into The Victory, The Victory that was it. When I first arrived, I went into the YWCA. I tried to get a contract with them for three months and I was refused and they recommended The Victory hostel to me, and then I went and did a trip, and … they sorted accommodation for me and it was a place called Littlehaven. It was a larger house, a type of manor house. And there were other youngsters there, younger than me and possibly one or two ex-criminals who had recently been released.

She found this house too regimented, with insufficient personal freedom, and left after six months, sharing accommodation with another ex-resident. She describes this period (around two and a half years previously) as positive and healthy. The whole interview reveals a sense of rootlessness, especially as she indicates some detachment from her family. Her parents live in Portugal; her brother, who was a Royal Marine in the Falklands War, is now married and lives locally; and her sister lives with evangelical Christians, 'so there's no chance of me living there'. The single theme running through this confused commentary is the notion of freedom, associated with healthy outdoor living and with swimming.

Geoff

I met Geoff, an itinerant seller of cigarette lighters and the like, at St Piran's as he was on his way to Cornwall. He comes from Basingstoke where his daughter lives in a caravan on a travellers' site, and where by implication, he lives too. His granddaughter was killed in a traffic accident three years ago (he mentions the date specifically), the day after her twelfth birthday; his two daughters travelling with her were also badly injured but have recovered. After the accident he went on holiday to Cornwall and is now repeating the experience. He says that he has tried talking to God about the accident but had no reply, so this time will talk to Amy, his (deceased) granddaughter instead.

He mentions in passing that he has been married but they have split up; that he is also illiterate. He talks about having a gift of second sight, but does not call this religious. He holds strong and often negative opinions – there is no point in feeling sorry for yourself, 'I've no time for robbers, murders, or child abusers. I've a better idea than throwing them in jail'. He doesn't like Myra Hindley's use of religion and thinks that charity should start at home before Christian Aid abroad:

> I don't drink, don't smoke, don't take drugs, I'm not a reformed addict. I've no time for wasters. Sometimes I think you encourage [it], I've no time for that. It puts nothing in. I am in receipt of benefits, do my own thing in the meantime. The vehicle is bought with my own sweat. It's not given me by the Social.

He has mixed views about the Church, strongly disliking his Catholic education, but speaking quite warmly about a recent visit to a URC church in Basingstoke where the Bible was taught clearly. He distinguishes this from religion.

Julie

There is little direct biographical material in this interview, although she speaks at length and with clarity about her beliefs and understanding of God. This is examined in more detail in a later section, but there is an outline of the major events in her life. Her early years (from 2 until 15½) were spent in a children's home run by nuns; she also refers to a Church of England school where she was educated until she left. Home had been problematic between mother, father and stepfather. On leaving she became homeless, was arrested for vagrancy and sent to a remand home. It is at this point (aged 16½), without real home or money that she turns to shoplifting and 'I haven't been out of crime since'. She refers to two other episodes in her life. She has been married three times, once to an alcoholic, once to a heroin addict, and has had children who went into care:

> I sort of wandered. I've been married a few times, been homeless as well. My marriages have broken up. Had three marriages so my children went into care, because there wasn't places that would take children in those days. Today, it's a lot easier for … one parent families to get accommodation than it was for, back in those days in the early 60s, late 60s, early 70s.

She mentions that she has worked in residential homes for the elderly in Weston-super-Mare, and is critical about the way these are run. Her kindness to the residents and her outspokenness did not endear her to her employers. Since she has been at Aubyn House, Julie has been attempting to reform her habitual shoplifting and in her own view is making some progress.

Jim

I first met Jim as an acute and voracious player of Scrabble. As a result of playing and losing many games with him I asked for an interview. When Jim tells his story, he mentions two significant events. He was in work as a steel fixer, but the end of a 'bad relationship' about 15 or 16 years previously led him to a series of bedsits and other temporary accommodation, having abandoned his house to his girlfriend. Ten years before on August Bank Holiday he had been involved in a near-fatal car accident, in which he had come drunkenly out of a pub in front of a car. He spent some time in hospital, and because of confusion with housing benefit while he was there, he lost the council house in which he was living. He spent another period of very insecure accommodation, preferring in the end to sleep rough with nothing, than to have the little he did possess stolen by others. He describes these times in this exchange:

> David. But have you ever been out on the streets?

> Jim. Yes, I have. At one time, it was about five years, sleeping anywhere, hedges, anybody's floor, in a bus, squats. I used to get drunk just to make me forget, so I could sleep. I was like that for about five or six years. Hell of a state.

He is currently living in a bedsit which is relatively satisfactory, but he hopes to have his own home again at some point.

He feels that he has started a process of recovery with the help of St Piran's and the National Health Service, and is beginning to be less numb, less blank, which is how he described himself before. He has also been receiving treatment for a form of obsessive compulsive disorder which expresses itself in habitual counting. He explains this by saying that he had been single for such a long time, that he had had no one to talk to. His former partner offered him a new start two years ago, but he refused – he has become distrustful of women. When asked about God, he expresses no particular belief except to suggest that at the time of his accident 'someone didn't want me to die'.

Marc

I had met Marc at least once before this interview and knew a little of his story, yet at first glimpse the transcript appears confused, with jumps backwards and forwards in time and in geography. The connections made are those of the speaker and rely more on emotions than logic, yet close attention reveals a clear series of biographical elements which will now be summarised.

Early childhood in Doncaster appears chaotic – a dysfunctional family where a drunken father physically, emotionally, and sexually abused him, and physically assaulted his mother. There is also mention of a stepfather and a stepmother, though when he refers to 'dad' it is uncertain exactly who is meant. He first attempted suicide at the age of 7 and at 14 left home. He returned at 18 as an openly gay man facing rejection by his family because of his sexuality. He spent some time living with Martin in Doncaster where there was a measure of reconciliation with his mother. His homosexuality still caused problems with the family. He was reluctant to tell his other brothers and sisters and was prevented from taking a partner to his stepbrother's wedding.

He moved from Doncaster to the South West, hoping to find work, but ostensibly to live with Andrew, a new lover. This relationship broke down almost from the outset, and with it went any secure home. Marc moved into The Victory hostel reluctantly, describing his surprise at shared rooms, drunk residents and the attempt to force him to smoke cannabis. At the evening meal he eats, goes to the nearest toilet and makes himself sick. He was at The Victory a number of months, tried a reconciliation with Andrew which failed, moved to a B&B in a local town with the same practice of making himself sick and taking laxative, then returned to The Victory for a second time. He started another relationship with John which went badly wrong, ending when he was stabbed and hospitalised. John reminded him of his father: 'it was like my dad because my father beat me up, laid me down on floor, smacked me in the face with his fist violently, because he'd been drinking. This is not for me'.

He agreed to give a statement to the police, but months went by before the court case and the whole incident preyed on his mind. He was shocked to read his name in a local newspaper report and this prompted another suicide attempt. It was at this time that he first visited Pete The Rock, a Christian cafe close to The Victory hostel. He was drawn more closely into the social activities and did some voluntary work there. Shortly afterwards he moved to Aubyn House and changed his name from Stephen to Marc. By the time of the interview he had been at Aubyn for 14 months and is looking forward to moving out into his own accommodation, describing this as 'the second thing I've done in my life', the first being when he left home aged 14.

Before the interview finished, he describes how he has written to his parents and started to renegotiate his relationship with them and the rest of his family. He wants to tell them what life has really been like, but worries that they will try to persuade him to return to Doncaster. Indirectly at this point, he also mentions that another man, Phil, had raped him and subsequently threatened him. This incident probably occurred before his arrival at Aubyn. The interview ends as Marc tells me that he is more able to tell people his story now, but that he recognises that he has to tackle problems for himself.

Pete

After some opening remarks, Pete begins the interview with a precise event and date, and in fact he says little about his life prior to that event: 'I lost my first wife, New Year's Day, thinking that when I lost her that as I was going to continue living, I was going to spend the rest of my life on my own'. This was followed three and a half years later by the death of his mother-in-law. At this point both his parents, his wife's parents and his wife were all dead. However, only a month later he met the woman who was to become his second wife and they were married. In the meantime, he had been forced to take early retirement from the dockyard on the grounds of ill health, and therefore spent a great deal more time at home. The story of the breakdown of his second marriage and his experience of homelessness began properly after about 11 years of married life. The reason he gives for the collapse of their relationship is the difference in their ages, yet he recognises later that she has had a difficult childhood, and needed a father as much as a husband. He describes their first encounter: 'At quarter to ten that evening I met the most beautiful 23-year-old, blue-eyed, blonde which any man could ever wish to meet and remember then at the time I was 47 years of age, which put an age gap of 24 years between us'. By this point, his wife was 34 and he was 58 – 'an old man who was quite happy to spend his time of an evening sat watching the TV ...'. They had two children from his wife's first marriage, who were now teenagers. This is how he describes life at that time:

> I'm afraid that my children were, by then, teenagers so my wife and my children used to disappear at seven o'clock of an evening, meet up with another crowd of youngsters and have an evening together, much to my regret, smoking dope and listening to reggae music. She used to come home with ten to a dozen of these youngsters every evening and I accepted that, I appreciated that my wife had to have friends of her own, the same as I did.

However, what he really objected to was that when he came downstairs in the morning, they were still a number of these friends sleeping in the sitting room. Eventually he gave his wife an ultimatum that it was either them or him. His wife preferred the friends, so Pete left home and moved into a local B&B. However, remembering his marriage vows, during the seven months he spent there, he continued to provide financial support for his wife and children. What he only realised later was that most of the money had been spent on providing amphetamines for his wife's increasing dependency. An attempted reconciliation failed when she appeared 'stoned out of her brainbox', so he was forced to spend the night in his car in a local car park. He was referred by his doctor the following day to The Victory hostel where he spent five weeks. A second attempt at reconciliation with his wife lasted two days, after which she told him without equivocation that their marriage was over. His reaction was rapid. He drove to Dartmoor, swallowed sleeping tablets, connected a hosepipe to the car exhaust and prepared to end his life. He woke up surprised the next morning.

Pete explains that on further examination the hosepipe was still connected, but the engine had broken down. He had to be towed back, discovering that the car was beyond repair. He first visited his wife, who promptly called the police, and so he was arrested and spent the day in the police cells before being released in the evening. He went to his house and his wife refused him entry this time, so he was forced to return to the police station. They arranged accommodation for him again at The Victory. A couple of days later he accepted a place in the Salvation Army hostel. While he is quite critical of the Salvation Army regime, this marks a turning point in Pete's life. He was still in contact with his wife so was able to give her the support she needed while her health and dependency worsened. After 10 months in the hostel, he was accepted at Aubyn House, where he has now been for 16 months. He is impressed that the staff there bent the admission rules to allow him in, since he was in some need of supervised care.

He believes his wife was close to death as a result of addiction, but she is now on her way to recovery. She visits him two to three times a week, spending the night with him. They hope to secure a bungalow from a local housing association, where they intend to live together again. Pete is realistic that the woman he married has changed considerably in the intervening years.

Two other significant factors are mentioned in Pete's story: his ability to sing, which he particularly made use of after the death of his first wife, and again now that his life is more secure. He is keen to share a gift which he regards as coming from God, especially at concerts for charity. Secondly, he describes himself as going to Church and Sunday School as a child. Although at 18 he decided that he had had his fill of church, he clearly retains respect for the clergy, speaking about the visit of a local curate after the death of his first wife, his friendship with the vicar who married him to his second wife, and his stay with the Salvation Army. After a long period of absence, he says that he has started attending services again in the Church of England.

Richard

When Richard left the Navy he moved straight to John Brown Engineering. He worked there for some years before sickness and an operation forced him to leave. It had been completely unexpected: 'Never had an illness, just that things came to a halt, which I've never experienced before'. He does not say how precisely he came to the town, or became homeless, but does describe where he is living now:

> A friend of mine, whom I've known for a number of years, has got like a conservatory place with pot plants and things, so I've got like a Z bed, so just sleep there. No cooking facilities. I'm grateful to St Piran's for meals cooked. Saves me a lot of money because if I was going to restaurants and things, I would say that I would never get through the week with what I get. Four to five days a week I get something inside me, heated up.

It is difficult to keep warm in the winter, and find somewhere to go on Saturdays and Sundays. He uses the swimming baths for washing.

Richard finds his present situation very restricting and is looking forward to getting well again. When he retires he would like to do some voluntary work with homeless people because he feels that he has some understanding of their experience. He feels strongly that more should be done about homelessness, 'because it's not like a thing crept up overnight'. He sees his present situation as a task or a test to gain experience, that this is part of a bigger plan which has been worked out in advance, with a purpose yet to be discovered. Richard is more philosophical now he is older, more accepting, 'you sit and listen more'.

Tim

A review of Tim's interview transcript reveals a loop-like structure in which certain themes recur and phrases are repeated often with no apparent connection to the question asked, but with a new piece of information added. Staff at St Piran's have said that his short-term memory-loss is due to diabetes and some alcohol dependency. The two main themes of his story focus on his working life and his divorce, both of which are connected to his housing problems, but with the exact sequence of events and precise links left vague. He worked for British Aerospace but implies that during a large-scale retrenchment he was made redundant. He then worked for the Government Information Service in conjunction with the Army, where his job was to interview serving soldiers for local papers and specialist publications. He mentions that once he took part in an exercise in Jordan:

> The British government was asked to provide assistance. If they had sent troops in it would have been an act of aggression, so some bright character thought of staging an exercise. 'Get someone like Timothy to walk into Jerusalem and get the parachute regiment to find him'.

He was already in his fifties at this stage and the fixed-term contract was not renewed because of his age.

Tim speaks of being forced into a marriage with the woman he was living with because of the traditional views of her father. He implies that not long after the marriage the relationship ended and the divorce was difficult. They did not own the house they lived in, and so to avoid paying alimony he simply disappeared. He comments adversely on his experience of bedsits and greedy landlords, preferring his present arrangements: 'I sleep in the doorway of a bank'. Rather charmingly, he makes these and other remarks as if they are quotations from his own autobiography. Although he has to sign on every day at the Benefits Office, he sees this as a way of being able to pay his debts off.

He says that his experience of homelessness has taught him the essentials of life, and that his Christian faith has been strengthened. While he was brought up in the Church of England, he now prefers to attend the Baptist Church where they take an interest in him while respecting his lifestyle.

Chapter 6
Themes from Homeless Lives: Biography

There was a rich man, who was clothed in purple and fine linen and who feasted sumptuously every day. And at his gate lay a poor man named Lazarus, full of sores, who desired to be fed with what fell from the rich man's table; moreover the dogs came and licked his sores.

Luke 16: 19–21

The previous chapter focused on 12 individual histories. By contrast, analysing vertically within a single interview and horizontally across interviews, similarities and continuities within the group emerge. So under the heading of Biography, I determine a single main theme and a number of sub-themes; under the heading of Emotions there are six themes, and under Spirituality five. For each theme I provide extracts of richly significant material from the interviews to illustrate and substantiate the points made, enabling the reader at the same time access to the language, tone and experience of the speaker. Additional quotations are included, some of which run counter to the prevailing argument, others of which show how themes merge and overlap.

The single main theme of this biographical section is that of arriving at a crisis point. This can be the stark issue of being without a home or more starkly of being faced with spending the night without a roof; or it may be the sense that something has to change. Some of the speakers talk of more than one crisis. The following extracts give examples of this.

Caroline is 20 years old at the time of the interview. She has been living at Aubyn House about a month having spent some time previously at The Victory hostel. She describes the culmination of a number of difficult experiences:

> That's the only time I got help. That's the first time, I never knew about The Victory, I never knew about hostels, I never knew about this place. I went down to the Health Centre because I was doing a lot of drugs and because I left my boyfriend. I went back, I had my own place, but the rent had been stopped and I was with my boyfriend and the landlord threw all my stuff out, moved somebody else in, so I go back, I got nothing, I'm homeless again. I met a few people but because they were doing all these other kind of drugs, giving it to me, I was taking it because I couldn't handle reality. I wasn't eating so I was in a state and one day I didn't have no drugs, I was screaming, crying, shaking, it was the worst day of my life, it really was. I was just slumped down, delirious. I went to the Health Centre, one of my friends took me to the Health Centre and they advised me to go to The Victory hostel. I stayed there, it was good, they helped me, really did help me.

Danni has similar issues of health, but recalls the moment in prison when she took a more active decision that she had to change:

> I was put in and out of prison all that time and that's when I got heavily into drink and my crimes got more serious and more often, and then in May, well January to May, I decided I knew I had to change. I couldn't go on like this anymore. I was in prison at the time and my health was really bad, and that's when I decided to try something else, you know.

Marc describes a series of crises throughout his life. His rapidly delivered story of himself, full of direct speech and repetitions and in the style of a stream of consciousness, recalls vividly and emotionally central events in his life:

> Anyway it built up and built up till Andrew said, 'Right you're on your own now'. I said, 'What d'you mean?' 'Well you're on your own'. I said I didn't know the city very well. 'You know the town, you know the Hoe'. I knew Hoe Gate, the bus station that's what I knew, the train station. He said, 'You've got The Victory [hostel:]' Anyway I said, 'Fair enough', and I went down on my hands and knees and said, 'Andrew we've got to work this out'. I was crying on my hands and knees. He said, 'Go on you silly devil'. Anyway I wiped my eyes and he said, 'Come on Stephen, go and cry at Social Services to see if you can get a loan back to Yorkshire', because I didn't want to live in there. So I did and they said, 'Can't give you a loan for about five weeks'. So I went back to Andrew's house, so he said, 'You've got to move as soon as possible, I don't want you here'. I said, 'Come on Andrew we've got to talk about it'.

By contrast, Tim is much calmer and it is possible to say there is no crisis point by comparison to the others. Yet there is still that moment of decision out of which flows a lifetime of experiences which focus around homelessness:

> Tim. I divorced my wife, it wasn't going to be a happy relationship. I had to pay her what would be an absolute minimum and since I've been as I am now, I've not bothered to pay it. I suppose I've always liked to do things properly, it was rather against me. I 'just disappeared' I've not a clue where she is now. We are properly divorced. I'm very lucky that the law hasn't arrested me or made me pay, what's the word?
>
> David. Alimony?
>
> Tim. That sort of thing.

It seems from these examples that the cause of the crisis is either health related or derives from a relationship problem. A more detailed consideration of the transcripts reveals that there are *causes* of crisis and *results* of crisis, and that some of the results are circular – in other words, they become causes in themselves. The causes of crisis may be subdivided into the two already mentioned, health and intimate relationships, with a further four: issues around childhood, the death of family members, sexuality, and crime. The results of crisis lie in two areas: self-harm including suicide attempts, and substance abuse including alcohol. It will be immediately observed that these are not wholly discrete divisions, but they are nevertheless helpful in understanding the lives of these women and men. Homelessness is thus the public presenting issue for a number of other serious concerns which have otherwise remained largely within the private domain.

Causes of Crisis

Health

Examples of health issues forcing a moment of crisis have appeared in the interviews with Caroline and Danni. For Danni this was a long-term problem which now requires immediate attention. She is forced to face reality by a doctor outside the prison:

> I got help because I've had a health problem with my kidneys since I was fourteen, and while I was in and out of prison, drinking, and I worked at my medication, so my kidneys were getting worse and I'd end up back in prison and they'd get me all better again. So I just felt I was being looked after. It was good, but it wasn't until the last sentence that my health really deteriorated while I was in prison and I had to go to an outside hospital. The doctor there just turned round to me and he said 'If you were released from prison now, what would you do?' So I said 'Go to a bar and get drunk'. And he said 'You'd best enjoy it that time, because you won't wake up in the morning, that'll be it'. And that's when I knew it was serious.

Charlie explains that while health is not the initial cause of his housing problems, it is the point around which any recovery and change must focus. Cause and result can overlap, with abuse of alcohol and pethidine being at the intersection.

> It's really more of a physical thing than anything else, because my body just wouldn't take a lot of the things I was doing to it ... I've always loved the West Country and I moved down here and at the time, I was in quite a state, drinking too much and everything else. And I moved down to the city about 4½ to 5 years ago. When I first moved there, I was really ill. I was feeling bad. Not only drunk, I was addicted to pethidine as well, which I'd been given too much of when I was in hospital having various operations that I've had. So I was in a bit of a state. The first six or seven months I was there, I was in trouble basically. I was drinking. I was getting pethidine off all the doctors in town, taking that,

and at one stage, I was really way down, rock bottom … I'd already made the decision that I couldn't run away from myself anymore and all this going from town to town, changing homes was running away from myself, and I was taking problems with me when I went. I'd already decided that, but it was basically a physical thing. I found that I couldn't drink any more, because my body just wouldn't take the alcohol.

A similar situation applies to Jim, for while it is a relationship breakdown which initiates a cycle of housing problems, the whole is exacerbated by a car accident, a period in hospital and the consequent difficulties in paying the rent. He is the only interviewee to mention issues of mental ill health for which he is receiving help:

> Treatment for habitual counting. If I'm bored and I'm doing nothing, I just sit down and count things. If it's wallpaper, with flowers, I sit and count all the flowers everywhere. I just sit there and count them. I didn't [worry] much when it first happened, but when it happens on a consistent term, it gets to you. It uneases you. I'm being treated for that now, different kinds of medications, not too bad, can't sleep. It keeps me awake all night, but I don't count. I play solo, I keep occupied. To keep on working … when I was earning … but I just sit there counting, it's horrible. At the time I didn't think nothing of it. … I can't stop it. I've done it in here many a time, just sit and count things, like all the straight edges and all the curves on your pillars. I suppose being single for a long time, there's nothing you could talk to, know what I mean?

A second crisis is precipitated for Pete when he is forced to take early retirement from the dockyard on the grounds of ill health. The effect of this is to put pressure on his marriage. He had already explained that his second wife is 23 years younger than him – they married when he was 47 and she was 24. One result of this is that he was four years older than his mother-in-law and seven years older than his stepfather-in-law. For Richard, who had worked in the Navy and then at John Brown Engineering, an unspecified episode of ill health had forced him into temporary accommodation: a foldaway bed in the unheated conservatory of a friend, with no cooking or washing facilities.

Relationships

A failure of intimate relationship causes crises in the lives of Marc, Tim and Jim. Sometimes this failure is accompanied by violence. Marc comes down to the South West from his home in Doncaster with Andrew his lover who then proceeds to evict him. He spends time in The Victory hostel, then nine weeks in a B&B in a local town, and returns to the larger city. He meets a man called John at The Victory. He describes this encounter as 'love at first sight, match made in heaven but it was, when I first met him I walked into this lamppost, hitting my head, great big black eye'. What he did not know at first was that John mixed alcohol and tranquillisers, becoming violent. Marc describes what happens on one particular occasion:

> This particular night it was our anniversary … that were it, I turned round and I thought, 'Slap him back, give him a surprise'. I turned round, hit the wall, I jumped on my back. Oh my back's sore. '[Has he] stabbed you?' I said, 'No I'm all right me'. Fell back on floor. I think I was shocked. Next thing I knew I went downstairs to Angela and I talked to her, 'Where's John, where's John, quick?' He was behind me, I didn't see him, like this black shadow. That frightened me actually, he was a bit taller. I sat down on bottom step and John passed me. Anyway he said to Clare, 'I've done it, I've done it now, I don't know how the hell I've done it'. And Clare said 'What you done?' 'I just stabbed Stephen'.

Marc was taken to Derriford hospital, discharges himself, returns to hospital, and is interviewed by the police. An earlier relationship is alluded to (Martin) in Doncaster which caused problems between Marc and his parents, and towards the end of the interview he refers obliquely to Phil as the man who raped him.

There is also violence in Caroline's marriage, a contributory factor to her crisis illustrated above:

> Caroline … my mum never told me about the facts of life so I had to find that out all myself. I started out going into relationships … they all broke up, got married when I was eighteen, he beat me up.
>
> David. So you got married and your, that didn't last very long?
>
> Caroline. No I left him, he beat me up. He broke my nose and black eyes and bruises everywhere. I went back to him after that [laugh].
>
> David. Really?
>
> Caroline. I did yes, believing what he said.
>
> David. Did it get better?
>
> Caroline. No.
>
> David. That's what he said he'd do?
>
> Caroline. Yes, he said that he would be all right.

A third crisis erupts for Pete when he has to spend more time at home having finished his working life. He jumps to a period 11 years into this marriage, with no description of the intervening years, except that it 'still went along very, very, well'. He fixes the problem around their disparity of ages, for at 58, describing himself as an old man, his wife is only 34. He prefers to spend the evening in front of the television, while she goes out with her teenage children (from a previous marriage) 'smoking dope and listening to reggae music'. He describes the domestic scene:

> So I used to go to bed about eleven o'clock and leave her down in the sitting room with the children and her friends. But the thing that always upset me was nine o'clock in the morning when I came down again from my bed, there were still six or seven of them sleeping on my floor, on my sofa, in my armchairs. And I gave her the option, that either stops or she could find herself minus a husband because I wouldn't tolerate it. I said this is our home. I'm the one who pays the mortgage, therefore I expect to be considered. However, her answer was that they were my friends and if come half past two, three o'clock in the morning because that was the normal time they stayed up to, they were, it was too late for them to go home, she was quite agreeable to let them sleep in my sitting room. So after giving her an ultimatum that it's either them or me, she said, 'Well they're my friends, I'm not going to throw them out'. So I said fair enough and went upstairs. I packed two suitcases, walked down to my car and drove away from her. [About seven months later] she decided she wanted to try again and I was quite prepared to because at the end of the day she is my wife and I love her very dearly. So I went home on a Monday lunch time remembering I had given up Patna Place then, so someone was going to move into my room when I left. So when I went home, there was this crowd of young people still all sat around smoking pot or whatever they like to call it. She came out to be in the kitchen, stoned out of her brainbox and she took out a packet of speed which cost, what, ten pounds, so naturally I just said 'forget it' and I got back into the car and drove up to Mutley Plane and I spent the night in the car park at Mutley Plane. I slept in the car.

So he then spent five weeks at The Victory hostel, and at the instigation of his wife, they tried again to save their marriage, this time with more disastrous consequences:

> … two days together, then she told me she no longer loved me. Our marriage was over and in the meantime, I had three beautiful rings, a wedding ring, an orange ring, a signet ring, which one of her so-called friends stole – presumably to buy stuff with. So I thought to myself, life isn't worth living, so I had a car and went to the garage and filled up with petrol and I drove out to the middle of Dartmoor. I took eight sleeping tablets, connected up the hosepipe to the back of the car, started the engine up and as far as I was concerned that was it, that was the end of my life.

Issues from Childhood and Adolescence

For her humour, energy and image-making, Julie is one of the memorable characters of this project. She refers to her early life both positively and negatively. Her family life was disrupted, but she talks with gratitude about the nuns who ran the home where she was brought up. She attended (and possibly lived in) a Church of England school from the age of two until leaving school at 15½, and says she was 'brought up in a children's home by nuns so I've always believed that God's been there'. The problem at home stemmed from a poor relationship with her mother, who although married to another man was still having a relationship with her former husband: 'while my stepfather was at work, my mother was knocking father off and totally confused my home'. She found her mother's deceit difficult, and worse, the expectation that she would collude with it. So Julie left home, was arrested for vagrancy and turned to petty crime as a means of survival.

Given what has been written already about Caroline and Marc, it is not surprising that they feature in this section about childhood problems. In a similar way to Julie, it is others' problems visited upon the child which are so detrimental. Caroline paints a bleak picture of family life and the relationship with her mother:

> Caroline. I didn't get on with my mum very well. When I was younger I was sexually abused … I think maybe from then, from the age of seven years old … my head must have been messed up, part of the reasons. Then mum used to go out drinking
>
> David. Was it locally?
>
> Caroline. Yes. She started going out drinking all the time, she always used to come back and start on me, say it was my fault and things were my fault and my dad's divorce was my fault, she wished she had an abortion on me and things like that, which didn't make me very happy.

She links this early experience with petty criminality from the age of 13, and then with leaving home at 15. She moved in with a friend, and around this period began taking pills as an escape route. Marc has a similar tale of childhood abuse, recalling his father bringing other men home to laugh at him while he was asleep, that he 'felt like a piece of meat, pushed this way, pulled that'. This was part of a wider context of violence within the home:

> I said, 'Look mother, when I was little, I saw you'd been beaten black and blue by the pinball machine and I didn't say a thing'. 'You knew when to keep your mouth shut when you were little; who put you in your bed when you'd been out and dying?' I said, 'You', because I remember sleeping in bus stations, subways and all sorts, because my father had been drinking, abusing me, beating my mum up.

Danni's first remarks speak of having lived in a children's home up until the age of 17. Although she goes into no details, she talks about her criminal behaviour then, and the fact that she was asked to leave the home involuntarily at that age. She attributes her later problems to the uncertainty about follow-on accommodation. She is unable to sign a tenancy agreement at the age of 17 and there was no local provision for those under 18.

Death and Bereavement

The death of a close family member and the unresolved grief around it is the primary focus of crisis for two of the people interviewed for this study, and important for a third. It appears that it is either multiple loss which causes difficulty or the randomness of an accident. Both Charlie and Pete speak of the death of their first wives as a turning point for them:

> I first became homeless … precisely two weeks after my wife died. I … how can I put it … I always had a home when my parents were alive. When my father died, I kept the flat on and then I got married. My wife lived in a flat with me, a council flat. Then she became ill with cancer. I won't go into the circumstances, but it got to a point where I couldn't look after her and work, so I moved in with my mother and father-in-law, who I didn't get on with terribly well, but nevertheless, it was an essential part of her recovery in trying to recover. But eventually she died, and they asked me to leave the premises within two weeks after her death, find somewhere else to live. And I found myself living in a bedsit in Wood Green, which I stayed in for a couple of months, then I just left there. I didn't want to hang around. I was, at the time, started drinking quite heavily. And that's when my life started virtually to fall apart. I moved up to London. I was living in a Salvation Army hostel, travelling, very, very, transient existence, never living in one place, a lost wandering lad, you know. Everything I had was in a suitcase. And that really was the start of more or less eight or nine years of transient existence.

Later in the interview, he admits to feeling 'let down' by God around the suffering of his wife, almost saying as an after-thought that he had already lost both parents, his father in a fire and his mother due to multiple sclerosis. Pete also starts his lifestory with the death of his wife and with a specific reference to the loss of all his family as being significant: 'because my mum had died, my father had died, my father-in-law, my mother-in-law, my wife, so all my connections with anything previous had come to a halt'.

A random car accident in which his granddaughter aged 12 is killed is significant for Geoff. He introduces the subject of his granddaughter's death almost immediately and a short way into the interview I ask for clarification. This extract shows strong opinions expressed quite aggressively. Geoff feels that he has every right to lead his life as he chooses and is answerable to no one. The close link into issues of spirituality is also revealed.

David. Can I ask you about your granddaughter – I don't want to upset you?

Geoff. My granddaughter was eleven, on 25th August she was twelve and killed the day after her birthday in a car accident. The car went out of control, hit a tree and she was killed outright. One of my daughters was on a life support machine and the youngest one had a six hour head operation. One of the two drug addicts said he would swap for her, but he was a waste of space.

David. Did the other two survive?

Geoff. Yes, but my daughter suffers physically and mentally through the accident. But life goes on. I ask him upstairs why he did it, her and not me, or one of those useless sods. There's no answer.

Sexuality

Marc's homosexuality has already featured in the context of a series of failed, often violent, relationships. However, he also speaks of problems at home as a direct result of his sexuality. He is the only person interviewed to do so, but the effect of this situation is significant enough to warrant consideration here. He talks of his relationship with his mother in particular; how it moved from outright rejection to a degree of tolerance. In recalling his experience of being an 18 year old in a family which rejects him, his description as usual is to the point:

My parents got their own life, I got my own. What worries me about my parents is that they're right old fashioned. Men have got to be men, women have got to be women, settle down, kids, work for a living. But when I told them I was gay that hurt them more because I was like the black sheep of the family. We're five brothers and four sisters. Out of five and four there's one brother who is gay. At the end of the day why should I have the problem on my own, it's them with the problem ... She says, 'Does he want gravy?' as if I'm a complete stranger. 'Tell her, I don't want bloody gravy'. Stephen says, 'He doesn't want bloody gravy'. It hurt me like the one instance as I said the dinner on Sunday, 'Don't wash your pots in my basin'. Fair enough, I'll wash them in my own basin. Something snapped, like the flash of a light. I said, 'Mother, I'm your flesh and blood'. She said, 'You're not my flesh and blood, get out!'

Marc indicates that some issues around this area have now been resolved. He is in contact with his mother by letter and is now able to have a less hurtful relationship with her.

Crime

The final subheading illustrates how criminal behaviour has contributed to a sense of crisis in the lives of Caroline, Danni and Julie. Caroline describes shoplifting clothes from the age of 13, and selling them in order to buy food. Danni recalls that in her childhood she had been in trouble with the police a lot, but it is primarily the ending of a short tenancy that led her to commit crimes more frequently. This became a way of life for her, so that the homeless 17 year old found home behind bars. Here is the sense of a moment of decision.

> So when the six months tenancy of this flat finished, I was homeless. I didn't get support from social workers or anything like that, they just couldn't be bothered. So I, I don't know whether it was desperation or what, I started committing crimes and ended up in prison. That's the only home I had, on and off for four or five years. I was put in and out of prison all that time and that's when I got heavily into drink and my crimes got more serious and more often, and then in May, well January to May, I decided I knew I had to change.

Julie too began shoplifting early on, saying that she started at the age of 16½ and has not stopped since. Her explanation, however, is one of survival rather than desperation, and it is this that enables her to say that she has strong moral convictions and a Christian faith at the same time as being a criminal. She calls herself honest in the sense that she cannot lie when caught, gives no violence or trouble to the police and will offer an 'honest opinion' when requested. This sense of morality and honesty is captured in the following remark:

> I was out there everyday. I used to shoplift for all the people on the dole. So they would get everything a third of the price because they couldn't afford to buy it. Most of the police officers in every town I go to end up calling me Robin Hood which is my nickname.

Now that she is living at Aubyn House she is able to receive more help from a key worker as well as from her probation officer. She is pleased that she has only relapsed twice; when I ask in how long, she replies: 'I've only been here a week'.

Fran is included in this section as a counterpoint since she is a victim of crime rather than a perpetrator; there is also much less of a sense of crisis in her story. Indeed I am surprised by how different she appears from the other subjects although she has lived at The Victory on four separate occasions. A few minutes into the interview I ask:

> David. Did you think of yourself as homeless? It might seem a funny question …

Fran. Not until this last time when I was attacked, and I had been doing karate, I stopped doing that for three months so my whole body had seized up. I'd stopped swimming so all the joints were stiff and I did have quite a hard time, this time … I've never met so many, what do you call them, tramps?

She had spoken before about a mugging on her way to see her parents in Portugal in which her belongings had been stolen apart from a return coach ticket. She returned to The Victory, and soon after that moved to Aubyn House.

Results of Crisis

Self-Harm and Suicide

The most extreme reaction to crisis or multiple crises amongst this group of people is to decide to end life itself. The crisis (or crises) seem so overwhelming to them that there is no alternative. Slightly less serious is the issue of self-harm, and I include in this section Marc's comments on deliberately making himself vomit. The repeated suicide attempts of which he speaks may be 'cries for help', but the evidence from his own words would suggest that Pete's attempt was serious, and that for Caroline the distinction between taking an overdose of tablets and simply blanking out life was a fine one. Marc says that he has tried to commit suicide six times, and in the course of the interview he seems keen to say that this was the first time, second time and so on, though not every incident is detailed. The number of attempts seems important, because he links this up with God (Jesus) and a sense of protection. It is when talking about his childhood that he first mentions suicide, recalling that at the age of seven he swallowed a lot of paracetamol tablets and was forced to have his stomach pumped. Much more recently, questioning by the police about his stabbing and the publicity in the local paper associated with it led to another couple of attempts to kill himself. His remarks are not without humour, of a very black kind – when the newspaper report appears again, he thinks of gassing himself, only to find that the fire is an electric one. If there is any pattern to these attempts, it is that panic and fear lead him to think about and attempt to harm himself. Similarly, when he stays at The Victory hostel for the first time, having been made homeless by Andrew, his reactions are directed against himself:

> Anyway I got my meal, [I was] like a child with food, I was. People watching you. [Someone] said, 'Here young one, d'you want a drink?' 'No ta. I only drink coffee'. 'The only time you get coffee is at night time'. There won't be night time here, I want to be out. Anyway, sat down to my dinner, had my dinner, I went to nearest toilet, I put my hand down my throat, made myself sick, physically sick. I felt frightened.

A failed attempt at reconciliation with his second wife leads Pete to try to kill himself on Dartmoor. As with Marc there is a certain black humour, but I also perceive that Pete tells a good story. Consciously or not he builds to this dramatic crisis, and then almost lets the listener down with an anti-climax:

> I took eight sleeping tablets, connected up the hosepipe to the back of the car, started the engine up and as far as I was concerned that was it, that was the end of my life. I woke up twenty to six next morning, rather astounded that I was waking up, because as far as I was concerned, I was dead [laugh]. And I got out of the car and couldn't understand why I wasn't dead. I kept falling over because, of course, the carbon monoxide fumes had taken some effect and I went round to the back of the car. The hosepipe was still on there, got back in the car and tried to work out – and the engine had stopped running. So I tried to start the car up. Needless to say, the car wouldn't start.

Later on in the interview, in a less polished way, he is talking about the death of his first wife. He had originally said that this event made him realise that he would spend the rest of his life on his own; now he suggests that his first reaction was to tidy up his affairs and then 'I contemplated finishing my life'. A local curate, calling on him, persuades him that this is not the right answer to his grief.

Caroline, aged 20 at the time of the interview, looks back to when she was 16 as the age at which she could not cope any more. She began to take tablets as a reaction, and mentions suicide at that age, and at 18 when her marriage became violent. She focuses also on the need to talk to someone:

> Caroline. I started to take pills, I tried to kill myself, I tried to kill myself when I was sixteen as well, because I couldn't handle life, it was just too much to cope with at that age I suppose.

> David. It seems ever so grown up doesn't it but you're actually very young.

> Caroline. I was, I don't know how I got through it. I started taking pills, well because I tried to kill myself, but it didn't work. I woke up the next day, I woke up and thought, Oh no, what's going to happen now? And I done it again, started taking more pills, it stopped the feeling, it blanked everything out and that's how I got addicted to them. I'm on a reducing script now, of valium. I nearly od-ed twice, on pills and drink. I never had no help, that's what it was, that's what I needed, somebody to talk to. I never had nobody to talk to.

It is her addiction eventually which leads people to listen to her and so she is able to begin a recovery process.

Substance Abuse

In the extracts already quoted, Caroline, Charlie and Danni have all reacted to difficulties in their lives by some kind of substance abuse: tablets, pethidine, alcohol. The substance abuse of others has affected the lives of Marc (in his relationship with John, and his initial experiences in The Victory hostel) and Pete (his wife's addiction to amphetamines). Charlie now feels that it is hard to make any assessment of his real emotional or spiritual state while he was drinking because he recognises that alcohol exaggerates and falsifies such experiences. Jim comments that he was getting drunk over a period of five or six years 'just to make me forget'. The person whose interview I should like to focus on more at this point is Danni, since she also describes her participation in a recovery programme. Her ill health forced her to address her alcoholism. Through her solicitor, while in prison, she made contact with Akron House which took her immediately on release. She spent nine weeks there, and while this was successful, she refused to continue in a secondary treatment centre feeling that she had had enough restriction on her freedom already. She describes the regime at Akron in two separate comments:

> It's a lot of group therapy work. And they look into the reasons why, because there are drink and drugs there and other addictions they do there, so they look into your addiction; the reason why you do it and your behaviour when you …
> It's shocking because when you're doing the things you are when you're drunk and stuff, you don't think about the consequences or what people are suffering, but when you're clean and you're looking back at it all, it's really terrible. There were some good times in Akron as well. They used to take us off on to the moors for walks and I like all that sort of stuff. And being from London, it was really different.

More specifically, Akron employs a 12-step programme similar to that of the Alcoholics Anonymous organisation. Danni refers to doing steps four and five, and when I ask for clarification on this she replies:

> I can't remember what the title was, but basically it's an inventory of your life and there's about thirty six categories and you have to do two examples of each category and it's basically about tolerance, impatience, like you get the bad side and the good side of each subject. Basically it's like a lifestory, in categories. You have to read through it with a priest. Some people were with the priest like seven or eight hours. It was a whole day thing. It wasn't just an hour and that was it, you know. Some of it was really heavy.

She also talks about the way alcohol numbed everything around her, so that without alcohol she is feeling less tough and 'I find it hard to deal with people now'.

This chapter has focused on the theme of crisis in the lives of those interviewed – the causes of crisis, the results of crisis and the circularity of the interaction between the two. From the field of applied social research, the preferred term to describe such crises (or turning points) is 'epiphanies'. Norman Denzin makes specific reference to the Christian feast of the Epiphany to include within his understanding the concept of 'manifestation', after which 'the person is never quite the same again'.[1] His location of epiphanies at the point when a private trouble becomes public is identified in this study by the way in which homelessness uncovers a number of other issues which have remained relatively hidden. Such epiphanies do not simply involve events but include strong emotions, the analysis of which in these interviews forms the subject matter of the next chapter.

---

[1] Norman K. Denzin, *Interpretive Interactionism* (London: Sage Publications, 1989), p. 15. See also pp. 129–31. For an example of epiphanies in the life of one individual, see Andrew C. Sparkes, 'The Fatal Flaw: A Narrative of the Fragile Body-Self', *Qualitative Inquiry* 2/4 (1996): 463–93.

Chapter 7
Themes from Homeless Lives: Emotions

And he arose and came to his father. But while he was yet at a distance, his father saw him and had compassion, and ran and embraced him and kissed him. And the son said to him, 'Father, I have sinned against heaven and before you; I am no longer worthy to be called your son. But the father said to his servants, 'Bring quickly the best robe, and put it on him; put a ring on his hands and shoes on his feet; and bring the fatted calf and kill it, and let us eat and make merry; for this my son was dead, and is alive again; he was lost and is found'. And they began to make merry.

Luke 15: 20–24

The previous chapter is a snapshot of biographical details of the homeless people interviewed for this study, schematised around the theme of crisis. The reader will already have an overview of each of these subjects, and equally importantly, by means of the various sub-sections, have greater insight into a shared history. At present this view is one-dimensional, since I have extracted out of a mass of information what is of interest almost exclusively as the plot of these life histories, answering the question 'How did you come to be homeless?' To add a second dimension I turn now to the various responses to the question: 'What does it feel like to be homeless?' These answers, for the most part, come from the benefit of hindsight; Charlie, for example, reckons that alcohol blurred and altered any emotions he may have had at the time. He is still able, however, to paint a graphic picture of what homelessness did feel like from the inside. Answers have been grouped into six themes under the following headings: Anger, Pain and Isolation, Independence, Love and Survival, Telling the Story, Incoherence and Order, and Coming Back to Life / Returning Home. I have also included extracts which run counter to these groupings.

Anger, Pain and Isolation

The title here is drawn from the interview with Marc who describes his feelings when he returns to hospital after he has been stabbed: 'I were angry, in pain, lonely, on my own'. Added to this for Marc and Danni is the sense of fear and panic. Marc uses the word 'frightened' or 'frightening' 12 times in relation to himself and twice about a friend. He is frightened when he first goes to The Victory, and at supper time there; John frightens him, Derriford hospital frightens him; he is frightened when he reads stories of the crucifixion, having his stomach pumped as a child is frightening, the thought that people know that he has been stabbed is frightening. Fear and panic lead him to make himself sick, as described previously. It can reasonably be inferred from this interview that fear is (or has been) a dominant feature in Marc's life. There is also a sense of pain throughout much of the interview. Extracts have featured a violent relationship with John who reminded him of his father – 'it was like my dad because my father beat me up, laid me on the floor and smacked me in the face with his fist, violently because he'd been drinking' – of a difficult home life as a child and as a young man, of suicide attempts, self-harm and male rape. What is surprising is that Marc also features in the final category of this section when he looks to the future with some confidence.

Danni links a sense of isolation with panic when she has to leave her children's home with no clear future. The result is almost predictable:

> Danni. And the children's home, because I was actually thrown out of there, not discharged, I did go to them for help, but they refused to help me because of my behaviour while I was living there. So I just felt alone, you know. I just didn't know where to turn.

> David. So in a sense, you turned to crime. You don't mind me putting it as bluntly as that?

> Danni. I had been in trouble with the police, like a lot, while I was in the children's home. I thought that when I got the flat, I'd be able to sort myself out and at that time I was heavily into drink, but I'd stopped. But when the end of the six months was getting nearer and nearer and there was nowhere I was going, I started panicking and started drinking and that led to crime again.

Caroline, like Danni, feels that there was no one to talk to at vital times, especially for those under 18. Her family were not much help and she simply did not know of the existence of other agencies:

> I had nowhere to go, nothing to do, no one to stay with, which I have now, which is a good thing, but if, I knew about counsellors, things like that years ago I don't think I'd have ended up like this, because that is what has helped me. That's what I needed years ago, which I never knew. There was no advertisement about it. All there was was Childline which I phoned up, couldn't get through, that was it. That was the only thing, I didn't know no other way; my mum never told me about the facts of life so I had to find that out all myself.

It is the possibility of talking her problems through with a key worker that contributes in a substantial way to her recovery. When I ask her later if she can recall how she felt through any of her earlier life, she replies: 'I tell you what it felt like, hell. You do live in hell because it's hell to live'.

   In counterpoint to these emotions, Charlie, in a speech containing negative views on homelessness and sleeping rough, also wants to put his finger on something different. Perhaps this sense of freedom overlaps with the following section on independence, but he is trying to understand some of the attractions of being without a home:

> It can be, believe it or not, it sound's stupid, but it can be quite an attractive existence to some people. That's why some people will never live in a house. You'll never get them to settle in one place, because there is a certain amount of, excitement is not the right word, but you're sort of fighting from day to day for an existence and it tends to add a new dimension, if you like. Instead of living in a house with a regular job and a mortgage and worry about the kids and this sort of thing, instead, you've got just yourself to worry about and you're fighting from day to day to exist, but it sounds worse than it is actually. It can be interesting, it can be an interesting existence at times, it can be a real pig in the middle of winter.

Independence

A mixed range of emotions is centred on the concept of freedom, independence or the search for an undefined goal. Some of these subjects talk of restrictions placed on their freedom by different institutions (Caroline, Danni and Pete) or by the limitations of poverty (Richard); others like Charlie and Tim point out a more positive aspect of homelessness and the disadvantages of some sorts of accommodation; Fran talks of freedom using the imagery of water, and Julie gives an impression throughout the interview of a fierce independence won with a struggle. This range of impressions highlights the tension between the desire for freedom and the equally strongly held wish to belong and feel at home. This tension is captured within a single interview in the case of Caroline. She describes leaving home at the age of 16 and escaping from her mother's abusive behaviour:

> I moved in with a friend, one of my friends from school, I enjoyed it at first, it was freedom but then I started to miss my mum. Things were going through my head, and I felt suicidal really.

But then after she collapsed in the Health Centre and moved into The Victory, she recognised positive and negative aspects to living there.

> I had a key worker, never had one before. I told him everything, from when I was young, from the age of six and upwards. It was the first time in my life, I got it out. I had someone to speak to, I had a roof over my head, my own room, meals everyday, what I always wanted. It was the only thing I really wanted. I had it but then it was my independence was getting between it, you know, 'cause

I was having friends in my room, and you're not allowed to have anybody in your room. So that's why they moved me into here.

For Danni, the thought of being 'banged up' in a secondary treatment centre for six months was not welcome after three months in prison and three months of intensive rehabilitation therapy. She discharged herself and returned, initially going to The Victory and then to Aubyn House. Six weeks at The Victory challenged her new-found freedom from alcohol. She describes her time there as a 'nightmare', trying to keep sober among a lot of drug takers. Pete felt the same sense of restriction living in the Salvation Army hostel. He is grateful for their concern for him, calling Brian, an assistant officer, 'A man put on this earth by God for his ability to care', yet at the same time saying:

> The problem with the Salvation Army is that they take away your independence. They do everything for you. You don't even have to think for yourself, and to me, a man who has always made his own thoughts in life, as I said, with a very responsible job when I did work, it wasn't the right thing.

He stayed there 10 months before moving on to Aubyn House. Richard is the only person interviewed to mention directly the restrictions of poverty: 'at the moment I'm restricted in buying things or going to different places'. Ill health has forced his retirement, but he looks forward to getting better and doing the things he is 'yearning' to return to.

Charlie talked about the quasi-excitement of living day to day, when you 'lived and died' for the arrival of the giro cheque on Tuesdays, though, all things considered he does not recommend being without a proper roof over one's head. Tim is homeless because he does not wish to pay alimony after a difficult divorce. He feels he was forced into marriage by 'her old-school father' and now would rather remain sleeping in the doorway of a bank, and be effectively untraceable. He sees this as a temporary measure while he resolves his debts. He rejects any other form of assisted accommodation, though his health is not particularly good.

> I have tried to remain independent. I've had all sorts of offers but a lot of those characters are rather greedy, you end up with pennies as pocket money. The government has been very understanding. I have to sign on every day with them. They continue to pay me standard income support, what I suppose is the maximum they can. If I get involved, I only looked at one house with any form of person looking after me, what they wanted by money was astronomical. They also pay some sort of special housing allowance, the people who own these properties tend to be very greedy, they give you two or three pounds a week pocket money, like they're giving you the earth. Quite naturally this is not for the rest of my life. It's the only way I can get the financial side of my life squared up.

Fran has spent much of her adult life travelling in Britain, and emphasises the importance of fresh air and physical fitness. In between trips she has stayed at The Victory. When she was found other hostel accommodation by them she comments that 'I couldn't find my own space, that was all so controlled even doing the cooking so I still needed to get away from things and set up my own life'. The tone of the interview is of someone searching for the right path in life, but determined to do this as a free individual. She uses phrases like 'there's been loads of doors for me', and 'I realise there's a long road for me'. Other imagery will appear as a result of asking questions about spirituality, but she associates water with freedom. When I ask what it represents to her she replies: 'My eyesight, so I can see and drink, drink properly, and not get caught in any way, get tied up'.

This theme of identity is also present in Julie's interview, particularly in the style and tone of her conversation. She talks of her experiences with a freedom of expression which is fresh, direct, and full of memorable images. She is very willing to talk about God, to me and to others on the streets, but realises that this does not make her popular, nevertheless she continues in what sounds like a mission:

> We're in a dog-eat-dog world which I don't like. I don't want to be a dog and I don't want to eat dog. It's hard staying in the middle when you're a criminal, being a nice criminal doesn't fit down here sometimes. I accept quite a few hardened criminals because they don't like the way I talk, because I talk God and I talk nice and I talk love and a lot of criminals don't like that sort of talk and I have to suffer quite a lot down this end.

Her desire for independence and her survival as a free individual are linked to her criminal activities. She says at the start of the interview that leaving home at 16½ years old she had met many homeless people, but thought: 'I'm never going to be without money in my pocket and that's when I started turning to crime and I haven't been out of crime since'.

Love and Survival

It may seem odd to link these two themes together, yet an attentive reading of the interviews indicates that a closing down or suppression of all emotions, including love, is a key part of the survival process: of Danni in prison, Julie as a shoplifter with a conscience, and Caroline as an abused child. The opening up of love is part of the process of coming back to life which is the subject of a later section. There are close connections too with the spirituality of a number of these individuals. Absence of love or its withdrawal are characteristic of the lives of both Marc and Pete, where actual survival is in question.

Marc talks about the abuse of his childhood, and recalling an interview with a psychiatrist after his first suicide attempt aged seven, he remembers saying that he felt he had never been loved at home; so that now as an adult he finds love confusing:

> Saying that, when Tracy says, 'I love you' but I actually say, 'I love you Tracy', but what is love? I don't know what it is, I never found it. Saying that, if Jesus loves you, you love him don't you? It hurts a bit, like, I can't grow attached to too many people. With John I knew his faults, his drinking, his tablets, but he didn't love me, like … I don't know. I was in lust or whatever, I don't know, he said to me, 'You're too young to settle down', too young at twenty seven. So I still read Bible it helps me along.

A similar absence of love in early years is a reasonable interpretation of the opening remarks of Caroline's interview quoted above. By contrast, there are many expressions of love and affection in the interview with Pete. He talks about 'adoring' his mother-in-law, and meeting 'the most beautiful 23-year-old, blue-eyed blonde which any man could ever wish to meet'. When he first leaves his second wife he remembers his marriage vows: 'I promised in front of her that I loved her, honoured her, in sickness and all the rest of it, so even though I left home, I didn't lose contact with my wife or children'. After the serious suicide attempt described above and some rehabilitation work both at the Salvation Army hostel and at Aubyn House, he is hoping to re-establish a more permanent home and a reconciliation with his wife. He explains why:

> at the end of the day my wife loves me, for some reason I can't explain, but the thing is it's not just the fact she loves me, David, it's the fact that she needs me. You see I have a big advantage over my wife; although I love her, I don't need her. I can live my life without her. She cannot live her own life without me, so that's the difference. So we anticipate a reconciliation.

If this strikes the reader as ironic (especially given his suicide attempt) and in some ways as missing the point, a little later Pete contrasts the woman he married 10 years before with the 'vicious, nasty young lady' which resulted from two and a half years of drug abuse. He is sanguine about the reality of reconciliation but sees some hint of her previous character re-emerging. Towards the end of the interview he recalls a scene with his first wife, whom he names for the first time. At a regular social event, it was the habit of a group of friends to partner each other's wives for the last dance. Pete and Suzie would never do this because she always reserved the last dance for her husband. I wonder in the course of our conversation and in subsequent re-reading whether this emphasis on love moving into sentimentality is really part of Pete's character, or an attempt to recapture in words and memory the good days of his past and stable existence.

It is Julie who links up the two ideas of love and survival. She takes a traditional view of the family, seeing the father as the one who provides discipline and the mother who contributes love. When pressed to explain more fully about her image of God, she comes back quickly with the phrase: 'All I know is that God is love and that is all I need to know'. Her independent stance in talking about God and love leads to the following exchange where she recognises the paradox between love and survival:

> And I see so much that goes on down here that hurts me so much. I hurt a lot from what goes on down here. But you've got to be tough when you're down this end because if you're not tough, you've had it. [D. Very true.] Sad. I don't like life, but this is where I am. I help a few people somewhere along the line. I don't think we're judged on how much we love, but how people love us. [D. Interesting thought.] There's too many people out looking for love and they're looking for the wrong things. That comes from within you. It doesn't come from other people unless you earn it. [D. Don't you think we've got to try to love ourselves a bit?] Self love is the greatest love because we're in God's image. We're built in God's image and the first commandment is 'Love thy God' and then 'Love thy neighbour as thyself'. If everyone just lived by those two, the rest would fall into place.

Julie is much less willing than Pete to talk about her own emotions, preferring to talk about her opinions. She uses reflections about her understanding of God as an indirect way to say what she regards as important. When she talks about her own rehabilitation ('The behavioural therapy nurse told me that I had to shoplift to survive ...') she lets slip more personal information, but then reverts to the general comment:

> I've got a few friends who are helping me through it. I've been married to an alcoholic, I've also been married to a heroin addict. I've been through a lot of the programmes like Family Anonymous and things like that. So I'm doing a bit there and some of the things they come out with. I've read *Why am I afraid to love?* and *Why am I afraid to tell you who I am?* I read quite a lot of psychology, but as I said psychology is just common sense. You don't need psychology. You just need common sense in this life. And that's what a lot of people lack is common sense and a love for others. That's what's lacking today.[1]

The paradox of survival is also stated by Danni. She says that she does not feel as tough as in the past: 'because when I was young, in and out of prison, you have to be tough always, or you're not going to stand a chance'. Now that she has stopped drinking and is more vulnerable, she is aware of having to face problems directly, so her emotional sensitivity is heightened. Charlie also talks about living without the emotional crutch of alcohol. Caroline's answer to my question on survival points us to the final section of this chapter:

---

[1]   John Powell, *Why Am I Afraid to Love?* (London: HarperCollins, 1975) and *Why Am I Afraid to Tell You Who I Am?* (London: Fontana, 1975).

David. But you're a survivor as well aren't you? You personally are a survivor in this.

Caroline. I don't know how, but I am. The Victory, from going from The Victory I was in a bad state, I might as well have been dead really, but they brought me back, they brought me back to life, they brought me back to life now. I feel I've got a life, I feel I've got a future. I never did before. I never could see no future.

Telling the Story

There is a fourth theme here which engenders an emotional reaction, but one which is different to the previous three. There are moments when the subject wishes to comment on the process of being interviewed or how it felt on other occasions to speak of a difficult life history. There are also the interviewer's own (often untimely) interjections which, for the sake of completeness and honesty, I wish to include. This corresponds to previous comments about the ethics of the research and the involvement of the researcher. Caroline and Marc make the most explicit references to the interview process, with further statements from Charlie, Julie and Pete. My own involvement is seen in these interviews too and also in Fran's.

Part of Caroline's rehabilitation is having a key worker at The Victory to whom she is able to tell her whole history: 'I told him everything, from when I was young, from the age of six and upwards. It was the first time in my life I got it out'. Without the experience of telling her story at The Victory she would never have had the confidence to speak to me. I begin then to draw the interview to a close, but not before the following exchange in which the mutuality of this project is underlined. In some ways the tone is naive, but it does emphasise the engagement of the researcher and the necessity of such engagement. It also shows Caroline looking outwards beyond her own concerns to those of others like her.

David. Is there anything more you want to say, I'm really grateful, I mean, if I just, it doesn't matter if this is recorded or not, but this is very new for me and you're the first person I've done an interview like this, well it's not really an interview it's a chat and you, you've given me a lot of stuff to think about but given me some confidence that what I'm doing is actually quite a valuable thing to do.

Caroline. Yes it is, it really is. That's why I said yes right away because I'm speaking to you, because I know that there is people out there need help.

David. I'm really grateful because of that, because you've given me confidence.

Caroline. I'm glad you're doing it, I'm glad somebody's doing something, that and I'm glad somebody's interested in it, because it will help, it does help as well.

David. Yes I think so

Caroline. You may not think so, but it does. There's a lot like me out there.

David. We need to help together. Thank you very much indeed. I'm really grateful.

Caroline. Thank you. I'm glad I was able to help you.

There is a tone of heightened emotion throughout Marc's interview as evident in the extracts already quoted. There was a point at which the tape needed to be turned over when these feelings came to the surface and I noticed that I too have started to feel very nervous as Marc has been talking. I tell him this: 'I feel a bit, can certainly feel your ...'. He interrupts: 'Shakes?' He describes the process as 'nerve-wracking' and I agree with him. But it is towards the end of the interview that I make my own reactions clearer, almost involuntarily, and clumsily. Marc responds in a similar way to Caroline but there is an emphasis on self-reliance:

David. How do you, you said earlier, you know, you talked in a very moving way about lots of things, I'm very grateful, I feel quite moved by all that, well some of it you told me before, well I guess I am shocked in the sense of, I'm not shocked and outraged; I'm outraged that those things happened to you. Shocked about these dreadful things, I'm wondering how you're feeling now. You've said all this, it's all come out, are you feeling OK about that?

Marc. Yes, I couldn't talk about them, kept it all in; but now they're more open, it's Stephen, I can talk to anybody about them. I've seen shrinks from A to B to C. I thought I wasn't getting anywhere, I gave up, so you stick to one person, if they know and no one else knows you're all right. But it hurt though because like ... if you've got a problem like you've got to sort it out for yourself, you know.

Charlie too comments that previously he would never have had the patience to talk to an interviewer unless he was getting some benefit out of it. This interview also shows another aspect of my own feelings – a defensive reaction to a criticism of the Church. Charlie complains that at a Catholic convent in London he was forced to take part in what was (I assume) a recitation of the Rosary or the Angelus before he was able to receive any food. He was embarrassed to be reciting lots of Hail Mary's without really knowing the prayer at all. He links this with an implicit criticism of the sacrament of confession and I leap in defensively, breaking the flow of conversation. It is quite hard to return to the previous subject matter.

Charlie. What the hell is a Hail Mary. Hail Mary! I don't agree with the whole concept of being able to do virtually what you like and then go and confess your sins. I think that's very hypocritical to me. I think it is. 'I shot someone yesterday'. 'Well say ten Hail Mary's and'

David. I don't think it's quite as

Charlie. You get the idea of what I'm saying.

There is an opposite dynamic in the interview with Fran. She is talking about her sister whom she describes as a 'born again Christian' who tries to persuade Fran to have a full immersion baptism without which she is not properly Christian. Fran is resistant to this because she had been baptised already as an infant. Twice I make clear my support for Fran's position. Happily for the interview, it is an occasion for Fran to tell me that her baptism is significant to her. Both Julie and Pete refer at the start of the interview to telling the story of their lives; and my reaction is spoken explicitly again towards the end of the interview with Julie. I express my surprise and gratitude at the way in which she speaks of God, with a sense of freshness and urgency in her imagery.

Incoherence and Order

The previous section illustrated a conscious reaction to how it felt to be interviewed or tell one's life history. A second narrative element to these interviews is the extent to which they tell a coherent or a confused story. Shorter extracts from these interviews tend to imply a well-structured conversation, but in some cases it has been more like detective work to sift through hints to uncover the sequence of events. Three levels of order exist potentially: each interviewee will order events, feelings about events and so on as they speak; the questions I ask and the way they are asked apply another level of order; thirdly, data analysis imposes structure or order on very varied text. [']

Nigel Rapport's work with analysis of conversations cited earlier illustrates a degree of misunderstanding and failed communication from which he draws conclusions about conflicting world views, but at least superficially the conversations make sense. The same is not true for all the interviews that have been carried out here, recalling Frank's concept of the chaos story. I have indicated in the brief life histories where there is a degree of confusion; however, there is still an assumption that each person has told in essence a coherent story. The following two longer extracts contrast a relatively incoherent story with a well-structured one and at the same time allow the reader access to a greater stretch of text, from both the content and stylistic point of view. Each extract is followed by a brief analysis in which I suggest that the degree of order in the narrative is indicative of the order of their present lives. This partly exposes and counteracts the unconscious temptation to value the story and the storyteller in proportion to their clarity: I give value to that which is easy to understand, I dismiss the complex and confused.

The first extract is taken from exchanges of conversation half way through the interview with Marc, just after I have asked him how he is finding life at Aubyn House.

> Marc. I cried my eyes out for three days when I moved out of Victory and moved in here, just like you've got to meet new people, staff and everything. Aubyn House is different like, you've got your own key [pause]. I like Aubyn House because there's no people taking drugs and drinking. It's their life, they do it in their own bedrooms. I done that once, never again, didn't like it, I didn't. It did my head in. It frightened me because in Victory, I was telling you about Victory, I saw people taking drugs. In the morning they're nasty, but when they're down you take it good or bad. The one instance a lad called Nick he got hold of my throat, squeezing my Adam's apple. I was going redder and redder like a beetroot, I kneed him in the groin. As soon as I got in Aubyn House I got more hard, stronger than I did in Victory.

> David. Right.

> Marc. Like because in Aubyn House people didn't like push drugs on you, Take this, take that, but in Victory they do. I try and ignore it [pause]. Five suicides too much for me.

> David. Quite, for anybody.

> Marc. Like Jesus, somebody up there wants me alive.

> David. I think

> Marc. Certain things, … nice T shirts, that's all I need me.

> David. Right.

> Marc. I couldn't turn the clock back, no way. If I did I might have changed things about my own lifestyle, I wouldn't have had the rape, the stabbing, the beating up. Saying that, you can't, you can't dwell in the past, you have to dwell in the future. Before I lived in the past all the time, that's done my head in. I'm suffering from that now, like tension headaches all the time, that's … GPs and Samaritans and God and all that. I do it all off my own back … on my own plate … If I told my parents I'd been stabbed, 'Back to Yorkshire now Stephen'. You can move and move and move but you soon end up back here. You can't keep moving, can you? You can't. My parents got their own life, I got my own.

What worries me about my parents is that they're right old-fashioned. Men have got to be men, women have got to be women, settle down, kids, work for a living. But when I told them I was gay that hurt them more because I was like the black sheep of the family. We're five brothers and four sisters. Out of five and four there's one brother who is gay. At the end of the day why should I have the problem on my own, it's them with the problem, they can't … That hurt me in a way. I was hiding behind closed doors all the time, coming into the house at early hours of the morning, three o'clock, because I'd been seeing this fellow which I'm not ashamed of, but I was too young then, about seven years ago. Told them I was black sheep of the family. 'Get out, you're not my son'. I was pleading with her, knocked on the door five times. Got to the stage she rang the police twice to get me evicted. She didn't like Martin, he was too bold, always drinking all the time. She could see me going to fall in that trap. I could never do that. Moved in with him, he had his life, liked his drink. He said, 'Write to your sister'. Saying that she only lived next door but one! That hurt me because she's got two girls, I'm only one with no kids in the family. So I had to tell Laura about it, my homosexuality. I thought, does she know or doesn't she know? If they know, it's behind closed doors. When I told my mother, it was like she was panicking for weeks. It got to a stage at table, Sunday roast, 'Does he want gravy?' Does he want gravy, ask him? Like a complete stranger.

David. How old were you then, twenty something?

Marc. Eighteen, nineteen. She says, 'Does he want gravy?' as if I'm a complete stranger.

This extract illustrates not only some of themes already encountered in respect of Marc, but shows the way in which he moves from one idea to another. An initial question and answer about where he is currently living leads to a thought about where he had moved from and the people at The Victory, and then without a pause, back to his parents, their way of life and their treatment of him. This is the first time he has spoken about his parents, his relationship with Martin, and their reaction to this situation. He talks of looking more to the future now, but cannot help coming back to the pain and alienation of the past. He recalls very specific incidents (assault by Nick at The Victory, Sunday lunch with his parents) with a clarity and intensity which implies that they are still 'live' in his mind. He acknowledges that he has suffered from living in the past, and that he alone has to take some responsibility for himself, but he seems unable at this point to move forward.

This second extract is towards the end of Pete's interview. I have heard the basic account of his life and how he came to be living at Aubyn House. So I move into the second part of the interview process by picking up a reference he has already made to 'our friend upstairs' in order to ask about spirituality. This answer continues almost without interruption until the end of the interview.

My wife died New Year's Day, which was a Sunday. Of course, on a Sunday, you can't do anything because the Bank Holiday was on the Monday. There was still nowhere open or anything. So I spent the day with my younger brother and my uncle, and another relative, but I was no company for anybody because I had only just lost my wife, so I left them and went home to the empty house where I lived, as I was so used to going home and there being a very beautiful girl waiting for me. I was sat down having a cup of tea and my doorbell went about 8 o'clock in the evening. And I thought 'Oh no, not a visitor'. But anyway being courteous, I opened the door and there was this young man stood there in a long black cassock, very tall, young lad about six foot four inches. And he said, 'My name is Christopher Smith'. I said, 'Yes'. He said, 'I live in King's Road (just behind where I live) and I've heard about your great loss'. So he said, 'Would you mind if I came in and talked to you?' Always being a bit courteous I didn't wish to be rude, so I invited the young man in. And we had a most wonderful talk. He convinced me that suicide was not the answer. I wouldn't go straight to my Suzie, because the good Lord would keep me in limbo as long as if I'd earned a living on earth. So in the end he convinced me that that was not the answer and there was only one person gives life and only one person takes life away, so therefore if you take your own life you put yourself on a par with God, that's not allowed. So anyway, on the Tuesday, my GP, Dr Slater, came to visit me because he was very concerned because he loved my wife as well. The fact was that when she died she had forty-eight wreathes. She was only an ordinary girl, but everybody who met her, you had no chance, David, you had to fall in love with her. She was the most beautiful creature ever. I used to be envied by so many people because I had this young lady as my wife. So he said, he came in the door and I just spoke to him as I would normally and he said, 'It's amazing Pete'. And I said, 'What is?' And he said, 'When I came and you opened the door I expected to see a weeping, gibbering, idiot', he said, 'because I know how you felt about Suzie'. So I explained to him about the night before when this young man appeared on my doorstep and he said, 'If ever God worked in a mysterious way, he certainly worked that one, because there is no way unless something like that happened you would be as sensible or as sane as what you are at the present time'. That gave me a lot of goals, to think yes I never. It was my faith really in the end that kept me going for as long as I did. As I said prior, I've been very blessed. God gave me a voice which a lot of people seem to like here and I've sung in many pubs, clubs, raising money for charity, organizations, singing in people's homes. I've even sung in churches. And people appear to enjoy it, so I used to think to myself, maybe this is my purpose. But at the end of the day, David, I still didn't like going to work and leaving work at half past four, arriving home at about ten to five and walking into an empty house. And I used to sit there and think, why? And I used to go down to the theatre or the old Palace Theatre or the Athenaeum or the Globe Theatre and stand on the stage and sing and I used to get applause. And I used to think to myself, There's the answer, I can give people something that a lot of people can't. I can give people pleasure. But not only do I give people pleasure, I get pleasure out of it myself. And that's why I've tried to live.

By comparison with Marc's story, Pete presents a coherent account of a difficult period after the death of his first wife. New Year's Day, an evening visit by the curate, discussion about Suzie's death and a visit the next day by the doctor follow in clear temporal order. There is then a short reflection on how he feels blessed with the ability to sing, but still unhappy about the absence of his wife. While there are similarities with Marc's story (use of direct speech and very long answers) the way Pete has ordered the account of his life gives the impression that he has reflected on this already, decided what to include and exclude, and where humour might be suitable. In some ways this is not surprising since a key worker will focus on needs and their solutions, requiring some understanding of the context of the individual. Pete's is a genuine story, but I suspect that he has told it before and has in some ways even practised it. He has clarity about where he is going next. Marc's story is also genuine, but by contrast, he is still in the midst of it. The emotions which he still feels as he tells it, and which gives it such immense vitality, are witness to the way in which these events are not fully processed. His story is much less coherent because there is less coherence in his life and few firm foundations to build on. He has hopes for the future but they are as yet undifferentiated.

Coming Back to Life: Returning Home

Possibilities for the future summarise the final section of this analysis and point forward to the next chapter on spirituality. The sub-title here captures a dual approach – for Caroline, Fran and Marc the future is like virgin territory, an unexplored opportunity to achieve the things they had always expected; whereas for an older group, Jim, Pete, Richard and Charlie there is a stronger sense of life returning to how it was, to the comfort of the past, returning home. For many of these people their language takes on a freshness and originality as they look towards the future with hope. The four not included here – Danni, Geoff, Julie and Tim – are not without hope, but the future simply does not feature strongly in their interviews. Danni does mention her wish to move on in terms of housing, and Tim has a vague notion of clearing his debts though he says he 'tolerates' his present lifestyle; Geoff's short interview is not orientated around future plans and Julie seems content with plans to help her shoplifting, having only recently moved to Aubyn House.

Caroline sees her return to life in literal terms, as if without the help of The Victory her drug addiction would have proved fatal. But now with the support of counselling she has a very different outlook:

I can see a future for me now, it's good, it is, it makes me feel good, but it's bringing back my confidence and that as well. It's quite strange looking back on it feels weird now, my life seems to be coming together, like a jigsaw puzzle, all it was was in bits, but now all the pieces are coming together, you know what I mean … slowly but surely I know it takes time, because I'm quite an impatient person, but I'm learning, in spite of that.

Similarly at the end of Fran's interview, she comments that she has faith that places like Aubyn House can be successful; and then she uses the phrase 'my own spring, the light gets brighter for me as time goes on, and I keep seeing the light'. Home is significant for Marc, as we have seen when he talks of his childhood and the fear that possessed him when he was forced to seek out accommodation at The Victory hostel. When I ask him how long he has lived at Aubyn House and what he thinks of it, this is his reply:

Fourteen months, I love it. When I move out, February or March this month should be; it's going to be a big, open world, a great big hole in my life, because one thing you've got to start afresh again, buying new furniture, that's going to be frightening. No it's not going to be frightening, it's going to be great for me, because it's going to be the second thing I've done in my life. Left home at fourteen, come back at eighteen but now [you've got] to buy your own furniture, got your own key, saying all that, got to make a great big world for yourself. People that's left, people that's moved on. They've got their own life, got jobs which I should have eventually.

The positive and excited tone of this contrasts with the earlier sections about fear and isolation. It is also interesting to compare Marc's initial impressions as he arrives at The Victory with his reaction when he knows he is going to move on: 'I cried my eyes out for three days when I moved out of Victory and moved in here'. The Victory had clearly become some sort of a home to him.

Jim and Charlie, recovering from alcohol abuse, have a sense of feelings returning after years of confusion or blankness. Jim uses the phrases 'Something's coming back with the help of a lot of people, especially the NHS [National Health Service]' and 'I was totally numb, just blanked'. Charlie has a more imaginative expression for the same idea: 'At the moment, I'm still coming out of the fog of twenty years of living'. Jim hopes to return to his job as a steel fixer, get a house with a mortgage and contributions from lodgers. Equally Charlie recognises that he does not need alcohol any more, but that his new life will not be entirely a return to the past. He has learnt from these experiences:

If you can't look after yourself, you can't look after anybody else. I think that's where I went wrong with my wife to a certain extent. I wasn't looking after myself and I was trying to look after her. You cannot exist, just by saying, you can't say, 'Well my whole existence is looking after other people'. You've got to have an interest in yourself and be able to look after yourself before you can look after anybody else. You've got to have a stable platform to work from. That's not selfish, that's common sense. Also, you have to draw a line with people, I think, very much. There comes a point when you have to say, 'No, I'm sorry I can't do that'. If you've got, I try to live by my own set of morals and standards in life, which I think are fairly high morals and standards. And if other people want to step over the line, that's their fault, but they don't expect me to do it or to do things that would go against my own morals.

Pete has the strongest desire to return to life as it was, and in spite of what has happened to him, he volunteers the thought that he feels he has had a good life, and has no complaints. But he does isolate more than once in the interview 'the last three years' as being a highly problematic period. Perhaps his acceptance of life is linked to his hopes for a reconciliation with his wife, when she becomes again the kind of person he married, and the re-establishment of a home together. He talks specifically about his expectation of a housing association bungalow with disabled facilities. The only real change he is considering is that he is now able to cook for himself. He has also come back to the Church of England, calling himself an 'Anglican returnee'. Richard also hopes to return to work when he is well again, to regain his freedom and spending power. He says: 'At the moment, I think it's like a temporary thing which is an influence, but eventually I hope it will even itself out soon, later on, so I can go back to where I was before'.

Chapter 8
Themes from Homeless Lives: Spirituality

When Jesus heard the ruler's reply, he said to him, 'One thing you still lack. Sell all that you have and distribute it to the poor, and you will have treasure in heaven; and come follow me'. But when the man heard this he became sad, for he was very rich.

Luke 18: 22–3

Having designed an approximate schema for understanding biographical information and emotional commentary, the third element of the interviews concerns what I have loosely called 'the spiritual' or 'spirituality'. My aim is to produce a similar analysis, aware from the outset, however, that the material is even less precise than that which formed biographical or emotional content. This chapter focuses on a broad categorisation of the interview material taken under five headings, in part influenced by previously described concepts of spirituality and religious experience: Images of God, Experiences of Church and the Bible, Single Religious Experiences, Personal Theologies, and Humour. I wanted to include the idea of laughter somewhere in this analysis because it featured often enough during descriptions of traumatic events to be noteworthy and surprising. By placing examples in the section on Spirituality, I follow Michael Screech's *Laughter at the Foot of the Cross* which sees laughter as a significant element in a Christian understanding of God and human beings.

In general the reaction to my questions about God or spirituality elicited a wider range of responses than the previous areas of biography or emotion: wider in the sense that some individuals like Jim or Danni had almost nothing to say, whereas for Julie or Pete talking about God seemed part of their natural discourse; wider also in the sense of how the question was interpreted. Some opened by talking directly of God, others preferred the safer ground of assuming I referred to the Church. Some indicated from their initial remarks the kind of conversation we would have – 'I've never been a conventionally religious person' (Charlie) and 'Oh, I was very lucky. I was brought up in a children's home by nuns, so I've always believed that God's been there' (Julie). Others needed a series of specific questions. The following sections enable the reader a further glimpse into the world of these individuals and how they speak about the significance of spirituality in their lives.

Images of God

Swinburne's distinction between God 'being there' and God 'doing something or bringing about something' is one I shall maintain here particularly in reference to Julie's interview. The following gives an example of how she expresses herself about God:

> God's always with me, as bad as I am, which my probation officer says, 'You're not bad, you're only a shoplifter'. Though I steal, I believe that God will help me through it eventually, given a chance. And also that God's on my side and human beings shouldn't judge me anyway because I don't judge any other human beings. That's up to my Maker to judge me at the end of the day. When judgement day comes, I'll face what I've got to face.

From this I take God to be always present, supportive and helping, but also judging. The notion of the presence of God is re-enforced a little later when Julie declares that God is everywhere and it is human beings who lose God in the 'desolation' they have created. While 'my Maker' may be said without much reflection, God as creator is intended when she introduces this more theological point:

> The way I look at it is God gave us a beautiful garden and gave us lots of animals and trees, things and flowers, and we were supposed to be gardeners as far as I'm concerned and look after his world. We just turned it into a rubbish tip.

I ask Julie specifically to describe her picture of God and she replies without hesitation with the abstract: 'All I know is that God is love and that is all I need to know'. Towards the end of the interview she introduces the phrase Higher Power in reference to God, and explains that she uses this because of her experience with groups like Families Anonymous. Many people she meets prefer this phrase to talk about 'someone to belief in, that's greater than yourself'.

Both Charlie and Danni use the same or a similar phrase: 'as for there being a Higher Being, yes, I believe there is somewhere' (Charlie). He has read about the Big Bang theory of the creation of the universe so 'there's got to be someone who said "let there be light" if you like and started it all off in the first place'. Danni recognises the term Higher Power from her rehabilitation programme but it has no real meaning for her. Tim says that his image of God is 'as someone I've been able to turn round to in prayer, or talk to, quite a few times in my life, in sticky positions'. He is the only person to refer to prayer. Pete is another person whose easy talk about God produces a variety of different images. In describing how he met his second much younger wife he says that:

> God compensated me for the loss of everybody then because my mum had died, my father had died, my father-in-law, my mother-in-law, my wife, so all my connections with anything previous had come to a halt.

Another image of God as protector and life guide is seen in relation to his attempt to commit suicide. He concludes that 'our friend up there made the big-end on the car pack up because it appears he has further things for me to do in my life'. He is not clear what this might be, except that he recognises that his singing voice is a gift from God and best used for the benefit of others in charity concerts and for worship. Pete begins his story with the death of his first wife; she too is considered as a gift. God is also conceived of as someone who is testing Pete through the different experiences of his wives, so that he wonders if God exists at all, and if so why he is being tested. This made him reluctant to attend any formal worship. Charlie also blames God for a sense of isolation and abandonment. This is the answer to my question seeking to tease out any spiritual experience, however vague, during that period of his life:

> When my wife died, I felt I had been let down. Quite honestly, to an extent I thought, if there is a God up there, how the hell could he let this woman suffer like this. I had already lost my father in a fire and my mother with multiple sclerosis. I felt very sick with life, in general, you know.

Blame and anger with God are more clearly marked in the interview with Geoff. The death of his granddaughter in a car accident has left him with questions but no answers:

> Geoff. My granddaughter was eleven, on 25th August she was twelve and killed the day after her birthday in a car accident. The car went out of control, hit a tree and she was killed outright. One of my daughters was on a life support machine and the youngest one had a six hour head operation. One of the two drug addicts said he would swap for her, but he was a waste of space.
>
> David. Did the other two survive?
>
> Geoff. Yes, but my daughter suffers physically and mentally through the accident. But life goes on. I ask him upstairs why he did it, her and not me or one of those useless sods. There's no answer.
>
> David. Did you expect an answer?
>
> Geoff. No, not really [pause] I suppose at the time I did. Why did this happen?

His answer in terms of an image of God is to say that there is definitely 'something' there and he 'ought to come back and sort it out'. The image of God as protector is given an indirect reference by Jim. He describes a car accident which could have been fatal except that 'someone didn't want me to die'. He wonders why in his drunkenness he was able to escape the car wheels, and decides that 'destiny is in other men's hands … someone else is above me'.

God as abstract creator is the nearest Richard comes to an image of God, as he thinks about the beginning and ending of the universe; whereas Fran is much more personal. God for her is the power inside her to give life and energy: 'I know there's a God inside me all the time because that's what gives me power to be able to get up and go'. She also has this lovely image of the imperfection of living away from home, which yet contains something of God:

> The essence has gone out of it, as I say living in hostels and things, the essence is slightly taken away, but we're also given something which is more, which is close … to God … the silver is slightly tarnished, you know, it's not a complete home there's no home there so it's different.

Marc and Julie are the only interviewees who mention Jesus. Marc uses three images: Jesus in pain on the cross, Jesus as someone who loves him, and Jesus as protector and guardian. His comment on his multiple attempts at suicide is to say that 'I think Jesus kept me alive'. Julie's reference is of Jesus using the plain language of parables as the vehicle for his message. Suitable quotations are included in the section 'Personal Theologies' below.

Experiences of Church and the Bible

There are many comments about Church in the course of these interviews, covering a wide spectrum of opinions, both positive and negative. Caroline considers the thought that churches might be there to help people in her situation, but does not see in reality how they could have done so. Her actual experience of Church is as a child – 'I went to Mass every Sunday, I knew the words off by heart and I used to say it at the same time as the priest did under my breath'. She also recalls school assemblies and having her flat blessed. She does make some connection between Church and her own situation when she describes her feelings:

> I tell you what it felt like: hell. That's how, this is my … I think that we live in hell and when we die we go to heaven, see, because when we live we're worried there are always bad things that can happen but when we die, at peace, at rest, we don't need to worry you see, nothing can hurt you … I've always thought that, thought that ever since I left home, well I thought that all my life, really. So I must have thought about the Church because that's to do with the Church … you do live in hell because it is hell to live.

Danni also responds to the word 'spiritual' by remembering that she went to church when she was younger, but there was no opportunity at the children's home. In prison, faced with the choice of being locked up or going to the chapel, she chose the chapel. Her more recent experience of Church is attending A.A. meetings in church buildings. We then move quickly to a more blurred area in which she talks about her therapy. In the A.A. programme Steps Four and Five are reflective exercises about self-knowledge and moving forward. The link here is that the person who helped her reflect was a priest. God is not immediately there for her in this process, but her reaction is still interesting:

> Danni. You do, I can't remember what the title was, but basically it's an inventory of your life and there's about thirty-six categories and you have to do two examples of each category and it's basically about tolerance, impatience, like you get the bad side and the good side of each subject. Basically it's like a lifestory, in categories. You have to read through it with a priest. Some people were with the priest like seven or eight hours. It was a whole day thing. It wasn't just an hour and that was it, you know. Some of it was really heavy.
>
> David. Did you feel kind of, did you feel God was there at all, or was it just something you were sitting doing at Akron?
>
> Danni. I felt before I went in, I was really upright, really nervous about it all. When we started sitting down and talking, I didn't feel that at all. I did feel relaxed, comfortable with it all.

Church as an experience of youth is recalled also by Pete – three times a day on Sunday – until the age of 18 when he decided to stop attending. He describes some later visits to hear a Salvation Army band concert (where he met his first wife) but it was not until her death that, thinking back now, he was aware of the absence of God. A visit very soon after her death by the local curate is a significant event for him when Pete is persuaded that taking his own life is not a shortcut to being reunited with his wife. He is given the opportunity to reflect on what life means for him now and encouraged to find a new purpose. In retrospect now he comments: 'It was my faith really in the end that kept me going for as long as I did'. Yet the importance of this mourning for him can be seen in his memory of spending some period every day at her graveside and being there at midnight on each New Year's Eve following her death. The priest reminds him that she is not there, and he replies that he knows that, but it does not stop him. He has also experienced the other side of the Salvation Army as a homeless person himself, and is grateful for their help. They again encouraged him in the idea that 'there is a plan worked out for me'. He does not want to be thought of as 'a religious nut' but his 'creed in life … is to do as the good book says: to do unto others as they would do unto me'.

Of all the interviewees, Tim describes the most positive attitude towards the Church. During his experience of being homeless he has in fact become a 'regular church-goer', though he has moved from the Church of England to the Baptist Church. I enquire further into this:

David. So what do you get out of church, that's the $64,000 question?

Tim. You mean personal feelings? Financially nothing! Being able to have a fixed firm belief. I'm given a lot more strength, plus my local Baptist Church has never done anything to bring any fixed bearings on me. They took their own time to get used to me. It's difficult to generalise, it may well be that the C of E here is different.

David. You've been given a lot more strength, what sort of strength?

Tim. I'm given a lot more confidence to 'perpetuate the lifestyle I lead now'. Over a period of time they've never brought any pressure to bear. Other organizations have thrown cheap coffee at you.

Another positive though indirect experience of Church is described by Marc. He has visited a Christian cafe called Pete the Rock (a former butcher's shop called Pete the Meat) near the hostel in which he lives. He is encouraged to read the Bible and it is from these visits that Marc draws the images of Jesus around the theme of pain. He starts to help there – cleaning tables and serving meals – noting that the people at the cafe are friendlier than at The Victory and from more diverse backgrounds. He says later in the interview that the Bible helps him when he is feeling depressed: 'Even now, occasionally I read the Bible, when I want to read it, like if I'm down, deep down, I read it. That perks me up a little bit'. Some of his approach is fatalistic however. This is how he speaks of one way of reading:

Shut the Bible, where I shut the page, slamming down, I put my hand on a certain page, it opened on a certain page, I thought he wants me to read this, he must want me to read this certain page here, so I kept reading, reading it. You know I read the Bible occasionally, not very often; to start with it looked like a story to me, I enjoyed it. I thought, well they'll get to know me, they'll get to know people on streets like from Victory.

A more mixed response is seen in the interviews with Fran and Julie. Fran's view of Church is coloured by the relationship with her sister whom she calls a 'born again Christian', who insists that Fran is not properly Christian until she has been re-baptised. Fran's reply is that since she has been baptised once she is a Christian already, and that this is important to her. Another Christian has challenged her practice of martial arts accusing her of being 'with the devil'. Julie takes a critical look at Church in her usual sharp way, with an image of how different churches relate to one another. In the first extract below, she links Church to how she sees her role as a disciple, and in the second she gives an interpretation of ecumenism:

I've been to churches, lots of different churches in my life, when I'm doing down on church or whoever knocks on my door I think most of them have got certain things right, but they've got a little lost. The Mormons have got lost for a start, the Jehovah's Witnesses have got lost. They think they are the only ones going to heaven. They're really lost [laugh] … I talk about God to all my friends. I don't go to Church. I know I don't go to Church. I try and pass on my own messages and that's all the disciples did. They just stayed down there with the people – sometimes you can't reach the people at the top. Sometimes you have to stay down with them.

I go Christmas Eve to any church which is available because I don't believe that, I believe my only way of explaining is that, in a field you've got a tree and as a branch you've got, on one branch you've got apples, and on one branch you've got oranges, on one branch you've got lemons, on one branch you've got peaches, but it's the same stem … I always pop into the nearest church where I'm living. As I said it doesn't matter what church, so long as it's a church and I thank him for my year and I ask him to forgive me at the end of the year.

Lastly, Charlie and Geoff talk about Church more negatively. For Charlie it is a memory of going to a church for a free meal and being expected to repeat a Hail Mary prayer which he did not know. 'I mumbled something, God knows what it was, so awkward really'. This then is transferred to a wider comment on how much he dislikes the concept of sacramental confession. He names the Roman Catholic Church in connection with 'too much dressing up, too much pomp and circumstance in churches, far too much' and reckons the Church should be more like a communist state: 'Everyone should be equal within the Church. They're not, are they?' He also dislikes any form of fanaticism in organized religion. Geoff's criticism dates from his days at a Catholic school. He says that he could recite the catechism but not do simple additions or tell the time. He resents religion being 'jammed down my throat'. We end the interview with this exchange, which gives a fair reflection of the tone of the whole:

David. Does that wind it up?

Geoff. I don't like Myra Hindley's use of religion. God is just an excuse.

David. You don't like religion very much, do you?

Geoff. Not when it's used to manipulate people. Ask me about church?

David. When?

Geoff. Four Sundays ago. I just walked in and sat down.

David. Locally?

Geoff. No, in Basingstoke. It was URC, no particular reason for it. I had no vision of God to go on or anything.

David. How was that?

Geoff. It was different, it was explained. There was biblical explanation which I find interesting, not religion but explaining. One bit I remember was the crucifixion, not four foot in the air on a cross but at eye-level.

David. That was interesting?

Geoff. Yes, I always thought of it four foot in the air. I could see Peter's hair on fire. A lot of people interpret the Bible to suit themselves. Churches use lots of things to suit themselves on the day. We should get our own house in order before we have Christian Aid abroad.

Single Religious Experiences

Religious experience-as-event (in Beardsworth's definition) is mentioned in only one interview, and that briefly. When Charlie is first asked whether there has been anything spiritual in his life, his reply interrupts me:

> To a certain extent I've never been a conventionally religious person, because although I do tend to think … I've never had a spiritual or religious experience, OK? I've got to say, the only experience I've ever had which is out of the ordinary is my wife was somewhat of a healer. She was very good with animals, she was a very caring person. She died in a horrible way and it always seems to happen to the nice people in this life that they have to go like that. She was a really lovely person, very gentle. And she once, I used to suffer from migraines, and she literally lifted a migraine out of the top of my head with her hands, literally lifted it out of the top. I could feel it going out the top of my head, lifted and that's about the only spiritual experience of any kind that I've ever had.

When Julie is asked whether she has had any particular experience of God, she shies away from a concrete answer and prefers instead 'Sunrises and sunsets that's all to do with God … God's in everything I see'. Geoff describes a couple of experiences of second sight but refuses to call these religious experiences:

David. Have you had any other experiences?

Geoff. I don't know, but I can tell you nothing about religion. I'm not a crank. There was a big dance in France, it caught fire. All the exits were cemented up. I saw that happen. I knew it happened. A few days later in the paper it was all there. There was a witness, a young boy from Reading. He disappeared from home in a green anorak, everybody was looking for him. She came outside and asked what am I doing? I say that there's a young lad out here, he's drowned. I said he had blue anorak on but it was green. He walked into the mud and dropped through and drowned … Quite a few of things like that. I can't get the numbers in the lottery.

Personal Theologies

In re-reading these transcripts I am struck by participants attempting to express complex ideas without many of the tools to do so. It is important here to acknowledge this attempt and see beyond the difficulties of expression. Some concepts are explicitly Christian (Julie's for the most part), others are implicitly so, some people use the language of Christianity but produce a skewed result, and others again (Richard for example) are trying to describe their own ideas. Some of these examples have been used previously so need not be reproduced in full again.

The two theological motifs of Julie's interview are sin/forgiveness and discipleship, which are repeated in different forms a number of times. In the section Images of God, the idea of personal sin is linked to judgement and salvation, as well as the wider picture of God's creation spoilt by the greed of human beings. On another occasion I ask the question more directly:

David. When you ask God for forgiveness, what does God say to you?

Julie. I don't know if God forgives me or not, but I won't know until the end of my life. I mean, I think he understands. He's the only one who can look into my heart and know what I'm really like, so at the end of the day … [laughs] I haven't killed anyone yet. We weren't put down here to be perfect. We weren't perfect when we got here, you know. I try my hardest to do the best I can in this life. All right, so I have a problem with shoplifting, but I think apart from that, I'm not too bad a Christian, not too bad a person to a lot of people.

The last words here connect to the second element of Julie's personal theology: mission or discipleship. She imagines a definite role for herself 'in the underground of life', and while she does not feel it important to attend Church, she does want to 'pass [on] my own messages' like a disciple. Similarly she says: 'Because I talk God and I talk nice and I talk love and a lot of criminals don't like that sort of talk, I have to suffer quite a lot down this end'. By implication, the message she is passing on is the same as her root image of God: 'God is love'. The simplicity of this is important for her in contrast to the obfuscations of everyday life:

> God made life so simple. It was people that complicated it. We're losing each other with lots of big words that people don't understand. God spoke in ... Jesus spoke in parables and things like that and made it so simple. He took something from life to explain something. They don't do that here. They explain things with things that people don't understand. With jargon, people don't understand jargon. They don't need jargon.

Reflections on the nature of pain and suffering are common to three people here. Caroline, Charlie and Marc all place their comments within a framework of traditional religious language (heaven, hell, God) though it is only Marc who relates suffering to a theology of the cross. This same image of Jesus is mentioned twice in Marc's interview; the second time in a rich mixture of Bible, love, lust and friendship:

> Well, Jesus had pain for us, he died for us, had pain ... like when you cut yourself you can put a plaster on, well he feels it, he must do, because you can easily wrap it up in plaster and that's over and done with, but he felt the pain for us on the cross, must have done. Even now, occasionally I read Bible, when I want to read it, like if I'm down, or run down, deep down, I read it. That perks me up a little bit. I read a bit more ... when I first read it, Tracy said, 'Oh you don't want to read that, it's sloppy that'. I said, 'Look it's not, it's a story'. Weeks go by and if I'm down, deep down, I read it and it helps, he helps you along that road ... Saying that when Tracy says 'I love you' but I actually say, 'I love you Tracy', but what is love? I don't know what it is, I never found it. Saying that, if Jesus loves you, you love him don't you? It hurts a bit, like, I can't grow attached to too many people. With John I knew his faults, his drinking, his tablets, but he didn't love me, like ... I don't know. I was in lust or whatever, I don't know, he said to me, 'You're too young to settle down', too young at twenty-seven. So I still read the Bible it helps me along.

Elsewhere Charlie wants to escape the straight-jacket of religious language and concepts when he seeks to separate the notion of moral good from religion: 'I think you can be a good person without being a religious person'. He is tired of hearing comments which imply that you have to be a Christian in order to be a 'nice guy'.

By comparison, Pete freely uses theological language, but his concept of God in a Christian sense is limited and fatalistic. One interpretation would be that his image of God is as provider of wives who are there to ensure his comfort; his anger is directed to God when there appears to be an arbitrary removal of these either through death or drug addiction. He relies on there being a plan of life worked out for him, but he recognises that he is hardly in control of it. This contrasts to Julie's remarks about a God of love and forgiveness.

Richard suggests an alternative viewpoint without using traditional religious language. He too imagines that life is planned, but in the context of a creator who also plans the beginning and end of the universe, who is greatly more advanced than we are. There is a reason for all creation, and human beings have to find their purpose within this. He talks of a 'task' or a 'test' which we have to experience, and therefore learn the kind of gifts we have and how they might be useful. It is partly this philosophy of life which prevents him from being angry with his situation. When I ask him further about this he says that as he has grown older 'You've just got to sit there and mellow. You sit and listen more'.

Humour

Black humour makes light of the most serious events of life and risks being misunderstood or considered in bad taste. It is a mechanism by which we are able to approach the unapproachable in the speech of everyday, so it should not be surprising that in the seriousness of these interviews, the humour that is around is of this kind. Three examples suffice and in each the speaker laughed or smiled after their remark. Pete laughs as he tells the story of waking up in the middle of Dartmoor having assumed he was dead and finding himself still alive; Marc smiles at the recollection of trying to gas himself and discovering only an electric fire. Caroline laughs as she recalls a very young, unhappy marriage:

> David. So you got married and your ... that didn't last very long?
>
> Caroline. No I left him, he beat me up. He broke my nose and black eyes and bruises everywhere. I went back to him after that [laugh].

Pete lightens his story with less black humour, and jokes at my expense: 'So I bought the vicar his cup of tea and sticky bun because vicars have never got any money. David, you know that'. Danni laughs in a little embarrassment as she remembers being questioned about who her Higher Power might be and finding that she really had no clue as so what was meant, unless she could include her pets:

> They used to say to me that your Higher Power is someone or something you turn to for like guidance, or to talk to about problems. And apart from my probation officer or social worker, or something like that, the only person I turn to is my pets.

This kind of humour is different from the style of Julie's interview, which relies more on wit and juxtaposition of opposites, part of her mechanism for survival in a hostile world. This chapter ends with two examples:

God gave us a beautiful garden … We just turned it into a rubbish tip.

I was lucky to be brought up in a children's home. I might have been brought up in a family.

Chapter 9

Themes from Homeless Lives:
Reading the Bible Together

A lawyer stood up to put Jesus to the test, saying, 'Teacher, what shall I do to inherit eternal life?' He said to him, 'What is written in the law? How do you read?' And he answered, 'You shall love the Lord your God with all your heart, and with all your soul, and with all your strength, and with all your mind; and your neighbour as yourself'. And Jesus said to him, 'You have answered right; do this, and you will live'. But he, desiring to justify himself, said to Jesus, 'And who is my neighbour?' Jesus replied, 'A man was going down from Jerusalem to Jericho, and he fell among robbers ... '.

Luke 10: 25–30

Contextual Bible Study (CBS) is one of the outcomes of a theological concentration on place and space, framed by an understanding via liberation theology that context is all important. Where theology is worked out is neither random nor incidental; it is a significant determinant of what conclusions are reached. An understanding that this applies to how Christian scriptures are interpreted is captured in the notable phrase of the feminist theologian Phyllis Trible, describing certain biblical passages with reference to women as 'texts of terror'.[1] While reading the Bible in particular situations has been criticised as being little more than the finding of analogies, Lawrence comments that:

> In fact, it is only in the collision of various contextual readings that liberatory narratives have been constructed: master narratives couched in patriarchy, slavery and racism have been exposed as oppressive by those counter stories from below.[2]

Thus she assembles reading groups in various locations including a fishing village, an inner city parish, a rural village and with the deaf community. A reading group with a second set of homeless people was a natural development of hearing personal stories via interviews.[3]

---

[1]   P. Trible, *Texts of Terror: Literary-Feminist Readings of Biblical Narrative* (London: SCM, 1992).

[2]   Lawrence, *The Word in Place*, p. 126.

[3]   See also Cornwall and Nixon, 'Readings from the Road'. In the extracts Susannah refers to Susannah Cornwall, the lead researcher.

The outcomes of such reading are described in the sections which follow, again with extensive quotations to illustrate substantive points as well as to provide the reader with a sense of these encounters. In each case, the biblical passage to which participants were asked to respond is included first.[4]

Session 1: Jesus' Temptations and Early Ministry

> Jesus full of the Holy Spirit returned from the Jordan and was led by the Spirit in the wilderness. Forty days he was tempted by the devil. He ate nothing at all during those days and when they were over he was famished. The devil said to him, 'If you are the Son of God, command this stone to become a loaf of bread'. Jesus answered him, 'It is written one does not live by bread alone'. Then the devil led him up and showed him in an instant all the kingdoms of the world. And the devil said to him, 'To you I will give their glory and all this authority for it has been given over to me and I will give it to anyone I please. I you then will worship me, it will all be yours'. Jesus answered him, 'It is written worship the Lord your God, and serve only him'. Then the devil took him to Jerusalem and placed him on the pinnacle of the temple saying to him, 'If you are the Son of God throw yourself down from here for it is written He will command His angels concerning you to protect you, and on their hands they will bear you up so that you will not dash your foot against the stone'. Jesus answered him, 'It is said do not put the Lord your God, to the test. 'When the devil had finished every test he departed from him until an opportune time. Then Jesus filled with the power of the Spirit returned to Galilee and a report about him spread through all the surrounding country. He began to teach in their synagogues and was praised by everyone. When he came to Nazareth where he'd been brought up he went to the synagogue on the Sabbath day as was his custom. He stood up to read and the scroll of the prophet Isaiah was given to him. He unrolled the scroll and found the place where it was written, 'The Spirit of the Lord is upon me because it has invited me to bring good news to the poor. He sent me to proclaim release to the captives and recovery of sight to the blind, to let the oppressed go free, to proclaim the year of the Lord's favour'. And he rolled up the scroll, gave it back to the attendant and sat down. The eyes of all in the synagogue were fixed on him. Then he began to say to them, 'Today this Scripture has been fulfilled in your hearing'. All spoke well of him and were amazed at the gracious words that came from his mouth. They said, 'Isn't this Joseph's son?' He said to them, 'Doubtless you will quote to me this proverb 'doctor cure yourself' and you will say 'do here also in your home town the things that we've heard you did at Capernaum''. And he said, 'Truly I tell you no prophet is accepted in the prophet's home town.' (Luke 4: 1–24)

---

[4]   In this text the pseudonym Dan has replaced Danny in the original article to prevent confusion with Danni.

Initial discussion focused around the final sentence and the concept of going back, especially going back home. This led naturally to some thoughts about home: what it is or where it is. Dan talks about the freedom of 'roaming' but its disadvantages in terms of employment. He goes on to cite an example of someone who because of abuse was at home nowhere, not even travelling:

> Dan. So for her to go back home is not happening, do you know. She's never, wherever she's been, it's like, I've met her in a few different places and she's never at home wherever she is. If she went back to where her parents and her family are from, do you know, there is no comfort there. She's looking for that comfort. But she's never got comfort with a companion either because she's learned to distrust people.

> Susannah. So she's not finding that travelling around either really. No.

> Dan. No.

Fiona's understanding is slightly different: '[You] prefer travelling and then find somewhere and settle down. Well, I haven't found somewhere but I have found someone'.

Susannah returned the focus to the biblical passage and asked for more specific responses to the temptations of Jesus. The image of the devil asking Jesus to worship him in exchange for power over the whole world elicits a discussion about contemporary society and the bargain offered by the economic system:

> Niall. If you work you can have a car, if you work you can have this. It's all there, isn't it.

> Dan. From the day we're born it's been like that really. You are told you'll get an ice cream.

> Niall. It's the desire not to be equal, I think, isn't it. We want to be above somebody else.

> Susannah. Oh, that's interesting, isn't it. So almost here the devil is saying to Jesus well, you know, if you do this you're going to have more power than anybody else. I'm going to give you …

> Niall. Yeah, give you what technically you are not going be the same as everybody else, you're going to be above everybody else. And that's what the system basically tells everybody to be.

The third temptation brings reference by one speaker to the Second Iraq War and Tony Blair being the one who is tempted, but on further questioning he says that he is not convinced by his own argument.

Session 2: Jesus and the Fishermen – A Healing Miracle

> Once while Jesus was standing by the lake of Gennesaret and the crowd was pressing in on him to hear the word of God he saw two boats there at the shore of the lake. The fishermen had gone out of them and were washing their nets. He got into one of the boats, the one belonging to Simon, and asked him to put out a little way from the shore. Then he sat down and taught the crowds from the boat. When he had finished speaking he said to Simon, 'Put out into the deep water and let down your nets for a catch'. Simon answered, 'Master, we've worked all night long but have caught nothing. Yet if you say so I will let down the nets'. When they'd done this they caught so many fish that their nets were beginning to break. So they signalled to their partners in the other boat to come and help them. And they came and filled both boats so that they began to sink. But when Simon Peter saw it he fell down at Jesus' knees saying, 'Go away from me, Lord, for I am a sinful man'. For he and all who were with him were amazed at the catch of fish that they had taken. And so also with James and John, sons of Zebedee, who were partners with Simon. Then Jesus said to Simon, 'Do not be afraid, from now on you will be catching people'. When they had brought their boats to shore they left everything and followed him. Once when he was in one of the cities there was a man covered with leprosy. When he saw Jesus he bowed with his face to the ground and begged him 'Lord, if you choose you can make me clean'. Then Jesus stretched out his hand, touched him, and said, 'I do choose, be made clean'. Immediately the leprosy left him. And he ordered him to tell no one. 'Go', he said, 'and show yourself to the priest and as Moses commanded make an offering for your cleansing for a testimony to them'. But now more than ever the word about Jesus spread abroad. Many crowds would gather to hear him and to be cured of their diseases. But he would withdraw to deserted places and pray. After this he went out and saw a tax collector named Levi sitting at the tax booth and he said to him, 'Follow me'. And he got up, left everything and followed him. Then Levi gave a great banquet for him in his house. And there was a large crowd of tax collectors and others sitting at the table with them. The Pharisees and their scribes were complaining to his disciples saying, 'Why do you eat and drink with tax collectors and sinners?' Jesus answered, 'Those who are well have no need of a doctor but those who are sick. I have come to call not the righteous but sinners for repentance.' (Luke 5: 1–16 and 27–32)

Out of the four sessions reading the Bible with homeless people, this one provoked the most responses and the most interesting responses about the person of Jesus. The text tends to be heard and imagined in literal detail, so one participant suggests that his experience of fishermen is that if he talked to them like Jesus did, they would throw him over the side. How could a carpenter be telling fishermen what to do? But there is also:

> James. Maybe he were a better fisherman, maybe he had new ideas that he could introduce to the older guys who had the boats and they could listen and … I mean, there's always people with new and fresh ideas, isn't there.

Fiona chooses another aspect of this account and comments on Jesus needing 'time out'. She draws parallels with her own experiences of needing space for reflection or recuperation:

> I get a picture that Jesus, because he calls him Master and people ask him to do so many things but he wants to go away sometimes and withdraw, doesn't he, and just be on his own for a bit. Because you know, everyone is asking him and asking him and asking him. He needs his space as well, doesn't he. That's what I like about it, that's what's so human about him. Do you know what I mean? He needs his space as well so he can cope. Because it can get too much sometimes. But he still comes back and he still helps. But he needs that space as well to go meditate or whatever … Yeah, I think he needs to like sort of recoup. And also he's got to think about himself. If he's not sort of good within himself, and hasn't got that inner strength, he won't be able to help other people so much. It's nice to know you can connect with that. Sometimes with things, you know, everyone needs that, a bit of quiet time. So something you can relate to.

Susannah asks what meaning they ascribe to Jesus' instruction to Simon: 'from now on you will be catching people'. This evokes the kind of comment that with a less transient group might be explored more fully:

> James. Cannibalism. [laughter] Well, the fishing, when they're fishing they're fishing for food, aren't they? So I mean, they could assume that, they could think this guy is a bit of a cannibal.

Followed by Jesus as a fairground attraction:

> James. Like Ripley's *Believe It or Not!*[5] You know, have you seen them in Blackpool, one of them ones. 'Come and see a man who catches men, not fish!' [several laugh].

Meanwhile Fiona has a more conventional interpretation:

---

[5]   'Believe It or Not'. Available at: http://www.ripleys.com (accessed 26 January 2012). This site contains stills, videos, graphics and stories of the weird and wonderful, particularly in North America.

He just wants to spread the word. He wants them to spread the word, doesn't he ... They are going to well, spread the word. Yeah ... This amazing man is around.

In response to the healing miracle there is discussion about why Jesus asks the man with leprosy not to tell others. All participants are immersed in the story at this point, almost as if they are bystanders, or have a clear picture in their imaginations. Again the focus is on the person of Jesus:

Fiona. I just think he doesn't want to be big, it's a bit of a crap word but bigheaded. He doesn't want to be like, you know, I've done all this, I've done all that.

Tom [at same time]. He's obviously tired out from doing things, isn't he.

Fiona. He wants to do it in moderation. You know, don't tell everyone because it will spread in its own time, people in their own time will hear and see. He doesn't want to get swamped. Again this is the space thing, isn't it.

James comes back into the conversation at this point and wants to combine the two previous images, extending the idea slightly. He has little confidence in what he is saying but in the context of this study his remark is especially insightful:

Well, how you interpret it, there can be two different interpretations. One where you're looking at it sort of sensationalist sort of I am a fisher of men, he might be a cannibal, bogeyman. And the other side then is a modest person, saying 'Don't tell anyone I'm the bogeyman, please keep it quiet. Maybe I want to do good work and good deeds. But also I am a bogeyman, because I need to be, because I can change things'. I mean, I'm just going off the top of my head. 'I can change things ...'.

The final part of this reading considers why Jesus eats with sinners, and who might be viewed in the same way now. Participants mention traffic wardens, health and safety executives, wheel clampers, politicians, and also homeless people. These remarks are made with no self-pity:

James. Homeless people. They're unpopular with people. I used to hear comments by people. [Jim agrees] I don't know what it is but I've had some cruel words, I suppose. Vindictiveness.

Tom. Yeah, we're not here from choice, are we?

Fiona. It's like a stigma … And most people I've met, I mean, we've both had full-time jobs, but there's a lot of mental illness out there. And I've met so many people that have been, you know, like upstanding citizens and they've just fallen. It's not their fault, you know. And that's what angers me. But you do get some horrible comments, don't you. You just get, 'Get a job', 'Scum', 'Drug addict' – and you just think, you don't know me. Do you know what I mean?

Tom. Try wearing my shoes for a day.

Session 3: At Simon's House – Anointing and a Parable

One of the Pharisees asked Jesus to eat with him, and he went into the Pharisee's house and took his place at the table. And a woman in the city, who was a sinner, having learned that he was eating in the Pharisee's house, brought an alabaster jar of ointment. She stood behind him at his feet, weeping, and began to bathe his feet with her tears and to dry them with her hair. Then she continued kissing his feet and anointing them with the ointment.

Now when the Pharisee who had invited him saw it, he said to himself, 'If this man were a prophet, he would have known who and what kind of woman this is who is touching him—that she is a sinner'. Jesus spoke up and said to him, 'Simon, I have something to say to you'. 'Teacher', he replied, 'speak'. 'A certain creditor had two debtors; one owed five hundred pounds, and the other fifty. When they could not pay, he cancelled the debts for both of them. Now which of them will love him more?' Simon answered, 'I suppose the one for whom he cancelled the greater debt'. And Jesus said to him, 'You have judged rightly'.

Then turning towards the woman, he said to Simon, 'Do you see this woman? I entered your house; you gave me no water for my feet, but she has bathed my feet with her tears and dried them with her hair. You gave me no kiss, but from the time I came in she has not stopped kissing my feet. You did not anoint my head with oil, but she has anointed my feet with ointment. Therefore, I tell you, her sins, which were many, have been forgiven; hence she has shown great love. But the one to whom little is forgiven, loves little'. Then he said to her, 'Your sins are forgiven'. But those who were at the table with him began to say among themselves, 'Who is this who even forgives sins?' And he said to the woman, 'Your faith has saved you; go in peace.' (Luke 7: 36–50)

Responses to hearing this biblical passage weave backwards and forwards, focusing on the woman and her tears, on Jesus and the issue of debt, back to the woman, to Simon as religious leader and host, back to debt and finally back to Simon. Not all of this movement is directed by the session leaders. The very first comments relate to the strangeness of the story and why it is there at all; there are issues linking the ice breaker with the process of hearing and reading; there is a possibility of a group reading; and there is evidence that single speakers can have a disproportionate effect on outcomes.

Fiona's reaction to the meaning and history of the woman in the story shows an empathy and identification with her actions towards Jesus:

> She was a working lady and she doesn't want to be like that anymore … Well, she wants to be saved, doesn't she, and forgiven, and she was wanting to be normal … Doesn't want to. She wants respect and probably to be loved. Just. Someone just to say to her it's okay, you're just who you are and you're forgiven. You're … You know. So yeah. She just wants that comfort.

Later comments include:

> Glenn. Scorned by society. Feels bad about herself. Guilt ridden.

> Michael. A lonely old woman.

> Al. But then again she could be saying that I'm not bothered about you, I'll take you as I find you, kind of thing, do you know what I mean. I'm not bothered if you've robbed, broke or stole or whatever. I'm here to whatever. I don't care who you are, anyway whatever, do you know what I mean, it doesn't matter whose feet it was, I'd still wash them, do you know what I mean?

> Michael. She's quite confident though, isn't she?

There is some interest in the gesture of kissing feet, recognition of cultural and temporal distance, and the down-to-earth: 'Especially if he had boots on and his feet were stinking'.

The issue of debt raises a variety of responses, some of which challenge regular interpretations of the story and Jesus' own teaching. One participant indicates that it is the action of writing-off debts which is important, and not the amount, so in fact they are both equal. Another says that the one who has the smaller debt annulled will be disappointed he has not asked for more in the first place. Some of these debtors' reactions will also depend on their personal circumstances and why they were in debt: '[if] it was life or death time or whatever, then they'd feel more obliged than what he would [be] just putting it on the horses or whatever kind of thing'. The first speaker later links this story of debt to contemporary economic circumstances; description of the letter referred to dominates discussion:

So if they're paying 70 billion back, what's the debt? They didn't say what the debt was, just the interest, kind of thing. I was thinking to myself, Dear, Hiya Prime Minister, and I wrote him a letter, I've got 15 pages written now and I haven't finished it yet [several laugh].

Attitudes to Simon as host and religious leader are also instructive, including differing views about welcome and hospitality. There is humour as well.

Glenn. He's surprised that Jesus isn't revulsed [*sic*].

Al. I think he's put his car keys in the bowl the same as everybody else does [laughter from males].

Al. Say now, say like for example I was like planning on going to see the kids in Carlisle, so I've travelled 400 miles all the way to Carlisle, I would get there, which I was expecting But if I turned up and they thought 'Oh, it's only Dad', and carried on with whatever they were doing, that'd be like a disappointment kind of thing to have, do you know. It's like four years since I've been there and it's like … But anyway, so say I went up there tomorrow, knocked on the door, Deborah and Sean, 'Oh, it's only Dad', and carried on with their day-to-day life, so, bloody hell, I've never seen them for four years but yet they're still continuing as if I don't exist.

Michael. Coming back to what you were saying about knowing him, how long he's known him, see if you came round my house and I'd known you a year, and you've been coming round my house for a year, you know where the cupboard is, you know how to make yourself a cup of tea, I'm not going to offer you one. Same thing with the water and his feet, I'm guessing.

They return to Simon before the end of the session, and despite Al's attempts to monopolise the discussion with his own agenda, he also adds this perception: 'He was kind of like bigging himself up … Slagging off this, slagging off that, whatever'.

Despite the discontinuity of this conversation, the engagement with the event at Simon's house and the response to ideas about lifestyle, debt and hospitality include the potential for a group reading: that these homeless people have something particular to say about this biblical episode because of their common life experiences. It may be coincidental that the ice breaker for this session focused on optical illusions and at one stage Al had difficulties finding the sentence in the written text he wished to highlight. He says: I've got no glasses on … [reading] For I ask Jesus to be with him and he wants, went … I can't see without my glimmers'. Differences between hearing and reading texts and issues of literacy come to the fore.

Session 4: A Father and Two Sons

> Jesus said, 'There was a man who had two sons. The younger of them said to his father, 'Father, give me the share of the property that will belong to me'. So he divided his property between them. A few days later the younger son gathered all he had and travelled to a distant country, and there he squandered his property in reckless living. When he had spent everything, a severe famine took place throughout that country, and he began to be in need. So he went and hired himself out to one of the citizens of that country, who sent him to his fields to feed the pigs. He would gladly have filled himself with the food that the pigs were eating; and no one gave him anything. But when he came to himself he said, 'How many of my father's hired hands have bread enough and to spare, but here I am dying of hunger! I will get up and go to my father, and I will say to him, "Father, I have sinned against heaven and before you; I am no longer worthy to be called your son; treat me like one of your hired hands".'

> So he set off and went to his father. But while he was still far off, his father saw him and was filled with compassion; he ran and put his arms around him and kissed him. Then the son said to him, 'Father, I have sinned against heaven and before you; I am no longer worthy to be called your son'. But the father said to his slaves, 'Quickly, bring out a robe – the best one – and put it on him; put a ring on his finger and sandals on his feet. And get the fatted calf and kill it, and let us eat and celebrate; for this son of mine was dead and is alive again; he was lost and is found!' And they began to celebrate.

> 'Now his elder son was in the field; and when he came and approached the house, he heard music and dancing. He called one of the slaves and asked what was going on. He replied, 'Your brother has come, and your father has killed the fatted calf, because he has got him back safe and sound'. Then he became angry and refused to go in. His father came out and began to plead with him. But he answered his father, 'Listen! For all these years I have been working like a slave for you, and I have never disobeyed your command; yet you have never given me even a young goat so that I might celebrate with my friends. But when this son of yours came back, who has devoured your property with prostitutes, you killed the fatted calf for him!' Then the father said to him, 'Son, you are always with me, and all that is mine is yours. But we had to celebrate and rejoice, because this brother of yours was dead and has come to life; he was lost and has been found.' (Luke 15: 11–32)

Given the subject matter of this episode, it is perhaps not surprising that this reading prompts the most coherent conversation amongst these homeless people. It might be possible to say that there is a group reading which comes out of this, reflecting an ownership of the text and an engagement with the experiences of all the characters. Raymond immediately identifies with the family dynamic:

> Well, a similar thing happened with me and with my brother … While he was away, he was fighting in Japan at the time, but when he came back, he thought he should rule the roost kind of thing. And I'd been working all the time he'd been away, even though I was very young, and supporting me mother. And yet when he came back he thought he should take over, which I thought was wrong.

In this account, it is the older brother who returns, but Raymond is also the younger brother who spent a large sum of money quickly. Another participant describes a literal inheritance:

> Raymond. Went through the money quickly. I think I'm a record breaker with that … Six grand in a week … Well, I gambled a lot of it. I bought a lot of things, like clothes, I bought, a brand new piano and all that kind of thing. I didn't waste it all. I did have a lot back.

> Michael. On my 18th birthday I inherited £13,500 but it was too easily, and spent it in two weeks on crap. I haven't got one thing to show for it. If I knew now what I knew, even though it was only a few years ago, if I knew then what I knew now I wouldn't have done that. But you do these things. You've got a learning curve. And next time I get that amount of money … Because I will! [laughs] But yeah, no, and I would have, I was just about to say, I'm definitely the youngest.

The father's reaction evinces further comments about the verisimilitude of the story, with Glenn suggesting that the older brother will be more welcoming than the father, that as the younger son he would have too much pride to return like this; but his final comment relating to his own experience implies a greater truth in the biblical account than Glenn was prepared to allow. The memory he evokes parallels very clearly both the actions and emotions of the Lucan father:

> I don't think he would have gone home in the first place. He would have been too proud, he would have known he'd messed up. And if he had have gone home, the father would have been like, 'What the fuck are you doing here?', and the older brother would have been, like, 'Really good to see you'. He would have probably been the most accommodating … There's no way I could go crawling back as they say, you know. There you go. [laughs] … I would go grudgingly if I thought they were like completely accepting of the situation and I knew that I'd be saving myself a lot of aggro, I'd go with them, I wouldn't feel too bad about it. But if they tried to force me to go, then I would be like 'No, sorry, I'll stay and make a man of myself' and stay away … The only time my old man's ever told me that he loves me is that night when I got back from running away. He was crying and hugging me then.

At the end of the session, there is another parallel drawn, between the spendthrift son who is likened to indulgent bankers, and the hardworking older son likened to those who are now paying for the indulgence.

The story is brought into a contemporary focus with the reference to the family of Ozzy Osbourne of the rock group Black Sabbath. Discussion ranges across the potential similarities, explaining the story to those who do not see the connections, fragmenting into different side conversations before the session is brought to a close.

> Raymond. Ozzy Osbourne, yeah. That's the nearest to it in modern life, I think, isn't it. Pretty near. Because he'd got a son and a daughter and they both were wayward, you know, but I don't know how they are now. I think, I think …

> Dan. Okay, well, Ozzy Osbourne was a member of a rock band. Yeah … Sex, drugs, and rock'n'roll is what he stood up for. Since, he's probably given up on all of that because of his mental state. [laughter] He's gone from illegals to pharmaceuticals. But he's got two kids, I think it's two kids, and a wife. And they're all living off of his erm, yeah …

> Raymond. He's got three kids. Yeah, he's got two daughters and a son. The other daughter is out of it altogether. She isn't in it.

> Dan. Well, she's the runaway, yeah? She's the one who's living off his bank account, whereas the other two are in the spotlight, getting into it. He's gone from music to television, yeah. And then, yeah, there's a daughter gone off with his bank card.

> Tony: So who would Ozzy be in this story that Susannah talked about?

> Steve: He'd be the father. And then you've got the two kids there with him, they'd be like the eldest son, and then the one that's ran off would be the youngest one …

> Michael. Yeah. But actually, the other two kids that he has got, actually do work, because both of them have had their own TV shows, one of them's had, well, tried to get a number one hit and was useless.

The description of these four sessions illustrates the contribution of CBS as a method of reading, especially with groups on the margins. New, exciting, and perhaps unlikely images may replace tired, dull metaphors. However, it is not claimed that such a reading supersedes or improves upon other biblical readings; rather that it adds to what might already be known. Additionally, there can be no claim for universality here. This would run counter to any notion of contextual readings, and deny the specifics of this group, not least who took part and why, who left part way through, why one person did not give permission for his words to be used, and so on. These are the comments of a shifting group of homeless people at a particular time and place. In terms of this project aimed towards a theology of homelessness some questions remain: if not universal, then how far is it possible to say that there is something special or even unique about how homeless people might hear and read the Bible? How do such insights and images relate to the previous biographies and analysis of homeless narratives? Does starting with the Bible stories rather than the listener or reader affect conclusions, especially theological conclusions?

PART III
Conclusions

But he was pierced for our transgressions, crushed for our iniquities; the chastisement he bore restored us to health and by his wounds we are healed. We had all strayed like sheep, each of us going his own way, but the Lord laid on him the guilt of us all.

Isaiah 53: 5, 6

Chapter 10

Towards a Theology of Homelessness:
The Story We're In

It was the best of times, it was the worst of times, it was the age of wisdom, it was the age of foolishness, it was the epoch of belief, it was the epoch of incredulity, it was the season of Light, it was the season of Darkness, it was the spring of hope, it was the winter of despair, we had everything before us, we had nothing before us, we were all going direct to heaven, we were all going direct the other way.

Charles Dickens, *A Tale of Two Cities*[1]

The starting point of this book was a particular encounter with one individual, the story of his life and its effect on mine. The context was important: he had been a drug-user, I was a priest, the hostel was loosely connected with the local church. Writing from his experience in inner-city Leeds, David Rhodes echoes a similar sentiment:

> In this and many other ways it came to the priest that he was not bringing God to the homeless: it was the homeless and poor who were living and speaking the love of God to him in his need and his spiritual poverty. It was they who were the outward and visible expression of God's presence.[2]

An exploration of the meaning of this outward and visible expression is the subject matter of this book, together with an appreciation of the dialogue between those who are marginalised and those who listen to their lifestories. A theological route map proposed parallel paths. Practical theology implied an examination of the contemporary world in dialogue with different texts, including the Bible. It suggested that an inter-disciplinary method which paid heed to context and to the hidden 'others' created by Western modernity would yield an authentic theology of transformation. This led to a focus on the nature of the encounter – one story told to another person – and so to a theology of story. It was suggested that within certain criteria the stories of the poor can re-invigorate our Christian story and make these stories strange again. A second path was based on a desire to collect more stories and to analyse them systematically. Qualitative research methods applied to everyday life were the ones best disposed to achieve this task. The intersection of writer and those written about, together with issues of voice, point

---

[1]   Charles Dickens, *A Tale of Two Cities* (London and Glasgow: Collins' Clear-Type Press, no date), p. 8.

[2]   David Rhodes, *Faith in Dark Places* (London: Triangle, 1996), p. 18.

also to the influence of postmodern thinking and, as in a mathematical problem, the desire to show workings: what Jagose calls in relation to Queer Theory a display of exoskeletal support. This translates here to a recapitulation of the story in which we find ourselves, and in particular to a wish to isolate moments where previously held theory may be challenged by such empirical data that conversations and interviews have provided. A theology of homelessness is the destination to which these markers point.

A Theology of Story Revisited

Both a literary and a theological perspective saw story as fundamental to existence, a way of giving meaning and order to the confusion of human life. The stories which homeless people tell are particular evidence of this, where the search for identity and meaning is often sharper, perhaps unique. If the pain of homeless people is frequently centred around loss, including the loss of identity, then the story which begins to rediscover identity is all the more significant. The therapeutic dimension of storytelling exemplified by those with experience of the Alcoholics Anonymous organisation is also mirrored here, both consciously in those who acknowledge the power of the story, and unconsciously as they construct their lifestories in my hearing.

An understanding of liberation theology designated the poor as storytellers for God. While an analysis of the stories of these homeless people does not preclude notions of spirituality, with the possible exception of Julie's interview and Marc's experience of a Christian cafe, there is little evidence that they themselves have any concept that they are especially 'preferred' by God. On the other hand, there is ample proof to echo here Segundo's caveat that 'passive and fatalistic' imagery around God is not a helpful departure point for the evangelisation of the theologian by those who are marginal. It is certainly possible to affirm that a two-way traffic is desirable, but the evidence from this analysis points more in the direction of Rayan's 'latent' theology awaiting articulation perhaps by both specialist and non-specialist together. The theologian does indeed need to go outside the camp, and I believe that this was achieved in a small measure during these conversations.

Freire's more political language of oppressed and oppressor, and their entrapped reciprocity, leads to a wider critique. There is no evidence from any of the participants of an understanding of the Church as challenging the underlying causes of poverty and homelessness. It could be argued that there is not a lot of comment about the Church in any sense – where it is positive it is around personal support, non-interference in a lifestyle, and in reinforcing a conservative outlook on life. There are more examples of a negative apprehension of the Church. Yet added to this is my impression of a similar absence from the homeless centres I visited. They certainly attempt successfully to meet the changing needs of homeless people, but I question the degree of theological literacy in what are essentially Christian projects. In terms of the Good News as a loving response to those who suffer, there is no doubt that these projects tell out the gospel, but I wonder about the difficult task of a prophetic ministry which questions root causes of marginalisation. If, of course, the Church itself is weak in this role and prefers a quiet collusion, then it is hardly surprising that those who work within its broad margins are not encouraged to challenge the status quo. This is perhaps a concrete example of Myers' argument that the Churches have negotiated a withdrawal from the public, political domain in return for continued influence in individual lives. There is a concern here for non-persons (rather than non-believers) but much of the Church's resources and thinking about mission tends to marginalise connections with social justice.

Further insights into the nature of storytelling were provided by Buber, Wright and Hauerwas. While my intention was to create in the course of the interviews the I–Thou relationship which Buber describes, the interviewees witnessed to the significance of telling their stories whether it was to me or, more importantly, to a key worker. The therapeutic relief of 'getting the story out' for the first time is mentioned by more than one participant. Buber underlines the real gift of being able to listen to others, and the frequency with which nowadays conversations harden to an I–It status. This may explain partly explain why homeless people as experts on homelessness are so rarely consulted.[3] This would also extend to the insights of homeless (and other marginal) people when they read and interpret the Bible. Wright's notion that our stories carry our knowledge of the world, allowing new knowledge to be added, is supported here by the attempts of these storytellers to integrate their earlier lives with their present situations, and at the same time formulate plans and hopes for the future. They have already set up the beginnings of a third story, which shows a pattern of recovery and restitution favoured by Western narrative. If their first stories are an articulation of collapse then the intention is to move to reconstruction. Such a process is also supported by similar work amongst homeless people from a health perspective:

> The analysis of the transcripts indicated that homeless individuals strive to have valued lives and selves. Because of their homelessness, they experience disrupted plans and altered lives. The narrative text revealed that homelessness poses identity problems; positive former identities are preserved, current identity is devalued, and future identities are glimpsed. Past, present and future blends into one another as homeless individuals (for a number of reasons related to their biographies and context) cling to selves situated in the past or create selves oriented to the future.[4]

---

[3]   For an American example of this, see Alan Emmins, *31 Days: A New York Street Diary* (London: Corvo, 2006), p. 93.

[4]   K.M. Boydell et al., 'Narratives of Identity: Re-Presentation of Self in People Who Are Homeless', *Qualitative Health Research* 10/1 (2000): 30.

Stanley Hauerwas remarked on the same theme within a context of Christian storytelling, with the significant difference that he imagines that the Christian story is the vehicle through which the past and present are incorporated into the new self. It is not obvious from the interviews that the Christian story plays much part in the lives of these homeless people. It may be significant that Julie who articulates some clear Christian thinking appears as such a positive and energetic character, or that Marc speaks more positively than elsewhere in his interview of his time spent in a Christian cafe. But for the majority, a real hold on the powerful nature of the Christian story is absent.

Hauerwas' work on the loss of narrative is also reflected here. If the theme of loss in general is evidenced among this particular group of homeless people, then homelessness imposes another loss upon them: their place in the common societal story, or more likely their exclusion from it. They are outsiders to the story in which they once had a role. And so like the poor everywhere, they now they risk another alien story being imposed on them, via the labelling and prejudice against those who have fallen out of the system. They long to return to this old story, and recall the moments when they were part of it, trying to construct a future which allows for the awfulness of the present. The new story can never wipe out what is currently experienced but it may be able to mollify its effects. A more concrete loss of place is also emphasised in these stories, from Charlie's 'lost wandering lad' to Pete's descriptions of a disrupted marital home; from Danni's experience of prison to Fran's rootless searching. But equally, place is comprehend as a contested reality with different meanings ascribed to it, with home (and therefore homelessness) being loaded with ideology.

Three levels of loss or absence may be perceived here: a theoretical absence or exclusion from discourse concerning housing and homelessness, in other words a post-colonial erasure in social policy terms and in much sociological and theological study; a loss for specific individuals of their place in the story of the community, and the story they tell themselves about themselves; these two levels represented literally by the loss of a place of security, commonly summed up in the concept of home.

It is here that the Christian theologian wishes to intervene and say to homeless people: I know a story that can help you slowly to reconcile these things, to argue for real equality, to imagine a better future. Despairingly perhaps I ask: 'Why haven't you heard this story?' John Vincent has already provided some of the answer in his discussion about why poor people in Britain are rarely the instigators of a local liberation theology. But the message to the theologians is to ask themselves where they are situated in relation to the theology they are creating, and where this theology is being performed.

Collecting Stories Revisited

These biographies of homeless people and their analysis (including a reflection on reading the Bible together) need to be reviewed against the earlier decisions about how best to collect stories of everyday human life. The tensions between individual and group experience form one aspect of this, which leads neatly to a reminder about who constitutes a 'proper' subject for study. The way in which homeless voices are often ignored in terms of investigation is part of a wider cultural practice of marginalisation. The theme of spirituality forms the least 'good fit' and some reasons for this are suggested. Lastly, the important intersection between writer and subject is reconsidered.

The analysis of these interviews allows the current reader to have an understanding of these 11 homeless people (and to a small extent of one writer) in ways which respect both their individuality and at the same time their common experiences. While it is important not to lose sight of the particular against the universal, the idiosyncratic over against the stereotype, nevertheless this project also shows clearly the existence of a number of experiences, which many, but not all, of the participants share. These amount to a crisis or a series of crises often brought about by a major loss (by bereavement, of job, of partner, of health, and so on) which results in some form of abuse, of self or substance. At this point the story becomes public in the loss of home, and frequently in the loss of shelter. This is the first part of what might be described as a cycle of homelessness.

The second part is characterised by a paradoxical emotional reaction. Descriptions of pain, fear, suffering and isolation have usually accompanied this slide into homelessness; yet at the same time and within the same individuals there is a fierce will to survive, to remain independent and to preserve a measure of human dignity despite the circumstances. Ironically, such a combination may prevent a homeless person seeking outside intervention before further crises (for example, of health) develop.

The third part, occurring in varying degrees in these life histories, is an account of restitution or coming home. Drug and alcohol addiction is being controlled, marital reconciliation is underway, restoration of health is envisaged. Above all, the start of, or return to, a permanent and secure home is imagined. The manager of St Piran's remarks that this hope ranges from the realistic to the frankly fantastic, but such hope is present in almost all participants in this study, with the exceptions of Geoff and Tim. Both show a greater acceptance of their circumstances, though Tim's age and ill-health indicate that a change of lifestyle is required in the near future.

This process of homelessness has been presented as a linear one in accordance with the accounts of participants. Of those who were interviewed at Aubyn House, Caroline, Danni, Fran, Marc and Pete had also lived at the Victory hostel; Charlie and Pete had lived with the Salvation Army, and Danni had lived at Akron House on the outskirts of the city. This is implicit evidence of a resettlement policy: from short-stay hostels to a 'half-way house' like Aubyn to a secure tenancy.

The picture in the other town was less clear since St Piran's was a day-centre, but some of those interviewed there spoke of different hostels and bedsits. Resettlement work was part of St Piran's remit as evidenced by the employment of an outreach worker. Although there is only one hint of this (at the end of Danni's interview), what is presented here as primarily linear is often in practice cyclical: a cycle of homelessness. Before the appointment of resettlement or outreach workers, it was recognised that many who were simply rehoused came back to hostels quite quickly, unable to sustain independent living, and starting from a worse position of failure than before. Michael from St Piran's remarked that in dealing with a whole life and a whole person, provision of housing alone was not enough.[5] This points back to the concept of diversity – distinctive individual lives within shared experiences.

Diversity allows a challenge to negative labelling of homeless people, and sees instead individuals with a mixture of different characteristics and experiences. This undercuts any notion of respectable or unrespectable research subjects, and equally of respectable or unrespectable biblical interpretation. Of these participants, more than half, during a large part of their lives, would have been seen as respectable or middle class; of the others, the majority come from dysfunctional families and are too young to have established independent existence.

One of the things they may share is the common assumption of others about homeless people: a narrative which it is hard to contest. In the description of the humour of miscommunication between his speakers, Rapport suggests that the underlying cause is the unconscious attempt of speakers to impose different cultural concepts on one another, and the attempt's failure. He alludes to Wikan's work amongst the poor in Cairo, when she comments that the weaker groups in society have difficulty resisting an alien culture being imposed upon them. In respect of the homeless population the same phenomenon is apparent. Katherine Boydell comments that:

> the behaviour of … interviewees was better understood through an effort to understand the meanings that the homeless individuals themselves adopted rather than by concentrating only on the more unidimensional attributions made by others.[6]

The overall culture of the homeless people involved in this study reveals a tension or a paradox between suffering and survival. Though some of the actual descriptions seem to make light of the worst of the experiences described, the sum total for any individual, or for the group as a whole, amounts to serious degree of

---

[5]   See G. Randall and S. Brown, *Outreach and Resettlement Work with People Sleeping Rough* (London: DoE, 1995) and Pleace, 'Rehousing Single Homeless People' in Burrows, Pleace and Quilgars, *Homelessness and Social Policy*.

[6]   Boydell, 'Narratives of Identity', p. 28.

physical, emotional, psychological and spiritual suffering. Alongside this runs a powerful stream of fierce survival. Brett Smith remarks in his personal account of depression that 'the preference in Western culture for restitution narratives, in which the storyteller triumphs over her or his illness, reinforces a general aversion to hearing diverse and contradictory illness stories'.[7] Notwithstanding this preference, stories of survival may represent an unconscious attempt to resist the almost uniform negative images which are placed on homeless people, movingly described by those participating in the Bible reading experience. The fact that society at large continues in these images points to a public failure to make survival real. This supports the contention that these dialogues reflect the same phenomenon that Wikan describes – that the construction of culture is dependent on the relative power of different groups, and that homeless people have little with which to argue their case.

The category showing the least 'good fit' between theory and the data discovered by these conversations focused on spirituality and religious experience. The difficulties with terminology, especially in an empirical study, are best captured by the double recognition that while definitions of religious experience as both event and process are possible, an interviewee or respondent is quite free to choose their own understanding. Within this research I chose to emphasise the broader basis, with the use of the word 'spiritual' on occasions. However, as the results indicate, a very wide variety of response occurred, almost none of which fall into any of the categories previously designated. Such words and phrases as 'heightened perception', 'a sense of something dynamic, communal, mystical or numinous', 'God as Trinity', are largely missing from these transcripts. Instead, interviewees expressed a limited range of images and ideas associated with God, which include holding God to blame for their troubles. There was a range of expression about Church and the Bible, some interesting attempts to develop a personal theology and examples of black humour. It would be arrogant and misplaced to conclude that there is an absence of spirituality here, though there is little that is specifically Christian.

One explanation for this dichotomy between theory and practice is a methodological one. It concerns the difference between the purposes of the comparative studies and my own. Whereas they sought either to examine the religious experience of children or adults, or to approach these issues from a philosophical standpoint, my intention was to hear the stories of homeless people which might (or might not) include a religious or spiritual dimension. In view of this difference it is less likely that the resulting analysis will yield similar themes. It might also be argued that this study took a relatively small sample, focused on a group of people with some common experiences, and was not afraid to include 'negative' remarks. The insights of these interviewees can be included and valued by seeing them within the broader picture of the life history of each individual.

---

[7]   Smith, 'The Abyss', p. 276.

This also has the merit of avoiding a false separation between religion or spirituality and the rest of life.

The final part of this review concerns the relationship between writer and those written about. Qualitative research theory and postmodern methods both recognise a reciprocity of relationships inherent in this type of endeavour. The researcher will have an effect on the data and vice versa; just as the research subject will, to some extent, change the investigator, and vice versa. An awareness of this is essential, not simply in the sense that the data is not 'pure', but more positively that the honest involvement of the researcher brings a greater authenticity to the overall project. Such awareness is all the more necessary where there exists an imbalance of power with participants who are socially marginal. It is for these reasons that I have from the outset considered myself a participant in this research, albeit of a different character. I have touched upon questions of motivation in the Prologue; within the concept of life histories I have included some of my own, sharing a measure of vulnerability with the research participants. I hope I have shown that my sense of unease and of being 'on the edge' in the present Church of England may provide some tiny opening to access the lives of those who have suffered a great deal more marginalisation. Additionally, a longer-term involvement with these projects has provided a greater depth of understanding. It has also been noted where within the interviews themselves this writer felt more personally affected.

There was a similar sense of reciprocity in the experience of being a volunteer at St Piran's. Volunteers usually want to feel useful and be active doing things, yet often in these centres, there is not a lot to do except simply to be with the clients, the homeless people. The result is boredom and frustration on the part of the voluntary staff, and dissatisfaction. However, on reflection, these emotions probably mirror fairly closely those felt by the clients themselves; so the volunteer is drawn subconsciously into the world of the homeless person. It is from this point of greater equality that real dialogue can start.

A chance encounter and a private conversation soon took on a more public dimension following the first interview with Caroline. She was pleased that someone was going to write about her experiences and those like her. This reflected an unspoken moral bargain: homeless people would talk to me in intimate detail, but they wanted their stories heard. I hope I have kept my side of the bargain. On the other hand a growing familiarity with the transcripts and the need for a certain objectivity from them have sometimes blunted the sharpness of the stories they tell. I am grateful to others' accounts for reminding me of God's anger and human anger as a reaction to such suffering. Anger prompts engagement: the asking of difficult questions, or the advocacy of political action. Here I have chosen the task of reworking Christian theology so that it hears and honours the stories of homeless people, and contributes to the transformation of lives. In the course of this I too have had my consciousness raised about reading the Bible, about Church practice, about theology itself, in a way which is non-refundable. The exercise of writing this book becomes a part of my story, alongside the stories which homeless women and men have told to me. My future is not clear, but these 'events' will have to be incorporated into it.

Practical theology includes the argument that the disciplines of economics, sociology and psychology need to inform theology in its response to contemporary situations. This book makes a strong claim that such a theological method is both desirable and necessary. Without it, our theology of homelessness would be as empty of meaning as a fifteenth-century dispute into the number of teeth in a horse's mouth.[8] However practical theology 'must be prepared to admit to and live with huge black holes in understanding and experience'.[9] This book stands as an attempt to identify those black holes more precisely and begin to fill them in.

The findings of this investigation are summarised schematically below, in a way which allows departure points for the creation of a theology of homelessness. In particular, the discontinuity between theory and practice in the area of spiritual experience requires noting. Additionally, interviewees' critical appreciation of the Bible and the Church can now be placed in the wider context of how homelessness is understood in these two domains. The following chapter develops these insights at the level of both individual and society.

- Homelessness is the often the result of serious loss or losses – of close relative, of job, of partner, of health. The stories told by homeless people also record their loss of role in the common story of the society around them.
- Descriptions of pain, suffering and isolation co-exist alongside the will to survive independently and with dignity. Dynamic narratives of restitution also suggest that story has the potential for transformation and empowerment.

---

[8] 'In the year of our Lord 1435 there arose a grievous quarrel among the brethren over the number of teeth in the mouth of a horse. For thirteen days the disputation raged without ceasing. All the ancient books and chronicles were fetched out, and wonderful and ponderous erudition, such as was never before heard of in this region was made manifest. At the beginning of the fourteenth day a youthful friar of goodly bearing asked his learned superiors for permission to add a word, and straightway, to the wonderment of the disputants, whose wisdom he sore vexed, he beseeched them to unbend in a manner coarse and unheard of, and to look in the open mouth of a horse and find answer to their questionings. At this, their dignity being grievously hurt they waxed exceedingly wroth; and joining in a mighty uproar they flew upon him and smote him hip and thigh and cast him out forthwith. For, they said, surely Satan has tempted this bold neophyte to declare unholy and unheard of ways of finding truth contrary to all the teachings of the fathers. After many days more of grievous strife the dove of peace sat on the assembly and they, as one man, declaring the problem to be an everlasting miracle because of a grievous dearth of historical and theological evidence thereof, so ordered the same writ down.' Jack Priestley, Hockerill Lecture 1996, quoting Francis Bacon, 1602.

[9] Woodward and Pattison, *Practical Theology*, pp. 13–14.

- The diversity of the homeless population interviewed here and of their life experiences challenges a stereotypical view of homelessness.
- Distinctions between research subjects as respectable or unrespectable are undermined in terms of this data. Listening more attentively to those deemed socially excluded would be welcome.
- Traditional descriptors of religious experience are absent from this data, although this does not imply an absence of discourse about religion, the Bible, the Church or spirituality.
- For the majority of those interviewed, there is little comprehension that the Christian story is Good News for them.
- Within the particular Centres there is explicit focus on individual care, but little engagement with structural reasons for homelessness, from a theological or a political perspective.
- Insights from the study of economics, sociology and psychology can provide important material for theological reflection on current issues.
- Theologies of equality are worth restating as public theologies which lead to political action.
- Theologies of place are worth articulating because homelessness and homeless people are often at the sharp end of contested definitions of place and space. Reading the homeless city from the perspective of those on its margins can yield new theological understandings of home.
- Contextual Bible reading with those whose voices are less audible provide new images of Jesus in the contemporary world. Homeless people may have some insights which are especially valuable given their life experiences.
- Homelessness cannot be fully understood without an awareness of the society in which it is situated, including the political dimensions of a market in housing.
- An ethical framework includes not only the ethics of research into vulnerable individuals, but also the concepts of moral hazard and moral deficit as applied to recent economic crises.
- The vulnerability of the storied self allows some access to other more vulnerable groups. The recording and analysis of the stories of homeless interviewees are interactions between research subjects and researcher, which risk changing the lives of all participants.

Chapter 11

Towards a Theology of Homelessness:
A New Telling of the Story

There were two men in a certain city, the one rich and the other poor. The rich man had very many flocks and herds; but the poor man had nothing but one little ewe lamb, which he had bought. And he brought it up and it grew up with him and his children; it used to eat of his morsel and drink from his cup, and lie in his bosom, and it was like a daughter to him. Now there came a traveller to the rich man, and he was unwilling to take one of his flock or herd to prepare for the wayfarer who had come to him, but he took the poor man's lamb, and prepared it for the man who had come to him.

2 Samuel 12: 2–4

The prophet Nathan tells this story to shame King David after he has made Bathsheba pregnant and caused Uriah to die in battle. Tom Wright uses this example to show the powerfully subversive nature of story which can challenge and modify established world views. Nathan's words, 'You are the man' disclose the purpose of the little vignette, and bring David to a dreadful sense of reality. Homeless people have attempted to tell new stories as they envisage a better future. These stories identify differences between theory and practice, which lead to questions about the effectiveness of traditional theology in presenting the Christian story as one which contains meaning for homeless people. A theology of homelessness will be a new telling of the story which hopes to provide resonance for those who are rebuilding their lives, and to confront the myths and prejudices which attack them as they do so. Two theological texts stand as guides for this. Then an overview of how the Church has thought about and acted towards poor people over the last 25 years is contrasted with a biblical account of home. In a final chapter I turn to the image of the Trinity to refashion an understanding which provides a basis for a theology of homeless people.

The Disabled God by Nancy Eiesland discloses its purpose from the outset: that persons with disabilities should be able to participate fully in the life of the Church, and that reciprocally the Church should be able to gain access to the social-symbolic life of disabled people.[1] Her first step is to examine and challenge current views on the disabled body. Theologically this leads her to a taking a liberatory stance on disability. Her analysis of the life history of two disabled women through their autobiographical writing produces three themes, similar to those associated with homeless people: their ordinary lives incorporate contingency and difficulty,

---

[1]   Nancy Eiesland, *The Disabled God* (Nashville, TN: Abingdon Press, 1994), p. 21.

grief and creativity; they have an alternative understanding of embodiment which includes plastic and metal technology; disability is seen as part of ordinary life, but there is a distinction between the reality of disablement and its social construction. She examines changes in sociological methodology in respect of disability, and highlights the uncertainties, confusions and irony present in the Christian Church's attitudes. Her brief consideration of the Bible sees three themes again: the close relationship between sin and disability, with links to notions of impurity; the concept of virtuous suffering; that disabled people are recipients of charitable giving. She takes a close interest in the American Lutheran Church which wrote a theological text in support of persons with disabilities, but then, six years later, promoted the exclusion of disabled people from the ordained ministry. She summarises her intentions as follows:

> For people with disabilities, a liberatory theology draws together message and commitment. It acknowledges our struggle against the discrimination that is pervasive within the church and society as part of the work of coming to our bodies. A liberatory theology sustains our difficult but ordinary lives, empowers and collaborates with individuals and groups of people with disabilities who struggle for justice in concrete situations, creates new ways of resisting the theological symbols that exclude and devalue us, and reclaims our hidden history in the presence of God on earth.[2]

Eiesland's creation of a liberatory theology centres around finding new interpretations of old symbols and attempting to imagine new ones – she sees God 'in a sip-puff wheel chair, that is the chair used mostly by quadriplegics'.[3] With a sharper focus on Christology, she takes the resurrected body of Christ as the true response of the Church to disability. Jesus Christ, who is the disabled God, is symbolic of those who have been stigmatised as a result of their bodies and their colour, who have struggled to maintain their dignity in the face of physical suffering and ritual humiliation. Such a symbol brings realistic hope to persons with disabilities. In conclusion, she writes about how the Eucharist, as a celebration of Christ's resurrection, may also be a way in which both symbolically and practically disabled people are fully in communion.

God in South Africa by Albert Nolan was written before the end of the apartheid regime. It too focuses on a theology of liberation deeply rooted in a particular context. However, his starting point is to look at what is meant by the good news of the gospel, and how sin is described in the Bible. He draws a parallel between the holiness system of the Jewish Law and the total system of apartheid in South Africa, emphasising the indivisibility of sin, whether personal or corporate. The link between sin and suffering is his cue to speak more specifically about the South African people and their systematic abuse:

---

2   Ibid., p. 86.
3   Ibid., p. 89.

We have the beginnings of an answer to our question: where is God in South Africa today? God can be seen in the face of the starving black child. God can be heard in the crying of the children in detention. God speaks through the mouth of a person whose face has been disfigured by a policeman's boot. It is not their innocence, their holiness, their virtue, their religious perfection that makes them look like God. It is their suffering, their oppression, the fact that they have been sinned against.[4]

He writes further about the system of racial capitalism and how a cycle of sin and guilt operates in South Africa. A description of salvation in the Bible centred on a theology of the Kingdom is the opening for a discussion about where Nolan sees signs of hope. It is paradoxically by crushing all illusory hope and by becoming 'so evil, so manifestly evil' that the system begins to create its opposite – a sustainable movement for social change. Signs of hope are made more visible by the growing numbers of people engaged in the struggle, which itself is the practice of faith whether or not an explicit commitment is made to God or to Jesus Christ. Salvation is not simply another way of describing the struggle for liberation, it is the naming of God in the process of human affairs:

When we introduce God into the picture, or rather when we discover God already there in our world, it takes our breath away. When we begin to see God as the one who is sinned against and crucified in South Africa today, it makes us shudder. We are struck with the full impact of the crisis, the conflict, the struggle, the day of liberation, when we see them as wonderful works of God.[5]

He concludes by representing this Good News back to South African Christians and to the Church. Nolan recognises that for many in the Church such an analysis is challenging and painful, but he insists that hope and challenge go together. He is not aiming at renewal but at the kind of the new life of which the gospel speaks. He urges the Church not to take refuge in abstractions – that is, the preaching of a 'universal' gospel and the celebration of a liturgy which is divorced from the hard realities of ordinary life. These are the only ways by which the Church is maintaining its unity, but in doing so it stops preaching the gospel. Nolan considers that the unity of the Church is secondary to the demands of the gospel, and in this tension the Church itself becomes a 'site of struggle', just as Jesus made Judaism the site of struggle.[6]

These texts provide five themes which scaffold a building of a theology of homelessness. Firstly, they are concerned with a theology of liberation. Nolan in his focus on a singular geographical and economic context speaks of the 'Struggle' in which ordinary South Africans are engaged. Eiesland concentrates

---

[4]   Albert Nolan, *God in South Africa* (London: CIIR, 1988), p. 67.

[5]   Ibid., p. 193.

[6]   Ibid., p. 215.

on a particular segment of the American population and also speaks of a struggle for inclusion. Both have some of the passion apparent in earlier works cited here. They are concerned with liberation from something – suffering, oppression, exclusion, an erroneous social construction, a system. Although they arrive at similar conclusions, they do, however, engage with different theological methods. *The Disabled God* is much closer to the method employed here, though Eiesland uses lifestory in a less extensive manner. *God in South Africa*, more traditionally, starts with the scriptures and moves outwards to the sociopolitical context, more akin to the contextual Bible reading of the previous chapter. This may provide some balance in terms of arguments about where theology originates. Secondly, symbols are important. For Eiesland, symbolisation is the mechanism by which both able-bodied and persons with disabilities can communicate and challenge one another. A renewed set of symbols allows disabled people better access to the life of the Church. Though symbols do not play a specific part in the South African study, a similar role is played by the concept of 'signs of the times' and signs of hope in which God is at work. Thirdly, the Bible figures as the text for critical dialogue. Nolan launches his analysis of the evils of apartheid from a biblical basis, with an emphasis on the nature of sin, both individual and structural; Eiesland begins her critique of the Church's position on disability with a reading of the Bible which is less sympathetic, but shows parallels with those who believe individuals are primarily responsible for their own homelessness. Fourthly, as a consequence of how they interpret the scriptures, both are critical of the Church, but also understand the Church's role as critical. Both writers are clear in their belief that the Church is being less than it ought to be, in respect of the South African struggle or of the position of disabled people, that a diluted form of the Good News is being preached. Fifthly, both writers are engaged personally and us the personal stories of others. Human experience is described with aspects of tragedy and heroism intermingled. Nolan is a white South African, who admits that: 'Of real suffering I can only say that I have seen it, I have touched it and become marginally sensitive to it. Nothing more'.[7] Eiesland herself is disabled, though she never labours the point.

Against these five themes, a mapping of work so far looks like this. A theology of story allows access to life histories – the stories of individuals and communities. This is more than simply a literary account of story since the foundational quality of narrative in carrying our search for identity and meaning is likened to the search for God. A Christian theology of story involves juxtaposing and overlapping human life histories with God's story, as revealed by Jesus Christ in the scriptures, and including the stories of transformation told by Jesus himself. Without diminishing the role of the human story, it underlines our part in God's story, and sets limits to what can be claimed about this. A theology of story also gives permission to the researcher to work out of his or her own faith commitment as one lifestory among many. Liberation theology asserts that the stories of the

---

[7]   Ibid., p. 51.

poor, and therefore of homeless people, are especially significant since these men and women have privileged access to God's story. It is therefore possible that the stories of the poor re-invigorate the Christian narrative by making it strange again, by recalling its sense of shock, by prompting a righteous anger, and by envisioning transformation.

The specific lifestories of homeless people analysed in detail here show a pattern of individual and group experiences, and a paradoxical account of suffering and survival within a cycle of homelessness and resettlement. They challenge the separation of high-status and low-status research subjects, but support the 'fuzzy' boundaries between researcher and researched. They recognise the therapeutic nature of listening to and valuing the story of another person (especially a suffering person), and they illustrate the way in which homeless people seek to redress power imbalances by the creation of a new story which will re-insert them into mainstream society.

The introduction of contextual material to understand how God's liberation touches those on the margins of society has focused on theologies of equality and theologies of place. Homelessness is at the conjunction of both these, but like the negative of an old photographic image. At the sharp point or the public disclosure of both inequality and placelessness, a theology of homelessness makes a test case for both. If a new theological understanding cannot work for homeless people, then it probably will not work for other vulnerable groups. Equally, a critique of the market in general will be well served by examining, as an example, the way in which housing had been commodified.

There is one important disjunction between these lifestories and the theology of story outlined above. Homeless people may be the storytellers of God, they may bear God's message to the well-housed and comfortable, but, for the most part, they have little awareness that this process is taking place. They may bring new life to the Christian story, but (with the exception of Julie) this does not seem to translate into new life for the storyteller. The ethical question of investigating vulnerable research subjects from a position of strength was treated earlier. I hope I have shown that a respectful dialogue is a pointer towards God, and that vulnerability on the part of the researcher is a way of being open to other vulnerable lives. However, a much sharper ethical question is begged by use of these stories of homelessness in the restoration of the Christian faith of the comfortable, if homeless people themselves seem to have little or no part in it. Are we not guilty of imposing another loss on those who have experienced so much loss, of perpetuating disempowerment? Is this theft of deeply disturbing stories not equivalent to the stealing of a soul? There is also the suspicion voiced already that the gospel as a radical and transforming discourse for homeless people (at the level of individuals and of society) has not been heard because it has not been preached. Gutiérrez's original question (Given these conditions, how can we tell the poor that God loves them?) becomes: 'If the Church and theologians do not bear an explicit message of God's love for poor people, then who does?' Perhaps such questions can be summed up and answered by ensuring that the stories of homeless people presented here are honoured in general and in particular.

Stories of Church, Poverty and Home

In describing how the Church in Britain has approached poverty and homelessness in the last 25 years, a useful distinction can be made between 'what matters' and 'what works', recognising that the tension between these two is both practical and theoretical. 'What matters' is the theology which underpins whatever is done in the name of the Church; 'what works' is the Church's engagement in particular social issues.

The Church of England's 1985 report *Faith in the City* wished to challenge two understandings of theology: that there is a dichotomy between the practice of personal charitable acts towards the poor and social and political action against the causes of poverty. Secondly, and more importantly, that a deductive way of doing theology, which tends to favour those with high levels of literacy and academic ability, is the only way to do theology. While the report affirms the value of traditional theology, it supports the liberation model of an inductive theology. There is recognition that South American thinking cannot be transferred uncritically to Britain, nonetheless it is possible to start from 'the personal experiences, the modes of perception and the daily concerns of local people themselves'.[8] Starting from a description of Urban Priority Areas as characterised by economic decline, physical decay and social disintegration, the first two chapters are themselves examples of the methodology which the report is quietly favouring. *Living Faith in the City* five years later is much less optimistic about the reality of the Church's general response than it is about the development of theological thinking. It describes the period as one which is 'deeply flawed' during which 'little progress' has been made. It ascribes these faults to three reasons: that the structures of the Church do not reflect a liberative gospel, but rather focus around power and control; that the message of the Church is not good news to the poor; that the work which the Church undertakes originates from a powerful and privileged minority.[9]

Ken Leech (*The Sky is Red*) is critical of the Church's theological approach, especially of what he sees as assumptions in *Faith in the City*, but his own theology of the East End of London at least begins from that report's reflections. His criticisms are two-fold: that the Church of England is essentially reformist; that is, it cannot envisage any other political system than the present one. It fails to question whether market capitalism is consistent with Christian values, and so remains reliant on a generalised sense of goodwill, that we are all somehow 'on the same side'. Leech doubts this is true, and would like the Church to be more confrontational. Secondly, he criticises *Faith in the City* for being 'implicationist',

---

[8] ACCUPA, *Faith in the City* (London: Church House Publishing, 1985), p. 65.
[9] Ibid., p. 14.

that the gospel is one thing and its implications for society are another. He sees 'no distinction between the gospel and the vision of a transformed human society'. His East End theology, therefore, is orientated towards the future: liberatory, mystical, localised. It is a theology based in the community, a street theology, valuing the oral above the written. For Leech, the disappointment lies in the distance between such theoretical work coming out of his own ministry in London and the reality of most of the actual practice of the Church of England.[10]

This democratic theology is likened to a detective story – a Christian community trying to discover what God is doing and meaning in a particular place. David Rhodes from Chapeltown, Leeds begins from a similar experience to my own, that the priest has something significant to learn from the homeless person. He grounds this understanding in a reading of the parables of Jesus, and especially in the story of the Gerasene demoniac. He recalls that Jesus denies the man permission to be one of his disciples, but instead insists that he 'Go home to your friends, and tell them how much the Lord has done for you, and how he has had mercy on you' (Mark 5: 19). Similarly, Mary Magdalene carries the news of the resurrection to the other (male) disciples. Vulnerable people are the best preachers of the gospel in their own communities.[11]

This notion of a 'theology in the vernacular' is one of the key components of the report *Faithful Cities: A Call for Celebration, Vision and Justice* (2006) which came out of the Church of England's Commission on Urban Life and Faith (CULF), set up to mark the twentieth anniversary of *Faith in the City*. This builds on the deductive method of the first report, but while there were good intentions, especially in how the report was presented (for example, illustrations and side-bars for quotations and case studies), it was ultimately no more successful in achieving this breakthrough. Elaine Graham suggests that the result appeared 'fragmented, anecdotal and piecemeal', largely because a collaborative method gave way to writing by committee.[12] However, in posing the question, 'What makes a good city?' *Faithful Cities* was much more effective in advocating a spiritual dimension of urban regeneration, and in showing how religion and religious organisations might promote the 'soul' of the city:

> Strategies for regeneration frequently coalesce around four key principles of a good or successful city: economics; environment and infrastructure; politics and governance; and culture. These four 'pillars of regeneration' relate to questions of physical resources, wealth-creation, sustainability and political structures. What they don't do is to take into account less quantifiable questions such as quality of life, wellbeing—happiness even—what we might term the 'human

---

[10]   Ken Leech, *The Sky Is Red* (London: Darton, Longman and Todd, 1997), pp. 50–56, 107, 108, 135.

[11]   David Rhodes, *Faith in Dark Places* (London: Triangle, 1996), pp. 62–3.

[12]   Elaine Graham, 'What Makes a Good City? Reflections on Urban Life and Faith', *International Journal of Public Theology* 2 (2008): pp. 7–26.

face' of the city. We have to ask questions about the *soul* of the city as well, and how faith communities can help develop this.[13]

It coined the term 'faithful capital' (derived from concepts of social capital) to describe how a moral dimension of human worth and dignity originating in beliefs about God was intrinsic to urban life and development. This meant that cities as places of meaning embodied values open to theological critique. 'Faithful capital' also reminded government of the contributions made by faith-based organisations.

These theological developments were themselves put under pressure by political and cultural changes during the New Labour government. *Moral, But No Compass* (2008) argues for a much greater engagement between churches and the public service reform of the period, while also being critical of government's practical and theoretical understanding of faith communities, particularly Christian ones. At the same time, however, *Faith in the City* and the theology which undergirded it comes in for some sharp words: 'the old wineskins of post-war theology were being split apart by the force of new developments in thought and policy, and the Church was simply hiding its head in the sand'.[14] Those who rejected working critically alongside government commissioning services in favour of the prophetic voice and advocacy were often vague about what this meant in policy terms, as well as weak in their comprehension of social realities. But there was room for a distinctive contribution from the churches: 'Christians need to discover and re-invent the "mission-shaped church" as much in the sphere of social action and engagement as in any other area of activity'.[15]

The more recent development of Queer Theology, growing out of and arguably away from liberation theology and drawing insights from Queer Theory, would argue the presence of differential discrimination across various strands, seeing here distinctions within the population of homeless people, and setting aside once and for all the moniker of 'the homeless'.[16] In addition, queer theology pays attention to the way in which ideologies are constructed to maintain and exclude certain social groupings; Laura Stivers (*Disrupting Homelessness*) prefers 'a picture of Jesus who promoted compassion for the downtrodden by disrupting the structural and ideological systems that create and justify poverty

---

[13]   Archbishops' Commission on Urban Life and Faith, *Faithful Cities: A Call for Celebration, Vision and Justice* (Peterborough: Methodist Publishing House, 2006), p. 11.

[14]   Francis Davis, Elizabeth Paulhus and Andrew Bradstock, *Moral, But No Compass: Government, Church and the Future of Welfare* (Chelmsford: Matthew James Publishing, 2008), p. 32.

[15]   Ibid., p. 91.

[16]   For example, E. Stuart, *Gay and Lesbian Theologies, Repetitions with Critical Difference* (Aldershot: Ashgate, 2003).

and oppression'.[17] While homeless people are both victims and agents depending on circumstances, an analysis which depends on individual narratives will tend to support the status quo, leaving unexamined the underlying power relationships. The social dimension of homelessness frames analysis by posing questions about poverty and excessive wealth, about inequalities in housing, about political treatment of private ownership in contrast to social housing. Within the United States, Stivers also identifies the part housing played (and plays) in the establishment of the American Dream: the wholesome picture of the ideal homeowner as a middle-class, heterosexual, father of a nuclear family. Various attempts to remove homeless people from city streets reveal a disturbing discourse of purity/pollution based perhaps in biblical texts. Again, home is shown to have multiple connotations beyond shelter.

What liberation models and queer theology have in common is their desire to envisage a different future, and therefore the potential to be 'praxis-orientated'[18] The practical realisation of inductive theology is the subject of Laurie Green's *Power to the Powerless*, which describes the particular experience of the parish of Erdington in Birmingham. The book is much more a report on a specific project than a detailed theological reflection, though it contains more trenchant criticism of traditional theology than does *Faith in the City*. Green calls for the democratisation of theology and an end to 'a scholarly or priestly elite', admitting that 'our theological reflection relied far too much on verbal articulation and much more could have been accomplished had we explored earlier non-verbal ways into our theologising'.[19] This focuses the hermeneutical issue at the root of his quest into inner city life:

> How could western, white, wealthy students of the Gospel text ever be able to get into the mind of the eastern, poor, first century people who recorded in the Gospels their experience of Jesus of Nazareth?[20]

Leech also suggests reasons to explain the ineffectiveness of the Church's response to *Faith in the City*. He sees the Church of England as quintessentially bourgeois in respect of the majority of clergy and laity, who have simply shared no experiences with those from the inner cities. While he has some hope for the future, he is also concerned that behind the façade of financial constraint, a lack of nerve and a commitment to safety will blight the creative efforts he favours:

---

[17] L. Stivers *Disrupting Homelessness: Alternative Christian Approaches* (Minneapolis: Fortress Press, 2011), p. 8.

[18] A. Davey, *Urban Christianity and Global Order* (London: SPCK, 2001), p. 12.

[19] Laurie Green, *Power to the Powerless* (Basingstoke: Marshal Pickering, 1987), pp. 10–11.

[20] Laurie Green, 'The Jesus of the Inner City' in Ian Duffield (ed.), *Urban Christ: Responses to John J. Vincent* (Sheffield: Urban Theology Unit, 1997), p. 26.

My sense is that many clergy, and many lay Christians, come from precisely those groups in society who have never faced despair, and have somehow managed to avoid the upheaval which the existential crisis of meaninglessness and hopelessness brings to individuals and communities. They are the very people who will not understand how to respond. Yet I hope there will be some in the Churches who have faced the darkness of nihilism, and who have encountered it with radical faith.[21]

Structurally, he is keen to encourage the Church to challenge the myths he sees as currently associated with poverty: for example, that poverty and wealth are unconnected and that the Church's task is simply to care for marginalised people and not ask why they are marginalised. He praises the Church of England for the depth of its concern for the poor, but it has been largely top-down: a socialism which is 'aloof, genteel, polite, detached … not in fact socialist at all, certainly not revolutionary'.[22] Good work can be much in quantity, but in quality, patronising and dehumanising.

John Vincent's answer to this 'suburban captivity of the gospel' is to seek closer contact with those in the inner cities by living and working there. There is then the possibility that the voice of poverty is heard, if only those who interpret can stay quiet long enough to listen. He is both hopeful and critical of the role of theologians:

British liberation theology has been happening in the cracks and crevices of the land more or less for a decade. Its practitioners are not people with much time for reading and research, much less reflection and writing. Most of those well versed in liberation theology in general, in universities or colleges or churches, do not themselves practise it, and therefore cannot and should not write about it.[23]

In the same volume, Rowland reminds us that, while St Luke's Gospel challenges and discomforts a nation which seeks to be 'at ease with itself', the Bible still offers hope to rich and poor alike when 'vulnerability strikes home and we become people who suddenly find ourselves on the margins of normality'.[24]

Anne Morisy, writing about community ministry and mission, seeks to bridge the divide between thinking and action. *Beyond the Good Samaritan, Community Ministry and Mission* is a combination of theological reflection and practical guidebook, but she is firmly rooted in a liberation tradition and echoes much of what has been said here already:

---

[21]   Leech, *Red*, p. 91.

[22]   Ibid., pp. 106–1077 and 159.

[23]   Vincent, 'Liberation Theology in Britain, 1970–1995', p. 29.

[24]   Christopher Rowland, 'The Gospel, the Poor and the Churches', in Christopher Rowland and John Vincent (eds), *Liberation Theology UK* (Sheffield: Urban Theology Unit, 1995), pp. 41–54.

> The poor and the needy may be the recipients of care through a church-run community project, but they are not the primary object of active mission, because the poor, as Jesus insisted, are the likely trigger for the transforming of those who put themselves in the position of caring.[25]

She comments on the low level of religious literacy in British society, so community ministry supports the occasional use of 'apt' liturgies. These provide a framework for individuals to move beyond their limited horizons. Liturgy also emphasises a priority of discipleship over against doctrinal belief, and may also act as a counterbalance to 'secular drift' within Christian projects. Community ministry also encourages volunteers from outside the immediate faith group, provided that 'we' are open to learning from 'them'.[26]

Morisy develops ideas about literacy using Paulo Freire's concept of 'deep literacy': the ability not simply to read and write, but to comprehend the forces which shape lives often detrimentally. Dialogue and humility are at the core of this process, especially the humility which understands that the wealthy need to be alongside the poor more than the poor need the wealthy. She imagines that Freire would criticise community ministry for being a development of institutional church, but counters this by saying that to challenge the domestication of the gospel is a gradual process, initiated from where people are situated currently. But she does agree that there is a need to go 'beyond the Good Samaritan' by dialogue and posing questions.

Her practice of community ministry and mission is underpinned by a theology which observes the disjunction between a persistent thirst for spirituality and the inauthentic response of the Churches. The concept of people as empty vessels to be filled is replaced by the understanding that 'we need to walk gently because God has been there before us'. Discipleship is more readily envisaged as a matter of faithful action rather than doctrinal assent, and echoing Nolan, it is the struggle for the Kingdom of God which helps many articulate an implicit faith. The cross remains a significant challenge for the 'respectable', reminding them that the method of Jesus' execution allied him with the most degraded. A theology which continues to discomfort the powerful and unmask denial and delusion is a natural corollary. Anne Morisy is less gloomy than Leech, calling on God's grace to nurture trust and hope that 'makes it possible to hold on to the Christian calling to envisage a radically different future'.[27]

The postmodern approach of queer theology allows a different analysis of practical solutions to problems of housing. Stivers compares three American responses, asking the extent to which each one leaves intact dominant power structures. A rescue and recovery response favoured by more evangelical churches

---

[25]   Anne Morisy, *Beyond the Good Samaritan, Community Ministry and Mission* (London: Mowbray, 1997), p. 6.

[26]   Ibid., p. 62.

[27]   Ibid., chapter 7, pp. 105–21.

is based on individual responsibility for homelessness, even to the extent of identifying connections to sin and wickedness. While not at all disrupting existing systems of power, and ignorant of a race or gender dimension, the programme she visits treats homeless people with dignity, provides free addiction services, and opens up a spiritual perspective. Low income home ownership schemes provide no interest loans and volunteer help to provide housing for those at the lower (but not lowest) incomes levels. There is an emphasis on individual and community transformation via home ownership, and families tend to be idealised. This is intended to be 'a hand up, not a handout', but although there is a desire 'to break into the consciousness of the rich', there is little challenge to structural inequities. A recent turn to ecological concerns among low income housing schemes is welcome. In place of these two, Stivers prefers advocacy towards a social movement to bring about a compassionate community under God, adding that 'it is always easier to deny complicity in oppressive systems if we have done individual good deeds and have not been overtly discriminatory'.[28] Hospitality and justice rooted in scripture are key themes for individual Christians and Christian communities with a practical commitment to education, working amongst churches and other religious and secular groups, and supporting particular self-help projects – for example tent cities which have sprung up as a result of foreclosures. The aim is ambitious and widespread: 'The goal of a prophetic response is to prevent homelessness by changing policies and structures that cause poverty'.[29]

This overview of policy and practice now prompts some revision of the argument advanced earlier that a radical and transforming gospel has not been heard by homeless people because it has never been preached. *Faith in the City*, more than 25 years on, remains a bold document witnessing to a moment in Church of England history when the Kingdom breaks through, a rare kairos for an established church. What is dated now is the social context it describes, not the theological method it hopes to promote. Leech is right to call it a reformist document, but it was an adventurous first step, especially in the admission of long-seated difficulties in inner city areas. The tradition of reform is seen again in the proposals of Anne Morisy. It may be noted by contrast, that given the then South African situation of apartheid, Nolan calls not for renewal, but for something completely other: the new life of the resurrection. However, on the issue of housing itself, there is little attempt to see home and homelessness as a theological issue per se. Laura Stivers in America and this book in Britain intend to fill that gap.

Some encouraging and exciting examples of liberation theology in practice are realised in the work and writings of Green, Rhodes and Morisy. It is significant that two of these are rooted in the parables of Jesus. Morisy's work on 'apt' liturgy and religious or theological literacy supports previous contentions about story, and echoes the conclusions of Nancy Eiesland. All three agree that the gospel is revitalised for those who choose to minister among poor people, and that,

---

28   Stivers, *Disrupting Homelessness*, p. 121.
29   Ibid., p. 146.

paradoxically, it is the priest or Christian layperson who is evangelised by those on the margins. This recalls Myers' treatment of the gap between the understanding of First World theology and the experience of those living in the Third World, and his encouragement for theology to return home. However, where my critical view above is depressingly supported is within the structures and personnel of the Church itself. Green, Leech, Rhodes and Morisy have visions of a transformative gospel preached by a more radical Church; but they are exceptions. Leech in particular sees the future survival of the Church of England as dependent on its shift from the status quo to an overtly confrontational role, in which ministry to the wider community is only authentic inasmuch as the poor are at the heart of the Church's life.[30] The question raised by *Living Faith in the City* 'Is this good news for the poor?' might well be asked of recent Church of England emphasis on mission, which seems largely undefined, and focused more on Church maintenance and finances than the Kingdom.

It is here that postmodern analysis is helpful in discovering what discourses underpin ideologies and structures, suggesting where practical responses have in reality supported a discriminatory system, and equally where liberation theology has left unexamined concepts like social justice. A postmodern Jesus is even more challenging and radical than a modernist liberatory one. What this overview omits, however, is the urgency of the contemporary task, in terms of poverty in general and housing in particular. The current nexus of events in Europe and the United States, where government-directed austerity is affecting poorer people and poorer nations disproportionately, requires a re-emphasis on theologies of equality, liberation and hope, with a keen awareness of how political ideology tends to hide behind 'common sense' economics. The extreme commodification of the housing market in the US (matched to some extent in the UK by the residualisation of the social housing sector) means that the financial and credit crisis leading into recession and perhaps stagnation was no accident or coincidence. It was the outcome of a poisonous alchemy which allowed resources to be transferred from the poorest to the richest, of a dream turned sour. I wonder if an instructive parallel can be evinced here between the South African struggles against Nolan's apartheid 'System' and the present system of market dominance; and whether increasing numbers of 'ordinary people' just surviving and the increase of those seeking food handouts might prompt a serious revision of how capitalist political and social economy is constructed.[31]

Both practical church-sponsored action and its related theology need to protest loudly about these continuing inequalities. Such is the tenor of two recent publications: the statement from the Common Wealth Network and Archbishop Rowan Williams' *New Statesman* leading article. The opening sentences of the statement shows a tone of anger, urgency and engagement with the public realm:

---

[30]   Leech, *Red*, p. 248.

[31]   Jay Rayner, 'Sharp Rise in Demand for Food Handouts from Poverty-Stricken Families' *Observer* newspaper, 1 October 2011.

Christians in Britain today are called to take a stand. Faced with the biggest cuts to public spending for over a generation, it is not enough to retreat into the private ghetto of religious consolation. As Christians, we are convinced that the actions of the current government are an unjustified attack on the poor. The rhetoric of necessary austerity and virtuous belt-tightening conceals a grim reality: the victimisation of people at the margins of society and the corrosion of community. Meanwhile, the false worship of markets continues unchecked and the immorality of the growing gap between rich and poor goes unquestioned.[32]

Less stridently and with slightly different nuances, Williams places government policy in a wider perspective, at the same time as criticising 'a quiet resurgence of the seductive language of "deserving" and "undeserving" poor':

For someone like myself, there is an ironic satisfaction in the way several political thinkers today are quarrying theological traditions for ways forward. True, religious perspectives on these issues have often got bogged down in varieties of paternalism. But there is another theological strand to be retrieved that is not about 'the poor' as objects of kindness but about the nature of sustainable community, seeing it as one in which what circulates – like the flow of blood – is the mutual creation of capacity, building the ability of the other person or group to become, in turn, a giver of life and responsibility. Perhaps surprisingly, this is what is at the heart of St Paul's ideas about community at its fullest; community, in his terms, as God wants to see it.[33]

Perhaps this is what is meant by Eiesland's 'radical symbolic sedition'; in the debate between reform, renewal and revolution in the Church, she does not propose a separatist, symbolisation, but one that connects into history and tradition. These commentaries have only alluded to religious symbols in reference to liturgy, and in the opportunity for hearing the stories of the congregations of inner city churches, but these are not linked into any reformulation of the symbolic life of the Church. Nor is it clear that without a recognition of the open and hidden system of symbols which are used in church life, apparently small changes can be either completely insignificant or wildly revolutionary. The shock of new symbols is exemplified by the new images of Jesus which the contextual Bible study has evinced. Eiesland does comprehend how important religious symbols are for a liberatory theology, but she also sees the limits of change. In her search for empowering symbols, she turns first to the Bible and out of an unpropitious start develops a theology of Jesus

---

[32]   Common Wealth, 'Christians for economic and social justice', 16 November 2010. Available at: http://www.ekklesia.co.uk/CommonWealthStatement (accessed 26 January 2012).

[33]   R. Williams, leader 'The Government Needs to Know How Afraid People Are', *New Statesman*, 9 June 2011. Available at: http://www.archbishopofcanterbury.org/articles. php/2066/new-statesman-leader (accessed 26 January 2012).

Christ, the disabled God. After this review of the stories which the Church tells of poverty and home, it is appropriate to return to the Bible and see there the symbols which underpin the attitudes of Christian faith to those who have no home, and how those symbols might be renewed.

Biblical Stories of Home

An earlier route map posited a three-fold use of the Bible: as the significant text for critical dialogue; as reflecting the story of God in which as human beings we situate our own stories; with reference to the parables of Jesus, as transformative narrative for marginalised people. With these in mind, how does the Bible treat the theme of home and its close relations: absence of home, homecoming, and homelessness?

The absence of home is given a prominent and positive place in both Old and New Testaments. In the founding myths of the Jewish people, Abram is instructed by God to 'leave your country, your kindred and your father's house' so that his descendants will be blessed (Gen. 12: 1). Jacob journeys from Canaan to Egypt on the Lord's command, responding to the promise that he will see his son Joseph again and that the Lord will make of them a great nation (Gen. 46: 1–7). After the escape from Egypt, Moses and the Israelites spend many difficult years in the desert before they finally reach the land promised when God first saw their oppression:

> Then the Lord said, 'I have seen the affliction of my people who are in Egypt, and have heard their cry because of their taskmasters; I know their sufferings, and have come down to deliver them out of the land of the Egyptians, and to bring them up out of that land to a good and broad land, a land flowing with milk and honey …'. (Ex. 3: 7–8)

The Israelites are required in Deuteronomy to present the first fruits of their harvest to the Lord, and in doing so to recall their past and declare: 'A wandering Aramean was my father …' (Deut. 26: 5). The notion of separation from home – exile – is treated as both a fictional and actual occurrence. The book of Ruth, a likely fiction in a historical setting, pays tribute to Ruth's qualities of steadfastness in personal exile with her mother-in-law: 'for where you go, I will go, and where you lodge I will lodge; your people shall be my people, and your God my God'. (Ruth 1: 16). The reality of national exile in Babylon reflected in the words of Psalm 137 ('By the waters of Babylon, there we sat down and wept, when we remembered Zion') adds to the sense of a people who are homeless.[34]

---

[34] Andrew Bradstock in his essay 'Liberation Theology after the Failure of Revolution' advocates the use of the Babylonian captivity as a new or additional paradigm for those whose hope in revolution and the Kingdom of God have been frustrated. The dream of liberation can be realised in the rebuilding of community rather than in the pursuit of new territory.

The literature of the new Exodus and the restoration of the Temple (Deutero Isaiah, Ezra and Nehemiah) does not detract from this sense of dislocation, not least because Yahweh was also a God without a fixed home. When King David speaks to the prophet Nathan about his desire to build God a house since 'I dwell in a house of cedar, but the ark of God dwells in a tent', God's word comes instantly to the prophet. God rejects this form of house, and in a play on words which works equally well in Hebrew as in English, declares that his house will be a covenant with his people, the house of David, with whom he will dwell for ever (2 Sam. 7). The restored Temple of Third Isaiah is enlarged to a cosmic dimension, but retains echoes of the original Davidic covenant: 'Thus says the Lord: 'Heaven is my throne and the earth is my footstool; what is the house that you would build for me, and what is the place of my rest?'' (Isa. 66: 1).

In the New Testament, the reality of the birth of Jesus in a stable, the divine declaration of this event firstly to shepherds (not to prince or priest), and then exile into Egypt to escape Herod, have been obscured by a thick layer of popular sentiment, posing as faithfulness to the biblical account.[35] But they are consistent with a radical prophet, taking disciples from their homes for an itinerant ministry in which he makes himself intentionally homeless: 'Foxes have holes, and birds of the air have nests; but the Son of man has nowhere to lay his head' (Matt. 8: 20). Family too are rejected, or rather, there is the suggestion that the true family which Jesus envisages are those who turn to his Father in heaven (Matt. 12: 48f). The parallel in the New Testament to God's rejection of a fixed abode in Samuel and Isaiah is the account of Jesus' transfiguration. Peter's idea that they should build three booths on the mountain top for Jesus, Moses and Elijah is made out of surprise and fear, and is ignored. They come down off the mountain to face the reality of the future, with the instruction to tell no one about the vision until after the resurrection. The culmination of this journey with his disciples is the arrival in Jerusalem. The city signals a deep ambivalence: holy Zion, home to the faithful Jew, and yet the place where Jesus overturns the tables in the Temple courtyard; welcomed with palm branches, executed on a cross.

Absence of home is closely associated with rethinking God's meaning and purpose. In the desert the early Israelites face challenges to their faith and are often found wanting. The exile forces the Hebrews to rethink their theology and practice of worship. Jesus is forced to respond to the questions of the devil in the wilderness before the start of his ministry, and at the end of his ministry in the garden of Gethsemane his own doubts surface to question him. Gethsemane and Golgotha represent the degradation of Jesus, the God who has had nowhere to rest, the homeless God. The isolation of the cross is compounded by the desertion

---

[35] I remember the horrified reaction of a primary headteacher when I proposed that in the school Nativity play we should say that Jesus was born in the garage at the back of the local pub – this in a UPA parish. For a more detailed description of the Nativity in relation to liberation theology, see Rayan's account of the 'dalitness' of Jesus, *Dalits and Women*, p. 125.

of virtually all his friends and family, and by the sense that his heavenly Father has deserted him too. His only companions are the equally marginalised and condemned thieves. Rhodes makes Luke's repentant thief the first messenger of the resurrection, to the dying Jesus himself: 'Jesus, remember me when you come into your kingdom'.[36] So wilderness, exile, abandonment, have been regarded in Christian thinking as places where God is especially present, for it is 'at the heart of pain and apparent emptiness that the community of the resurrection often emerges'.[37]

If the absence of home for the people of God or for Jesus himself is presented in a relatively positive light, or at the very least as a fundamental part of their communal history, then the denial of home to the sojourner or the poor is against the express wishes of Yahweh (Lev. 19: 33f, Isa. 58: 7). In Leviticus and Amos (2: 10) treatment of poor and homeless people is linked specifically with the experience of Israel's escape from Egypt and God's promise. In Third Isaiah the New Jerusalem is a place of refuge and security:

> They shall build houses and inhabit them; they shall plant vineyards and eat their fruit. They shall not build and another inhabit; they shall not plant and another eat, for like the days of a tree shall the days of my people be, and my chosen shall long enjoy the work of their hands. (Isa. 65: 21)

Nor is home given a 'puritan condemnation' in the New Testament. It is in the home that Jesus, according to Mark's Gospel, dines with tax collectors and sinners (2: 15 and 14: 3), teaches his disciples (7: 17, 9.33 and 10: 10) and heals the sick (2: 1 and 5: 38).[38] What is condemned, however, is the unnecessary extravagance of luxury building, Solomon's palace for example, and the selfish possession of land and property. The apparent ambivalence of these attitudes towards home and homelessness is only superficial. The experience of the early Israelites led them to value both the security of home and the reality of their own itinerant homelessness. By contrast, it seems that it is the contemporary world, including Western Christians, who are so bound by an attachment to home and its weight of meanings as to prejudice its opposite, the absence of home.

The second theme is that it is God who provides the home, whether the Promised Land of the Exodus people, a land flowing with milk and honey, or the house of many rooms, prepared for the disciples of Jesus (John 14: 2f). God is homemaker from the moment a garden was prepared in which humans might dwell; 'This is a God with perpetually dirty fingernails, a God who is always playing in the mud'.[39] The parable of the Prodigal Son is the best New Testament

---

[36]   Rhodes, *Faith*, p. 70.

[37]   Leech, *Red*, p. 252.

[38]   Myers, *Strong Man*, p. 151.

[39]   Steven Bouma-Prediger and Brian J. Walsh, *Beyond Homelessness Christian Faith in a Culture of Displacement* (Grand Rapids, MI: Wm B. Eerdmans, 2008), p. 14.

expression of this. Subtitled 'A Story of Homecoming', Henri Nouwen's analysis is both devotional and theological, drawing together three different stories. There is firstly the parable told by Jesus as part of a series which includes the Lost Sheep and the Lost Coin. Nouwen's own lifestory is wrapped up in the story of the two sons and the father; and thirdly there is the story of the reader as she engages with the biblical text and is challenged by Nouwen to follow the same path of discovery. I intend to look at Nouwen's treatment of this parable at some length.

A fourth 'story' is introduced from the outset when Nouwen describes the inception of the book as an encounter with Rembrandt's picture 'Return of the Prodigal Son'. It is a dialogue with this painting, which he views in its original in the Hermitage Museum in St Petersburg, that gives him the inspiration to turn to St Luke's parable. He describes returning to the picture a number of times to refresh his ideas. The painting is also iconic inasmuch as it 'has become a mysterious window through which I can step into the Kingdom of God'.[40] Personal narrative thus becomes an effective tool for theological reflection. The two major themes focus on the identity of self and of God – Who am I and Who is God for us? Nouwen finds that he is both the younger and the elder son, and more surprisingly he is called to be the father too. As younger son, he finds in the painting 'something which represents the on-going yearning of the human spirit, the yearning for a final return, an unambiguous sense of safety, a lasting home'.[41] He likens the boy's lostness in a distant country to the addictions of modern life from which we long to be delivered. The younger son seeks forgiveness of the father as he prepares his speech: 'I will say to him, "Father, I have sinned against heaven and before you; I am no longer worthy to be called your son; treat me as one of your hired servants"' (Luke 15: 18). Nouwen's reflection on this combines an insight into our limited understanding of forgiveness with a personal engagement which draws the reader into the frame:

> There is repentance, but not a repentance in the light of the immense love of a forgiving God. It is a self-serving repentance that offers the possibility of survival. I know this state of mind and heart quite well. It is like saying: 'Well, I couldn't make it on my own, I have to acknowledge that God is the only resource left to me. I will go to God and ask forgiveness in the hope that I will receive a minimal punishment and be allowed to survive on the condition of hard labour'. God remains a harsh, judgmental God. It is this God who makes me feel guilty and worried and calls up in me all these self-serving apologies. Submission to this God does not create true inner freedom, but breeds only bitterness and resentment.[42]

---

[40] Henri Nouwen, *The Return of the Prodigal Son* (London: Darton, Longman and Todd, 1994), p. 15.

[41] Ibid., p. 5.

[42] Ibid., p. 52.

Nouwen is slightly surprised when a friend suggests that he is much more like the elder than the younger son, but agrees that this is likely. Nouwen is the one who has stayed faithful to the Church, worked hard, has been praised and admired; yet he detects in himself the same pride, resentment and selfishness which feature in the reaction of the elder son to his father's joy. It is a refusal to share joy which characterises both the elder son and the writer. Nouwen's own reaction here is to rename the parable that of the Lost Sons, both of whom in different ways have to come home. Yet the return of the elder is harder and can only be achieved through God's grace. His own poverty is revealed to him when he realises that he is totally unable to root out his resentments, and that 'Trust and gratitude are the disciplines for the conversion of the elder son. And I have come to know these through my own experience'.[43] Jesus takes on the role of both the younger and the elder son; he becomes the true prodigal in order to take us home, that his broken body may become the broken body of all humanity which longs to re-enter the lost paradise. He is also the elder, offering God's love to all his resentful children to bring them home too. Lastly Jesus shows us how to become the Father, and it is this which is the goal of Nouwen's account.

In writing about the father he posits a third title for the parable – The Welcome by the Compassionate Father – for he sees contained here an appropriate image of God and the whole of salvation history. Into his development of acceptable images he weaves a meditation about his and others' relationship with God, and our sense of coming home. The only authority which the father of the parable can claim is that of compassion, so that Nouwen is able to write:

> Here is the God I want to believe in: a Father who, from the beginning of creation, has stretched out his arms in merciful blessing, never forcing himself on anyone, but always waiting ...[44]

He writes too about the feminine aspect of God who is freely linked in love and compassion with all her children, and only rests when she has welcomed all of them home around the table prepared for them. The parable is one of a series of three in which Jesus answers the Pharisees' question about why he eats with sinners. The Lost Sheep, the Lost Coin and the Lost Son all suggest that it is God who takes the initiative in the search; rather than the person searching for God, it is God who is searching and we who are hiding. This change of viewpoint makes Nouwen reflect: 'Can I accept that I am worth looking for? Do I believe that there is a real desire in God to simply be with me?' His work in a community of adults with learning difficulties suggests that they are demanding of fatherhood, but they also show how to be a father, for 'a true spiritual homecoming means a return to the poor in spirit to whom the Kingdom of Heaven belongs'.[45]

---

[43]   Ibid., p. 84.

[44]   Ibid., p. 95.

[45]   Ibid., pp 107 and 135.

This long excursion into a single parable illuminates certain significant concepts. Like Eiesland's image of the crucified Jesus in terms of the disabled body, so Nouwen talks of the broken body of Jesus representing broken humanity's search for home. He also outlines a three-part movement: from a God who provides a home (a Promised Land) to a God who is home, to a God who is searching for us in our hiddenness. Lastly, there is the call for us to be home, to be Father, especially for the most vulnerable people who show us the means of achieving this.[46]

The doctrine of the incarnation gives us a third and final theme, a twist to the story, like the endings of the parables Jesus told. The start of John's Gospel tells us that 'The Word became flesh and dwelt amongst us' and later in Jesus' own words, 'If someone loves me, he will keep my word, and my Father will love him, and we will come to him, and make our home with him' (John 14: 23). In an extended metaphor about the Church, the letter to the Ephesians speaks of the community of faith as the temple of God:

> So then you are no longer strangers and sojourners, but you are fellow citizens with the saints and members of the household of God, built upon the foundation of the apostles and prophets, Christ Jesus himself being the corner-stone, in whom the whole structure is joined together and grows into a holy temple in the Lord; in whom you also are built into it for a dwelling place of God in the Spirit. (Eph. 2: 19–22)

Not only does God provide a home in the sense of a Promised Land, or become home in the sense that we return with Christ to the Father, but God answers our deepest human yearnings for transcendence in a completely original way. In the incarnation of Jesus, God reverses the order of homecoming and, to extend Nouwen's view, makes God's home with us. Jesus offers a new vision of homecoming in his public ministry of healing, casting out demons and restoring those who have been made ritually homeless: 'The homemaking glory of God has returned, "moved into the neighbourhood" and taken up residence with us. Homecoming is possible again'.[47]

The homeless God of Samuel, in an act of solidarity, comes home most intimately to God's own creation. The psalmist imagines the Lord as a refuge from pestilence, a shelter from the terrors of the night and the arrows of the day (Ps. 91); whereas in the Catholic litany of Our Lady it is Mary who provides

---

[46]   John Navone uses these same biblical examples and refers to travel stories in the Bible. The outer account of travel is matched by an inner journey of change, since 'travel stories tell of a particular search for personal wholeness, of people who are modified by their experiences, of catalysts of change, of horizon shifts.' Homecoming in the Bible reflects the deepest levels of our existence, our search for recognition and authenticity. Navone, *Theology of Story*, pp. 58–6.

[47]   Bouma-Prediger and Walsh, *Beyond Homelessness*, p. 24.

shelter for Jesus – she is described as 'Spiritual vessel, Vessel of honour ... Ark of the covenant'. This solidarity with humanity is by virtue of the birth narrative a solidarity with poor and homeless people in particular. Jesus was not made flesh in the womb of the wealthy, nor by some fairy-tale turn of fortune did Mary suddenly become rich. Instead she specifically sings in the Magnificat of her material poverty and of God's rejection of the powerful. There is a story told in the apocryphal *Acts of Thomas* that Thomas, when he first landed in India, collected large sums of money from the king in order to build him a magnificent house. When this failed to appear and he was arrested for fraud, he explained that the house had indeed been built, a 'house in heaven' for the king. The money had all been given to the poor.[48]

[48]   M.R. James, *The Apocryphal New Testament* (English translation. Oxford: Clarendon Press, 1924), pp. 371ff. The story goes on to recount that when the king's brother dies, he sees the palace which Thomas has built in heaven for the king, but is refused entry. He is allowed back down to earth to explain this to the king, who then releases Thomas from prison and is converted to Christianity.

Chapter 12
Stories of a Homeless God

Christimian I love you
not because you descended from a star
but because you revealed to me
that man has blood
tears
anguish
keys
tools
to open the doors closed to light
Yes! You taught me that man is God ...
a poor God crucified like you
and the one who is on your left on Golgotha
the bad thief
is God too!

These images from the Bible of home, homecoming and homelessness are complex rather than ambivalent, giving complementary value to those with homes and those without. The incarnation of Jesus illustrates a radical inversion of the concept that it is God who provides us with a home, as human beings learn what it means to be home to God, and so paradoxically, also come home to God. Similarly, the Church's attitudes to poor and homeless people are complex, but have tended in the direction of providing much-needed practical help (shelter, food and so on) rather than being welcoming and inclusive to the insights of the marginalised within the Church itself. The theological parallel is a preference for systematic deductive theology over against an inductive, liberatory method which places poor people at its centre. This preference is also apparent in a reluctance to question theologically and politically the structural reasons for poverty and homelessness.[1] By contrast, the reading of the Bible adopted here focuses on Jesus' ideological challenge to the inequalities of his own culture. The disjunction between theory and practice described earlier is matched therefore by another disjunction: ecclesial practice has not followed biblical example. This is different from Nancy Eiesland's analysis of biblical images as largely inimical to disabled people, but her desire to re-craft religious symbols is matched here by my suggestion that the old story needs to be

---

[1]   See for example The Church Urban Fund's 2011 report *Tackling Homelessness Together: A Study of Nine Faith-Based Housing Projects*. The summary includes very little that asks structural or ideological questions. Available at: http://www.cuf.org.uk/research/tackling-homelessness-together (accessed 28 May 2012).

told anew. This theology of homelessness opens up the possibility of a creative dialogue between the noisy Church and the silent poor.

Homeless people in this account have spoken of breakdowns of health and relationships, both as a cause and result of why they are without homes. Experiences from childhood and adolescence, and the discovery of sexuality have fed into these reasons, with crime, self-harm, substance abuse and mortality also apparent. A wide range of emotions coloured these experiences, including the deadening of feeling as a means of survival and as the result of drug-taking. Amid the darkness of fear, pain, anger, isolation and chaos, a faltering light of independence and love points to the return to a more orderly life. God is absent and present, and sometimes bizarrely so as in the case of the contextual Bible readers. The Bible is occasionally less of a sacred text and more of a lucky dip horoscope. The Church is treated warily and fondly, and also ignored. People have their own creeds and beliefs which they follow, with some tenuous links to a more traditional Christian faith. Their laughter sounds in the blackness as well as in the light of envisaging a new home.

The desire to read these stories alongside Christian theology, without incorporating them wholesale or blunting their sharpness, encourages a new reading of the old story. However, just as Eiesland was at pains not to create a new symbolic order, so it is open to question just how original this new telling of the old story may be. On the one hand, Barth says that even if God speaks 'through Russian communism or a flute concerto, a blossoming shrub or a dead dog' there is hardly a warrant for the Church to proclaim this;[2] on the other, there is almost childish pleasure in Zipes' examples of changed endings in folk tales. The rather meek maiden in the story of Rumpelstiltskin by the Brothers Grimm becomes in the late twentieth century a strident feminist: '"You're crazy!" the miller's daughter yelled. "I'll never marry this horrible king. I'd never give my child away".'[3] Rayan's theology of the dalit people contains a reworking of Matthew 23, the woes Jesus invokes against the Pharisees:

> Woe to us who have ignored, even distorted Christ's disclosure of the Fatherhood of God, and elaborately buried his vision of the family of God on earth. Woe to us who have solemnly introduced inequalities and master-slave relations where Christ had established a fellowship of brothers and sisters and co-learners, co-workers and comrades ... Woe to us who close our eyes to the light and weave in the dark theories of pure and impure bloods and births while ignoring the obvious and vital, the values of justice and mercy and equality and freedom and friendship and faithfulness to one another.[4]

---

[2]   Barth, *Dogmatics*, I.1, p. 60.
[3]   Zipes, *Magic Spell*, p. 180.
[4]   Rayan, *Dalits and Women*, pp. 135–6.

The endings of the parables of Jesus, as Herzog has shown, confound the astonished disciples, while Auerbach has argued that Christian literature itself challenges and overturns the norms of a high classical style. Theology's point of departure is important, but never to begin with those on the margins risks further exclusion; some balance has been attempted here with contextual Bible study and reference to Nolan's reading of the South Africa polity through a biblical lens.

There is no clear cut answer to where the boundaries of this story lie, but one approach is to look again at metaphor and symbol. A metaphor starts its life as appearing inappropriate and unconventional, becomes alive with a dual and tensive meaning, and dies dangerously when it becomes literalised.[5] Symbols 'grow organically in the soil of the unconscious and they die when they can no longer find sustenance there'.[6] The God of surprises encourages risk taking with the nourishment of the unconventional if the Christian story is to be enlivened once more. Maria Clara Bingemer from a feminist perspective uses the image of the woman at Bethany pouring ointment on the feet of Jesus to show women's theology competing in a male dominated world. She urges readers to have 'the courage to pour out the perfume at someone else's party' as they develop new theological insights.[7] Eiesland warns that there will be criticism for creating a chaos of different theological models, but offers the defence that 'The body of God is becoming alive, vivified by an insurrection of subjugated knowledges'.[8]

The implied references here to the body which is incarnate and the Spirit which is alive focus back on the concept of Trinity for a final outline of a theology of homelessness. It is the Father who welcomes the Son's return, it is the Son who makes his home in an uneasy humanity, and the Spirit who renews the life of the Church in the image of the poor. Gerard Loughlin explicitly links the doctrine of the Trinity with the concept of telling God's story. The stories of Father, Son and Holy Spirit are linked to three ways in which God's story is passed on. The story of God and the Hebrews, the story of God and God's Christ, and the story of God and the Church recounted by the community of the faithful 'are the reason for any talk of Trinity at all. It is the experience of God with God's people, as Father, Son and Spirit that impels the Trinitarian naming'. The process of telling the story of God is a dynamic one which imitates the restless ordering of the Trinity itself in its life of new creation. The story of Israel retold by Jesus becomes a new story, a second story, which in its turn is retold by the Church to form a third story. The Church's passion is to tell these other two stories together, which alone brings them to life. If 'the Church is the community that is called to stage the Trinity' then each storytelling is a singular performance which continues the event of God.[9]

---

[5]   McFague, *Metaphorical Theology*, p. 41.

[6]   T.R. Wright, *Literature*, p. 140.

[7]   Cited in Andrew Bradstock, 'Liberation Theology after the Failure of Revolution', p. 103.

[8]   Eiesland, *Disabled God*, p. 105.

[9]   Loughlin, *God's Story*, pp. 190–97.

In his book on the environment, community and ecology, Tim Gorringe anchors his theology in the persons of the Trinity:

> In relation to the built environment we can say that God the Creator is the one who brings order out of chaos … God the Reconciler is the one who 'breaks down the walls of partition' … God the Redeemer is the author of all dreams and visions …[10]

To adapt the names for the Trinitarian God is not to turn away from God: on the contrary, it is to name God as the true subject of the different stories Christians tell, perform and make in their imagining of God. The re-enchantment of these ultimate symbols of Christian faith is therefore radical without being revolutionary.

However, to conclude a theology of homelessness with a description of the Trinity, even one which is favourably reworked, looks uncomfortably like a return to the systematic method just criticised. Some earlier remarks give part justification. Samuel Rayan talks about a latent theology of marginalised people which requires the theologian to make it public. Segundo remarks that not all images of God are helpful ones: Gerard Hughes' Uncle George, and the rather limited range of ideas about God expressed in these interviews.[11] The introduction of Contextual Bible Study and Nolan's *God in South Africa* make a case for starting with established text rather than individual story, yet on balance, most emphasis here has been on the detailed stories of particular individuals. The experience of hearing and analysing these stories of homeless people has been the motivation for re-examining what both the Bible and the Church say. It is the sense that often there is little reciprocity between the official institution and the difficult lives of real people, that the pieces of the jigsaw are ill-matched, that prompts directly these suggestions about re-envisioning the Trinity. Equally, there is the irony expressed several times here that excluded as they are, it is in fact the poor who in practice evangelise those who have contributed (directly and indirectly) to their poverty. The God of Abraham, Isaac, Moses and Jesus demands that this inequality be redressed by offering as a gift another accessible way into the Trinitarian God.

---

[10] Gorringe, *Built Environment*, p. 5. See also T.J. Gorringe, *The Common Good and the Global Emergency* (Cambridge: Cambridge University Press, 2011).

[11] 'God was a family relative, much admired by Mum and Dad, who described himself as very loving, a great friend of the family, very powerful and interested in all of us. Eventually we are taken to visit "Good Old Uncle George". He lives in a formidable mansion, is bearded, gruff and threatening. We cannot share our parents professed admiration for this jewel in the family. At the end of the visit, Uncle George turns to address us. "Now listen, dear," he begins, looking very severe, "I want to see you here once a week, and if you fail to come, let me just show you what will happen to you." He then leads us down to the mansion's basement …'. Gerard W. Hughes, *God of Surprises* (London: Darton, Longman and Todd, 1988), p. 34.

Trinity Reworked

God the Father, Compassionate Father of Those Who are Homeless

As Leonardo Boff points out, 'Christian faith has no image of God the Father';[12] yet in a reading of both Old and New Testament stories, the Father of Abraham and the patriarchs, and the Father of our Lord Jesus Christ, is characterised by fatherhood towards people without homes. From the Hebrew slaves of the Exodus, to the exiled people of Israel, to the Jews who surrounded Jesus, to the Prodigal who dreams of home, all see God as the compassionate Father who provides 'recognition and acceptance of the truth about ourselves and our ultimate environment (home)'.[13] Yet if this compassion is characteristic of the Father, it must still be said that God the Father remains for ever a mystery. The concept of homecoming is one face of this mystery, for while there is a sense of home or homelessness, and some descriptors associated with both of these, yet the essence is still elusive. I offer two examples of this: from the writings of Oliver Sacks the neurologist, and from the novel *Staying On*. Sacks studies the recovery of patients from sleeping sickness and wants the reader to look beyond the diseased body to the diseased person:

> all of us have a basic intuitive feeling that once we were whole and well; at ease, at home, at peace in the world; totally united with the grounds of our being; and then we lost this primal happy, innocent state and fell into our present sickness and suffering. We had something of infinite beauty and preciousness – and we lost it; we spend our lives searching for what we have lost; and one day perhaps we will suddenly find it. And this will be the miracle, the millennium ... This sense of what is lost, and what must be found, is essentially a metaphysical one. If we arrest the patient in his metaphysical search, and ask him *what it is* that he wishes or seeks, he will not give us a tabulated list of items, but will say, simply, *My happiness, My lost health, My former condition, A sense of reality, Feeling fully alive* and so on. He does not long for this or that; he longs for a *general* change in the complexion of things, for everything to be *all right* once again, unblemished, the way it was.[14]

From a different perspective, Lucy Smalley is pictured seated on the 'thunderbox' adjacent to her bedroom in their bungalow in Pankot, India, mourning the death of her husband Tusker. They have stayed on in India after Independence. These are the final lines of the book:

---

[12] Leonardo Boff, *Trinity and Society* (Tunbridge Wells: Burns & Oates, 1988), p. 165.

[13] Navone, *Story*, p. 60.

[14] Oliver Sacks, *Awakenings* (London: Picador, 1991), p. 29.

but now until the end, I shall be alone, whatever I am doing, here as I feared, amid the alien corn, waking, sleeping, alone for ever and ever and I cannot bear it but mustn't cry and must must get over it but don't for the moment see how, so with my eyes shut, Tusker, I hold out my hand, and beg you Tusker, beg, beg you to take it and take me with you. How can you not, Tusker? Oh, Tusker, Tusker, Tusker, how can you make me stay here by myself, while you yourself go home?[15]

Both Sacks' patients and the fictional Lucy desire to return home, to how it was, even when the past was only barely satisfactory or thousands of miles away as in Lucy's case. There is some similarity here with one of Jon May's descriptions of the nomadic lifestyle of homeless people: 'Don's movements might therefore be understood as articulating what we can call a 'spectral geography' as he continually returns to places that were once meaningful but which now contain only the ghosts of previous relationships'.[16] The image of the innocence of the lost Eden remains deeply ingrained in the human psyche, and in Trinitarian terms is transferred to God the Father. It is the compassion of the Father to provide in Jesus a different way back home, for 'no one knows the Father except the Son and any one to whom the Son chooses to reveal him' (Matt. 11: 27); not the old paradise refound, but the new Adam.

God the Son, Radical Storyteller

The birth of Jesus, the Word of God, subverts the expectations of both priests and kings. No longer is home to be made with God, but God makes home with us, Emmanuel. But the cycle goes around again as the stable and the exile in Egypt foreshadow the exclusion and homelessness which Jesus was to experience throughout his life. The cross is the paradox whereby he suffers most distance from home and yet brings homeless humanity back to the Father. The homelessness of God is not diminished by this journey for Jesus takes birth again and again with human beings who continue to crucify him, and are thereby able to return to the Father. Like the air raids of 1940:

Still falls the Rain –
Dark as the world of man, black as our loss –
Blind as the nineteen hundred and forty nails
Upon the cross.[17]

---

[15] Paul Scott, *Staying On* (London: Granada, 1978), p. 255.

[16] Jon May, 'Of Nomads and Vagrants: Single Homelessness and Narratives of Home as Place', *Environment and Planning D: Society and Space* 18 (2000): 753.

[17] Edith Sitwell, 'Still Falls the Rain', in P. Levi (ed.), *Penguin Book of English Christian Verse* (Harmondsworth: Penguin, 1984), p. 293.

It is not only this cosmic cycle which shocks, Jesus is the Word who radicalises the word too. He unlocks the famine of hearing the word of the Lord (Amos 8: 11) by telling stories of everyday life, lulling the hearer into a false sense of security by sheer familiarity, and then overturning the tables of our expectation by showing what the Kingdom of God is really like. Barbara Hardy on the Sermon on the Mount explains that:

> The strange but illustrative treatment of the salt, the light, and the pearls is only appreciated when it is easily and implicitly referred to our memory of the normal way of treating salt, light and pearls. The memory of accumulated ordinary experience joins with the narrator's brilliantly bizarre invention to create the whole narrative in which salt, light, pearls and many other images are activated to instruct a humble and desperate audience in the ways of blessed righteousness and godliness.[18]

This return to the speech patterns and objects of daily life is the basis for the new religious literacy for which Anne Morisy calls. Speaking and living the vernacular implies a familiarity and a fearlessness with the ways in which ordinary people live, listening and observing respectfully especially if the environment is a strange one. It also means an openness to encourage and value the non-verbal communication to which Laurie Green refers, and which is central to Jenkins' analysis of the Kingswood Whit Walk. It is also the return to home territory which Myers encourages the theologian to make. When non-verbal religious communication becomes more structured, it turns into the 'apt liturgy' mentioned earlier; that is, liturgy which is better connected to the reality of the lives it seeks to touch.

The radical storyteller also leads his hearers on an unfamiliar and eccentric journey through the city, enabling them to look through the eyes of the homeless people who inhabit it and map it differently. The homeless city looks alien in this perspective as the prime retail space of shopping therapy becomes threatening, as the regulated paths of the homeless journey become more recognisable, and as once rejected spots become infused with elements of home. This storyteller does not refuse the images attributed to him however bizarre: bogeyman, cannibal, fairground attraction. He asks simply that they promote human flourishing and better relations with the God he enfleshes.

Jesus, the homeless God, empowers too. The incarnation of the Word does not leave humanity where it is, God does not become seduced by the comforts and temptations of God's new human home, but rather desires to transform the reality of the human person and the whole of humanity, 'until we all attain to the unity of the faith and the knowledge of the Son of God, to mature humanity, to the measure of the stature of the fullness of Christ' (Eph. 4: 13). The out-working of this desire in the life of Jesus is to tell stories of transformation to the women and

---

[18]   Barbara Hardy, *Tellers and Listeners* (London: Athlone Press, 1975), p. 5.

men in the society around him. Jesus' project is to build an inclusive community for those who are united by their suffering and exclusion within which there is the possibility of hope and healing. He reverses the rights of the powerful, so that it is the poor who inherit the Kingdom, receive satisfaction and go off laughing: the story of marginality becomes the story of entitlement.[19]

God the Holy Spirit, Power to Tell the Story Anew

The impetus for such empowerment comes through the working of the Holy Spirit who can 'make all things new' (Rev. 21: 5). The call from the more radical interpreters of the gospel like Nolan and Leech is not for incremental change, but for a much sharper re-orientation of the Church towards the poor, even at the expense of its own unity. Poor and homeless people become the centre and the measure of the activities of the Church, for like individual Christians, the whole institution is enabled to tell a new story if it is first able to hear the stories of the marginalised. But its hearing, as Buber asserts, is so often impaired. The wax in many Christian ears is the centuries-old accretion of comfort and affluence, which the Church of England reports correctly identify as being at the heart of its own structures. The Holy Spirit which blows where it wills needs to carry on its breath the lives of homeless people if it is to unblock the hearing of a bourgeois Church. Hans Anderson's story of *The Emperor's New Clothes* at the start of this book recalls the entrenched interests which prevent reality being named, even when the main protagonist is himself aware of the threadbare nature of the story. It takes the innocence of one on the edge, a little child, to speak out loud what all have suspected but been too frightened to articulate.

The Spirit also punctures our ethical certainties, placing under scrutiny again the inevitability of late capitalism and all its associated powers and dominions. It allows a comparison between the moral hazard of not assisting distressed tenants and homeowners, and the moral deficit between how rich and poor are treated in the marketplace.

There are signs of hope that this is happening, even in some parts of Britain. As Boff says:

> When the poor become conscious of their oppression, come together, organize their forces, throw over the taboos that held them in subjection, unmask the standards by which they were stigmatised, prophetically denounce those who kept them in chains ... when they are filled with creative imagination and plan utopias of the reconciled world in which all will have enough to eat and be able to profit from the bounty of nature, then we can say: the Spirit is at work there, being the catalyst in a conflictive situation.[20]

---

[19]   Davey, 'Being Church as Political Praxis', pp. 66–7.
[20]   Boff, *Trinity and Society*, p. 208.

The Spirit also breathes life into the two central images of Christianity. The birth of Jesus in a stable and the death of Jesus on a cross can be cleaned of their unhelpful patina and made to resonate again with their strange narrative. I hope it is possible to remove from the birth scene the away-in-a-manger imagery and memories of shepherd children in tea-towel headdresses, and to find again the surprise, the danger, the exclusion and the poverty of that birth. The many and well-publicised crises of refugees in the news media also find echo in the story of the flight into Egypt. The merit of the cross is that is it hard to sentimentalise it in the same way. Nevertheless the pietism which speaks of 'Jesus who died on the cross to save me from my sins' individualises the gospel to such an extent that any social and political impact is lost. Herzog gives the lie to this personalised view when he comments:

> If Jesus was a teacher of heavenly truths dispensed through literary gems called parables, it is difficult to understand how he could have been executed as a political subversive and crucified between two social bandits.[21]

The cross as a place of utter loneliness, complete isolation even from God, where the experiences of human poverty and homelessness are starkly drawn together into a single event, still has the powerful possibility of drawing together Christians of different life experiences. The homeless God is also therefore the crucified God. This is no new symbol, but an attempt to allow an old Christian symbol to be fashioned in a way which provides mutual access to the worlds of both those with homes and those without. The re-crafting of these two symbols is some of the ground work which enables the second sign of hope to be revealed. This is summarised in the words of John Vincent who urges the change 'from being a story-reader into a story-maker'.[22] When this is applied to homeless people, this process affirms the movement from the passivity of being recipients of charity to the activity of being agents in the growth of a Church to and with the most marginal. It recognises that homeless people have something of value to say which both theological and sociological research has often overlooked.[23]

Apt Liturgy

The last word in both Loughlin's account of God's story and Eiesland's vision of a disabled God is to focus on the Eucharist. Loughlin's on-going motif from Revelation of John eating the book ('bitter to your stomach, but sweet as honey in your mouth' Rev. 10: 8–10) becomes Eucharistic as the Word made flesh is consumed along with the divine *logos* of scripture.[24] Eiesland shows how the

---

21   Herzog, *Parables*, p. 9.
22   John Vincent, *Mark at Work* (London: Bible Reading Fellowship, 1986), p. 18.
23   Boydell, 'Narratives of Identity', p. 36.
24   Loughlin, *God's Story*, pp. 244–5.

Eucharist is a site for both inclusion and exclusion of disabled people, and finishes with a specially written Eucharistic Prayer.[25] Duncan Forrester reminds us of the centrality of eating and drinking in the ministry of Jesus, and the offence that he caused by sitting at table with those who were ritually impure and excluded. Jesus told stories of great feasts where street people were invited because others refused to come, of a banquet where a younger son was welcomed and an elder brother sulked; he fed the multitude when those who had come a distance to hear him were hungry and it was late. The Last Supper was therefore not an isolated incident in an otherwise food-free narrative, but the culmination of the challenge of Jesus to codes of purity and pollution. The way in which Christians have responded to Jesus' call for *anamnesis* have hardly reflected the open table which their leader promoted, with controversy over who could sit with whom part of Church history from the earliest days until the present. Yet the challenge goes beyond the Church to confront the inequalities of contemporary society too. Forrester writes:

> Eating and drinking and the way they are arranged have a very central place in Christian faith and life, as in most other religious systems. The practice and the theology of the eucharist cannot be separated from its ethical content, and that is very centrally egalitarian. When Christians gather to celebrate the Lord's Supper they not only present a challenge to racism, class and caste in the church, but very centrally to the inequalities of the world.[26]

For worship in this context to be authentic, whether Eucharistic or not, it might better reflect the theology outlined here. The Trinitarian God of homeless people finds concrete expression not simply in rituals of participation, but in the ordering of liturgical space and action which are inclusive rather than threatening. The Letter of James is quite specific:

> My brethren, show no partiality as you hold the faith of our Lord Jesus Christ, the Lord of glory. For if a man with gold rings and in fine clothing comes into your assembly, and a poor man in shabby clothing also comes in, and you pay attention to the one who wears the fine clothing and say, 'Have a seat here, please', while you say to the poor man, 'Stand there' or 'Sit at my feet', have you not made distinctions among yourselves, and become judges with evil thoughts? Listen, my beloved brethren. Has not God chosen those who are poor in the world to be rich in faith and heirs of the kingdom which he has promised to those who love him? But you have dishonoured the poor man. (James 2: 1–6)

So Liturgies of the Word include conspicuously the stories told in the Bible which value the absence of home as denoting the special presence of God, and allow room for those who have experienced homelessness to respond to these narratives

---

[25]   Eiesland, *Disabled God*, pp. 118–19.

[26]   Forrester, *Human Worth*, p. 211.

in verbal and non-verbal (symbolic) ways. The stories of Jesus which underline the generosity of God to the poor and marginalised and the reversal of contemporary values in the Kingdom become prominent for all parts of the congregation. However, for those who are not vulnerable and dispossessed, it is the call of Jesus for discipleship and repentance which matters. Myers contrasts his social location in the middle-class as one of entitlement with his Christian discipleship which 'represents my social dis-location'.[27] For Liturgies of the Sacrament, an emphasis on the transitory nature of the Last Supper replicating the hasty provision of the Exodus Passover (Ex. 12: 11) shifts the perspective of the Eucharist from a comfortable meal with friends to a preparation for a journey. Those with no home to receive friends and little food to distribute are implicitly excluded from a ritual which can easily mimic a middle-class lunch party. On the other hand, the concept of offertory in which the ordinary things of the earth (bread and wine) are made holy, at the same time as those who offer them are blessed, gives access to a simpler ceremony in which the excluded can take an equal part.

Worship which visibly fails to overturn the exclusion of homeless people is reduced to the status of worship of the *status quo* or of the present idol of the market. It is not the worship of the God whose story Jesus tells and which Christians attempt to perform in the community of faith. So an annual Service for Homelessness Sunday which included no homeless people among its main participants becomes another traditionally patronising act of charity.[28] In this way liturgy itself can become a site of struggle.

Liturgies of the Word and liturgies of the sacrament can be envisaged as food for the journey, nourishment for the creation of stories of hope and transformation. Viaticum is therefore required not only by those who face their final journey to God, but by all those who build new narratives of inclusion, and who have the courage to resist the temptation to build booths on the mountain of their transfiguration, and to follow instead the itinerant storyteller, Jesus the homeless God.

Many words have flowed from a reflection on why a chance encounter with Simon, a recovering narcotics user, should speak so distinctly of God. The desire to pursue this unexpected sense of holiness led to a theology of story. This was not simply a theoretical account of how and why poor people are the privileged storytellers of God, nor a comparison of different sociological studies of everyday life. A theology of story provides a sympathetic means to access ordinary lives, which respects both their triviality and their giftedness in the context of the Christian Trinity. Additionally, the lives of writer and reader are not allowed to stand completely apart from lives which are more microscopically examined. The critical tools employed here in particular respect of homeless people have

---

[27] Myers, *Stone*, p. 18.

[28] In fairness it should be added that one service of this kind included words from homeless people. The same church, it was reported to me, hosted a very positive funeral liturgy for the death of a homeless person, where friends were allowed to speak of their friendship and sadness.

uncovered certain mismatches between the stories recounted and what theory has proposed. In particular, while liberation theology speaks of privileged storytellers, the privilege still seems more weighted towards those who hear: poor people themselves are largely unaware.

Theologians with personal engagement and orientated towards praxis cannot be content to identify shortcomings without any attempt to provide remedies. This has encouraged a more profound examination of scripture and the Church, revealing a complex picture around the themes of home, homecoming and homelessness. The message of scripture which values the absence of home as part of Christian roots is only partly transferred to the practice of the Church. Churches and church-based organisations have been important partners in the relief of poverty, but the voices of poor people, in both suffering and recovery, have rarely been heard. With this in mind, the outline of a theology of homelessness which emerges from and honours the stories heard here is one way of asserting a proper appreciation of these life histories. The inclusion of remarks about appropriate liturgy is merely to scratch the surface of an application of such a theology of homelessness. Making theology real is more than simply recommending liturgical practice, but as a symbol for what the Church believes liturgy remains significant. It is in this context that negative images of homeless people can be balanced by a recognition of their strengths, and perhaps promote enough theological literacy to bring to light the hidden symbols of homeless Christianity.

Epilogue
Occupy

In October 2011 Occupy London set up its camp outside St Paul's Cathedral in London, following other such occupations in capital cities across the world. Though not directly related to issues of housing and homelessness, this protest nevertheless illustrated and responded to some of the same ideas highlighted here. What seems to have galvanised people is the juxtaposition of the many who are paying economic and social costs for the errors (greed?) of the few: this is summarised in the slogan of 99 per cent versus 1 per cent. Church of England bishops have also been at the forefront of objections to reform of welfare benefits, particularly those that cap total household incomes, believing that this will disproportionately affect families and children.

However, the protests in London also demonstrated the kind of tensions referred to here, in which the Churches and particularly the established Church are deeply enmeshed in national structures. This enables bishops' voices to be heard, but also places the Church as landowners on the opposite side to demonstrators when evictions are contemplated. This complexity of values became uncomfortably focused for St Paul's when a plan to move the camp forcibly was not supported by all its senior staff, resulting in the resignation of the dean, a canon and a minor canon.[1] In the South West, Occupy sites were established in Exeter also next to the cathedral, in Bristol on land jointly managed by cathedral and city, and in Plymouth in a disused benefits office. At the start of 2012, Exeter Cathedral was in negotiations to move the camp with a resort to law a distinct possibility, Occupy Bristol had decided to move, the Plymouth camp was evicted before Christmas and may well return to tents in front of the university building. Another sort of tension is revealed by a recent report from the Church Urban Fund which suggests that 'three quarters of clergy said they think poverty is mainly due to social injustice, but only one fifth of regular churchgoers agree'; indeed there is little difference in attitudes to poverty between those who attend church and those who do not.[2]

It is interesting that cathedrals have featured in such protests. Perhaps it is simply the availability of open land in a city centre, or the reckoning that objections will be more muted or disorganised, or the high-profile contrast between the tents

[1] Peter Walker and Riazat Butt, 'St Paul's may seek injunction to move Occupy London activists' (2011). Available at: http:// www.guardian.co.uk/uk/2011/oct/23/st-pauls-occupy-london-protest (accessed 24 October 2011).

[2] Church Urban Fund, 'Tackling homelessness together: A study of nine faith-based housing projects' (2011). Available at: http:// www.cuf.org.uk/research/tackling-homelessness-together (accessed 26 January 2012).

and ecclesial towers; more positively, perhaps there is some recognition that the Church as an organisation and the cathedral as its symbol represent an alternative world view: the city for people not for profit. The staff changes at St Paul's suggest that the Church's stance is more problematic. At least it seems that other cathedrals have learnt from St Paul's and perhaps have spent more time genuinely listening and negotiating.

If this is the case, that marks an important step. Otherwise my concern remains about the failure to listen to and value the stories of people on the margins, exemplified here by the narratives of homeless people; it is as if they could have no worthwhile insights into their own lives, their society or the faith they practise. There exists a similar failure to ask the structural questions demanded by both Christian faith and social reality. If these stories are not heard, and then retold within a new frame which provides hope and meaning, they risk festering in the storybag of society.[3] This book began with a reference to *Waiting for Godot*, recalling Vladimir and Estragon as they pass the time. My fear is that the homeless of our own day will continue to wait for change with diminishing expectation; my hope is that if only our listening informs our theology and social policy, then the heroic desperation with which Beckett's play ends may give way to an enlarged vision of the Kingdom of God.

---

[3]   Alida Gersie recounts a Korean folk tale in which the refusal to re-tell stories means that they are trapped and corrupted in a 'storybag', eventually seeking revenge on the man who refuses to let them out and be heard. *Earthtales: Storytelling in Times of Change* (London: Green Print, 1992), pp. 11–13.

Bibliography

ACAGUPA Archbishop of Canterbury's Advisory Group on Urban Priority Areas, *Living Faith in the City* (London: Church House Publishing, 1990).

ACCUPA Archbishop of Canterbury's Commission on Urban Priority Areas, *Faith in the City* (London: Church House Publishing, 1985).

Adams, Richard, *Watership Down* (Harmondsworth: Penguin, 1974).

Alcoholics Anonymous (3rd edn. York: A.A. General Service Office, 1976).

Anderson, Hans Christian, *The Emperor's New Clothes* (London, Blackie: no date).

Archbishops' Commission on Urban Life and Faith, *Faithful Cities: A Call for Celebration, Vision and Justice* (Peterborough: Methodist Publishing House, 2006).

Auerbach, Eric, *Mimesis* (Princeton, NJ: Princeton University Press, 1968).

Augé, Marc, *Non-Places: Introduction to an Anthropology of Supermodernity* (English translation. London & New York: Verso, 1997).

Augustine, *Confessions* (English translation. Harmondsworth: Penguin, 1970).

Barr, James, *The Bible in the Modern World* (London: SCM, 1973).

Barth, Karl, *Church Dogmatics* (English translation. Edinburgh: T&T Clark, 1936–77).

— *The Humanity of God*. London: Collins, 1967.

Beardsworth, Timothy, *A Sense of Perception* (Oxford: Religious Experience Research Unit, 1977).

Beckett, Samuel, *Waiting for Godot* (2nd edn. London: Faber and Faber, 1965).

Bellah, R., Madsen, R., Sullivan, W., Swidler, A. and Tipton S., *Habits of the Heart* (Berkeley: University of California Press, 1985).

Boff, Leonardo, *Trinity and Society* (Tunbridge Wells: Burns & Oates, 1988).

Bouma-Prediger, Steven and Walsh, Brian J., *Beyond Homelessness Christian Faith in a Culture of Displacement* (Grand Rapids, MI: Wm B. Eerdmans, 2008).

Boydell, K.M., Goering, P. and Morrell-Bellai, T.L., 'Narratives of Identity: Re-Presentation of Self in People Who Are Homeless', *Qualitative Health Research* 10/1 (2000): 26–38.

Bradstock, Andrew, 'Liberation Theology after the Failure of Revolution,' in Christopher Rowland and John Vincent (eds), *Liberation Theology UK* (Sheffield: Urban Theology Unit, 1995).

Brown, David, *God and Enchantment of Place* (Oxford: Oxford University Press, 2004).

Buber, Martin, *Between Man and Man* (English translation. London: Routledge & Kegan Paul, 1947).

— *I and Thou* (English translation. Edinburgh: T&T Clark, 1958).

Burrows, R., Pleace, N. and Quilgars, D. (eds), *Homelessness and Social Policy* (London and New York: Routledge, 1997).

Church Urban Fund, 'Tackling Homelessness Together: A Study of Nine Faith-based Housing Projects' (2011). Available at: http:// www.cuf.org.uk/research/ tackling-homelessness-together (accessed 26 January 2012).

Church Urban Fund, 'Bias to the Poor? Christian Attitudes to Poverty in this Country' (2012). Available at: http://cuf.org.uk/research/bias-to-the-poor (accessed 27 January 2012).

Clandinin, D. Jean and Rosiek, Jerry, 'Mapping a Landscape of Narrative Inquiry,' in D. Jean Clandinin (ed.), *Handbook of Narrative Inquiry* (London: Sage, 2007).

Cloke, P., May, J. and Johnsen, S., 'Performativity and Affect in the Homeless City', *Environment and Planning D: Society and Space* 26 (2008): 241–63.

Common Wealth, 'Christians for Economic and Social Justice' (2010). Available at: http://www.ekklesia.co.uk/CommonWealthStatement (accessed 26 January 2012).

Cornwall, Susannah and Nixon, David, 'Readings from the Road: Contextual Bible Study with a Group of Homeless and Vulnerably-Housed People', *The Expository Times* 123/1 (2011): 12–19.

Creswell, Tim, *Place: A Short Introduction* (Oxford: Blackwell, 2004).

Crossan, John Dominic, *The Dark Interval: Towards a Theology of Story* (Niles, IL: Argus Communications, 1975).

Cumbria Action for Social Support (CASS), 'A Guide to the Homelessness Act, 2002' (2011). Available at: http://www.cass-cumbria.co.uk/guide-homelessness-act-2002 (accessed 26 January 2012).

Cupitt, Don, *What is a Story?* (London: SCM, 1991).

Daly, Gerald, *Homeless, Policies, and Lives on the Street* (London and New York: Routledge, 1996).

Davey, Andrew, 'Being Church as Political Praxis', in Christopher Rowland and John Vincent (eds), *Liberation Theology UK* (Sheffield: Urban Theology Unit, 1995).

— *Urban Christianity and Global Order* (London: SPCK, 2001).

Davis, F., Paulhus, E. and Bradstock, A., *Moral, but No Compass: Government, Church and the Future of Welfare* (Chelmsford: Matthew James Publishing, 2008).

Denzin, Norman K., *Interpretive Interactionism* (London: Sage Publications, 1989).

Dewar, A., 'Will All the Generic Women in Sport Please Stand Up? Challenges Facing Feminist Sport Sociology', *Quest* 45 (1993): 211–29.

Dickens, Charles, *A Tale of Two Cities* (London and Glasgow: Collins' Clear-Type Press, no date).

Duffield, Ian (ed.), *Urban Christ, Responses to John J. Vincent* (Sheffield: Urban Theology Unit, 1997).

Eakin, Paul John, *How Our Lives Become Stories: Making Selves* (Ithaca and London: Cornell University Press, 1999).

Eiesland, Nancy, *The Disabled God* (Nashville, TN: Abingdon Press, 1994).

Emmins, Alan, *31 Days: A New York Street Diary* (London: Corvo, 2006).

Ford, David, *Barth and God's Story* (Frankfurt am Main: Lang, 1981).

Forrester, Duncan, *On Human Worth* (London: SCM Press, 2001).

Frank, Arthur W., *The Wounded Storyteller* (Chicago and London: Chicago University Press, 1995).

Freire, Paolo, *Pedagogy of the Oppressed* (Harmondsworth: Penguin, 1972).

Gersie, Alida, *Earthtales: Storytelling in Times of Change* (London: Green Print, 1992).

Glastonbury, Bryan, *Homeless Near a Thousand Homes* (London: Allen & Unwin, 1971).

Gorringe, T.J., *A Theology of the Built Environment* (Cambridge: Cambridge University Press, 2002).

— *The Common Good and the Global Emergency* (Cambridge: Cambridge University Press, 2011).

Graham, Elaine, 'What Makes a Good City? Reflections on Urban Life and Faith', *International Journal of Public Theology* 2 (2008): 7–26.

Green, Laurie, *Power to the Powerless* (Basingstoke: Marshal Pickering, 1987).

— 'The Jesus of the Inner City' in Ian Duffield (ed.), *Urban Christ, Responses to John J. Vincent* (Sheffield: Urban Theology Unit, 1997).

Gutiérrez, Gustavo, *A Theology of Liberation* (London: SCM, 1988).

Hardy, Barbara, *Tellers and Listeners* (London: Athlone Press, 1975).

— 'Narrative as a Primary Act of Mind' in Margaret Meek, Aidan Warlow and Griselda Barton (eds), *The Cool Web* (London: Bodley Head, 1977).

Hauerwas, Stanley, *A Community of Character* (London: University of Notre Dame Press, 1981).

Haw, K.F., 'Exploring the Educational Experience of Muslim Girls: Tales Told to Tourists – Should the White Researcher Stay at Home?', *British Educational Research Journal* 22/3 (1996): 319–30.

Hay, David with Nye, Rebecca, *The Spirit of the Child* (London: Fount, 1998).

Herzog II, William, *Parables as Subversive Speech* (Louisville, KY: Westminster/ John Knox Press, 1994).

Hughes, Gerard W., *God of Surprises* (London: Darton, Longman and Todd, 1988).

Hughes, Richard, *The Spider's Palace* (London: Chatto & Windus, 1961).

Inge, John, *A Christian Theology of Place* (Aldershot: Ashgate Publishing, 2003).

Jagose, A., *Queer Theory: An Introduction* (New York: New York University Press, 1996).

James, M.R., *The Apocryphal New Testament* (English translation. Oxford: Clarendon Press, 1924).

Jenkins, Timothy, *Religion in English Everyday Life* (Oxford: Berghahn, 1999).

Jeremias, Joachim, *The Parables of Jesus* (English translation. New York: Scribners, 1963).

Lawrence, Louise, *The Word in Place: Reading the New Testament in Contemporary Contexts* (London: SCM, 2009).

Leech, Ken, *The Sky is Red* (London: Darton, Longman and Todd, 1997).

Levi, Peter (ed.), *Penguin Book of English Christian Verse* (Harmondsworth: Penguin, 1984).

Lindbeck, George A., *The Nature of Doctrine* (London: SPCK, 1984).

Loughlin, Gerard, *Telling God's Story* (Cambridge: Cambridge University Press, 1996).

Malpas, Peter, *Housing and the Welfare State* (Basingstoke: Palgrave Macmillan, 2005).

May, Jon, 'Of Nomads and Vagrants: Single Homelessness and Narratives of Home as Place', *Environment and Planning D: Society and Space* 18 (2000): 737–59.

McFague, Sally, *Metaphorical Theology* (London: SCM, 1983).

Milbank, John, *Theology and Social Theory* (Oxford: Blackwell, 1990).

Moltmann, Jürgen, *Experiences in Theology* (English translation. London: SCM, 2000).

Moore, Basil (ed.), *Black Theology: The South African Voice* (London: Hurst, 1973).

Morisy, Anne, *Beyond the Good Samaritan: Community Ministry and Mission* (London: Mowbray, 1997).

Myers, Ched, *Binding the Strong Man* (Maryknoll, NY: Orbis, 1988).

— *Who Will Roll Away the Stone?* (Maryknoll, NY: Orbis, 1994).

Navone, John, *Towards a Theology of Story* (Slough: St. Paul Publications, 1977).

Nolan, Albert, *God in South Africa* (London: Catholic Institute for International Relations, 1988).

Nouwen, Henri, *The Return of the Prodigal Son* (London: Darton, Longman and Todd, 1994).

Orwell, George, *Down and Out in Paris and London* (Harmondsworth: Penguin, 1987).

Patton, Michael Quinn, *How to Use Qualitative Methods in Evaluation* (London: Sage Publications, 1987).

Plymouth Access to Housing (PATH), Homepage (2012). Available at: http://www.plymouthpath.org (accessed 26 January 2012).

Powell, John, *Why Am I Afraid to Love?* (London: HarperCollins, 1975).

— *Why Am I Afraid to Tell You Who I Am?* (London: Fontana, 1975).

Randall, G. and Brown, S., *Outreach and Resettlement Work with People Sleeping Rough* (London: DoE, 1995).

Rapport, Nigel, *Diverse World-Views in an English Village* (Edinburgh: Edinburgh University Press, 1993).

Rayan, Samuel, 'The Challenge of the Dalit Issue: Some Theological Perspectives' in V. Devasahayam (ed.), *Dalits and Women* (The Gurkukul Summer Institute, 1992).

Rayner, Jay, 'Sharp Rise in Demand for Food Handouts from Poverty-Stricken Families', *Observer* newspaper, 1 October 2011.

Rhodes, David, *Faith in Dark Places* (London: Triangle, 1996).

Richardson, Lisa, *Writing Strategies: Reaching Diverse Audiences* (London: Sage, 1990).

Riches, John, 'Worship Resources: Contextual Bible Study: Some Reflections', *Expository Times* 117 (2005): 23–6.

Ricoeur, Paul, *Time and Narrative* (Chicago: Chicago University Press, 1984).

Ripley's 'Believe It or Not' (2012). Available at: http://www.ripleys.com (accessed 26 January 2012).

Rowland, Christopher, 'The Gospel, the Poor and the Churches', in Christopher Rowland and John Vincent (eds), *Liberation Theology UK* (Sheffield: Urban Theology Unit, 1995).

Rowling, J.K., *Harry Potter and the Philosopher's Stone* (London: Bloomsbury, 1997).

Sacks, Oliver, *Awakenings* (London: Picador, 1991).

Scott, Paul, *Staying On* (London: Granada, 1978).

Screech, M.A., *Laughter at the Foot of the Cross* (London: Allen Lane The Penguin Press, 1997).

Segundo, Juan Luis, *Signs of the Times* (Maryknoll, NY: Orbis Books, 1993).

Shakespeare, William, *Hamlet* V.ii, in *Complete Works of William Shakespeare* (London: Abbey Library, 1978).

Sheldrake, Philip, 'Spirituality as an Academic Discipline' in Adrian Thatcher (ed.), *Spirituality and the Curriculum* (London: Cassell, 1999).

— *Spaces for the Sacred* (London: SCM Press, 2001).

Shelter, 'Homelessness up 10%' (2011). Available at: http://england.shelter.org.uk/news/june_2011/homelessness_up_10 (accessed 26 January 2012).

Simon, Ulrich, *Story and Faith in the Biblical Narrative* (London: SPCK, 1975).

Sitwell, Edith, 'Still Falls the Rain', in P. Levi (ed.), *Penguin Book of English Christian Verse* (Harmondsworth: Penguin, 1984).

Smith, Brett, 'The Abyss', *Qualitative Inquiry* 5/2 (1999): 264–79.

Sparkes, Andrew C., 'The Fatal Flaw: A Narrative of the Fragile Body-Self', *Qualitative Inquiry* 2.4 (1996): 463–94.

Stiglitz, Joseph, *Freefall: Free Markets and the Sinking of the Global Economy* (London: Penguin, 2010).

Stivers, Laura, *Disrupting Homelessness: Alternative Christian Approaches* (Minneapolis: Fortress Press, 2011).

Stuart, Elizabeth, *Chosen* (London: Chapman, 1993).

— *Gay and Lesbian Theologies: Repetitions with Critical Difference* (Aldershot: Ashgate, 2003).

Swinburne, Richard, *The Existence of God* (Oxford: Oxford University Press, 1977).

Trible, Phyllis, *Texts of Terror: Literary-Feminist Readings of Biblical Narrative* (London: SCM, 1992).

Vincent, John, *Mark at Work* (London: Bible Reading Fellowship, 1986).
— 'Liberation Theology in Britain, 1970–1995' in Christopher Rowland and John Vincent (eds), *Liberation Theology UK* (Sheffield: Urban Theology Unit, 1995).
Walker, Peter and Butt, Riazat, 'St Paul's May Seek Injunction to Move Occupy London Activists' (2001). Available at: http:// www.guardian.co.uk/uk/2011/ oct/23/st-pauls-occupy-london-protest (accessed 24 October 2011).
Webster, John, *Barth's Moral Theology* (Edinburgh: T&T Clark, 1998).
West, Gerald and Ujamaa Centre staff, *Doing Contextual Bible Study: A Resource Manual* (The Ujamaa Centre for Biblical and Theological Community Development and Research [formerly the Institute for the Study of the Bible and Worker Ministry Project], 2007).
Wikan, Unni, *Life among the Poor in Cairo* (English translation. London: Tavistock Publications, 1980).
Williams, Rowan, 'The Government Needs to Know How Afraid People Are', *New Statesman*, 9 June 2011. Available at: http://www.archbishopofcanterbury.org/ articles.php/2066/new-statesman-leader (accessed 26 January 2012).
Witvliet, Theo, *A Place in the Sun* (English translation. London: SCM, 1985).
Woodward, James and Pattison, Stephen (eds), *The Blackwell Reader in Pastoral and Practical Theology* (Oxford: Blackwell, 2000).
Wright, N.T., *The New Testament and the People of God* (London: SPCK, 1992).
Wright, T.R., *Theology and Literature* (Oxford: Blackwell, 1988).
Zipes, Jack, *Breaking the Magic Spell Radical Themes of Folk and Fairy Tales* (London: Heinemann, 1979).

Index

Note: numbers in brackets preceded by *n* are footnote numbers.